MASSACRE OF THE INNOCENTS

Sir Morgan Crofton, 2nd Life Guards, 1907.

MASSACRE OF THE INNOCENTS

The Crofton Diaries, YPRES
1914–1915

EDITED BY GAVIN ROYNON

FOREWORD BY
SIR MARTIN GILBERT

SUTTON PUBLISHING

First published in the United Kingdom in 2004 by
Sutton Publishing Limited · Phoenix Mill
Thrupp · Stroud · Gloucestershire · GL5 2BU

Gavin Roynon has asserted the moral right to be identified as the editor of this
work.

British Library Cataloguing in Publication Data
A catalogue record for this book is available from the British Library.

ISBN 0-7509-3739-4

Front endpaper: Desolation of Ypres. *(UPP, Paris)*
Back endpaper: Ypres receives the French Croix de Guerre, 28 January 1920.
(Antony of Ypres)

Typeset in Goudy 10.5/14pt
Typesetting and origination by
Sutton Publishing Limited
Printed and bound in England by
J.H. Haynes & Co. Ltd, Sparkford

To my son Nicholas
who shares my love of history
and accompanied me
on my first visit to Ypres

In Flanders Fields

—

In Flanders fields the poppies blow
Between the crosses, row on row,
That mark our place; and in the sky
The larks, still bravely singing, fly
Scarce heard amid the guns below.

We are the Dead. Short days ago
We lived, felt dawn, saw sunset glow,
Loved, and were loved, and now we lie
      In Flanders fields.

Take up our quarrel with the foe:
To you from failing hands we throw
  The torch; be yours to hold it high.
  If ye break faith with us who die
We shall not sleep, though poppies grow
      In Flanders fields

Punch
Dec 8. 1915

John McCrae
—

CONTENTS

VOLUME I: OCTOBER 27 – DECEMBER 3, 1914

Sir Morgan Crofton leaves for the Front – arrival at Le Havre – continues
via Rouen and Hazebrouck to Ypres – rejoins severely depleted 2nd Life
Guards – put in command of Machine Gun Section – plight of horses – take-
over from Somersets in the trenches – hauling out the corpses – death of
Trooper Boyce – Dick Deadeye – wreckage of Zillebeke – new billet in Girls'
School at Eecke – ancient Cloth Hall at Ypres destroyed – three prisoners
court-martialled – visit of HM The King and HRH The Prince of Wales.

VOLUME II: DECEMBER 4, 1914 – JANUARY 5, 1915

French 75mm field gun 'the best in Europe' – Archie Sinclair meets
Churchill – battle-cruisers lost at Coronel – future of cavalry debated –
organises new billets at Staple with the 'Ancient Mariner' – another girls'
school commandeered – 'nothing succeeds like excess' – visits Lt Col
Trotter in hospital – officer casualties – news from the Eastern Front –
three days' leave – attends Hilaire Belloc lecture – his third Christmas on
active service – receives presents from Princess Mary – aeroplane raid on
Cuxhaven – New Year's Eve 'banquet' – football against the Leicesters –
Auld Lang Syne – bathing parade in the brewery – institution of the
Military Cross – New Year greetings from Joffre.

VOLUME III: JANUARY 6 – FEBRUARY 18, 1915

Rides to Cassel, where Foch has his Headquarters – censors men's letters –
experiments by French artillery – effects of the blockade within Germany

– à Court Repington's article in *The Times* – Russian victory and huge Turkish losses at Sarakamish – resignation of Count Berchtold – shooting pheasant unpopular with French – outbreak of enteric – new French uniforms – returns to ruins of Ypres – sees carnage at first hand – wreckage of the Cathedral – criticism of the Belgian authorities – the British soldier as souvenir hunter – sleeps in nuns' dormitory – direct hit on 1st Life Guards' billet – terror in the rue des Chiens – a joke gets out of hand – Gen Kavanagh's anger at surfeit of mail.

FOREWORD

Ninety years have passed since the First World War began, amid an upsurge of confidence that it would be over within a few months – over and victorious; a confidence felt by all the warring nations. The fascination with that war has never faded: a fascination derived from our ever-growing knowledge of the scale and nature of the conflict. The diaries of Sir Morgan Crofton are an important addition to the contemporary literature of the war years, presenting many facets of an officer's experience and emotion.

Sir Morgan Crofton took part in the First Battle of Ypres, a nightmare of a battle in itself, and the prelude to more than three years of trench warfare in the Ypres Salient, the linchpin of the Western Front. His descriptions of what he saw and experienced are graphic and revealing: a powerful testimony to the endurance and perception of a professional soldier, who showed wisdom and sensitivity amid the pressures and turmoil of war. His diary entries are by turn laconic and outspoken. They give a remarkable picture of the rumours and expectations, the daily drudgery and wry humour, the burdens and terrors of trench warfare.

The diarist was well placed to record these scenes. Born in 1879, he entered the Army while Queen Victoria was still on the throne, being gazetted Second Lieutenant in the Lancashire Fusiliers in 1899. That same year he sailed to South Africa, where he was severely wounded during the campaign to relieve Ladysmith. For his war service in South Africa, he was awarded the Queen's Medal with five clasps. Returning to Britain, he transferred first to the Irish Guards in 1901 and then to the 2nd Life Guards in 1903. In 1902 he had succeeded his brother as 6th Baronet of Mohill, Ireland, a title that goes back to 1801. A Captain in the 2nd Life Guards, he retired in early 1914 and went on the Reserve of Officers. He could look forward to living on his estates in Ireland. There, and in Hampshire where he had his other home, he was a Justice of the Peace. He could not know that his military career would resume so swiftly. When the First World War broke out in August 1914 he was thirty-four years old.

Soldiering was in the Crofton blood. Sir Morgan's great-grandfather, also Sir Morgan (the 3rd Baronet), fought at the Battle of Trafalgar as a Lieutenant in the Royal Navy. The 3rd Baronet's son, Sir Hugh Crofton, fought in the Crimea, first at the Battle of the Alma and then at Inkerman, where he was severely wounded. He was awarded the Legion of Honour and the Order of the Medjidie. Almost a century later, Sir Morgan's eldest son, Major Morgan George Crofton, served with the 14th Army in Burma in the Second World War, and was twice mentioned in despatches; his youngest son, Edward Morgan Crofton, served for twenty-one years in the Coldstream Guards and his grandson, Henry Morgan Crofton, continues the family tradition as an officer in the same regiment.

The most dramatic and traumatic nine months of Sir Morgan Crofton's life are those covered by the diaries published here, from October 1914 to June 1915. His wartime service continued until the Armistice. During his service in the Ypres Salient he was twice mentioned in despatches, and was awarded both the Belgian Order of Leopold and the Croix de Guerre. From 1916 to 1918 he served as Provost Marshal in the East African Expeditionary Force, for which he was awarded the Distinguished Service Order and the French Legion of Honour. Later in 1918, he returned to the Western Front and saw active service as a Major in the Guards Machine Gun Regiment.

Crofton's six handwritten volumes of diaries have been impeccably edited by Gavin Roynon, and turned into a single volume. Harrowing in its detail, it casts much important light on one of the severest and most decisive battles of the First World War and its aftermath. His editor's note, 'Ypres Then and Now', is a fascinating survey of a small Belgian town that moved from relative obscurity to centre stage within a few months.

The power of these diaries is enhanced by Gavin Roynon's dedicated editorial work. He has included biographical notes for many of those who appear in its pages, including the colonel who was most probably the tallest man in the British Army; and he provides historical explanations that place the diary in its wider context; the context of an ever-present, all-devouring war, on several fronts, drawing in and wearing down the manhood of many nations.

Sir Martin Gilbert
Honorary Fellow
Merton College, Oxford

ACKNOWLEDGEMENTS

I am immensely grateful to Edward Crofton for entrusting me with the task of editing the first six volumes of his father's diaries which gave me three years of fascinating research. It has been a rewarding and enlightening experience. The diaries provide a first-hand record of the traumatic events at Ypres in 1914 and 1915, and show how a group of young cavalry officers faced up to a totally new and devastating form of warfare. As Sir Morgan Crofton kept himself informed about theatres of the war elsewhere, we also have his critical commentaries on such key areas as the Eastern Front, the ill-fated Dardanelles Campaign and the War at Sea.

It has been a privilege to have such a rare primary source at one's fingertips. I have tinkered as little as possible with the original, merely adding footnotes when a modicum of explanation is required, and endeavouring to avoid retrospective judgements. For the most part the text of this *tour de force* speaks for itself.

The photograph of the award of the French Croix de Guerre to the town of Ypres and the trio of photos showing the destruction of the medieval Cloth Hall are by Photo Antony of Ypres. Most of the other photographs are original and were taken by Sir Morgan Crofton. He was an expert cartographer and drew the sketch map of the position of the 2nd Life Guards in the trenches at Zillebeke. Sir Martin Gilbert kindly gave permission to reprint his maps of the First Battle of Ypres and of the Ypres Salient from his *Routledge Atlas of the First World War* and the maps of the Western Front, 1914–15 and the Eastern Front, 1914–16, from his *First World War*.

The map of 'The Fight at Klein Zillebeke' first appeared in *The Story of the Household Cavalry* by Sir George Arthur. Three maps illustrating the Neuve Chapelle offensive and the area given up as a result of 2nd Ypres are reproduced by kind permission of *The Times*. I am grateful to A.P. Watt Ltd on behalf of the Lord Tweedsmuir and Jean, Lady Tweedsmuir, for permission to print as an

Epilogue the extract from John Buchan's *The King's Grace, 1910–1935*. The 'Desolation of Ypres' illustration, inside the front cover, was first published by UPP Paris, and every effort has been made to trace the copyright owner and to attribute the 'Siege of the Empires' map, but so far without success. The aerial view of the centre of Ypres first appeared in the *Illustrated London News*.

Much of the research has been undertaken at the Imperial War Museum, and I am grateful to the team of historians in the Reading Room, who have been a model of courtesy and invariably helpful. I wish to record a special vote of thanks to Roderick Suddaby, Director of Documents, for his invaluable advice and warm encouragement. My neighbour Malcolm Brown willingly drew on his long experience for my benefit and provided informative and witty answers to my questions, however naive.

Christopher Hughes at the Household Cavalry Museum, Windsor, has been immensely patient. He has frequently dug into the archives at my request to trace the service records of individual officers and men in the 2nd Life Guards who served in the Salient. David Woodd kindly researched the polo-playing career of Captain Noel Edwards, who died from gas-poisoning. Michèle Pierron, Librarian of the Musée de l'Armée in Paris, provided exact information about the value of the French franc in 1914 and directed me to various French sources, not readily available in the UK.

I am very grateful to Dominiek Dendooven for his willing guidance during my visits to the Documentation Centre in Ypres. He is the author of *Menin Gate – Last Post*. Several other kind individuals have helped me along the way. Kerry Bateman, Secretary of the Leicestershire Yeomanry Regimental Association, provided me with a factual report on the heavy casualties suffered by the Regiment at 2nd Ypres. Anne Baker gave me an insight into the early months of the Royal Flying Corps by showing me the archives which belonged to her father, Air Chief Marshal Sir Geoffrey Salmond. Dr Peter Thwaites provided helpful information about the Royal Military Academy, Sandhurst, where he is Curator of the Archives.

My longstanding friend and mentor, Patrick Wilson, read the text and made several helpful suggestions. Major Douglas Goddard and Margaret Marshall also proof-read sections of the diaries. I am grateful for their painstaking efforts and for pointing out various errors. David Simpson and John Anderson came to the rescue when I was floored by Crofton's classical allusions. By recalling his father's experiences in the war, Sir William Gladstone threw helpful light on the shortage of interpreters in August 1914. Jean-Paul Dubois kindly settled any queries I had about France and so further cemented the Entente Cordiale.

My wife, whose father was gassed while serving in France in 1918, has given me great support in this venture and gallantly accompanied me as we tramped far and wide over the battlefields of Ypres. I am equally indebted to my daughter Tessa, who firmly persuaded me to aim high where publishers are concerned – and her advice has borne fruit.

Finally, I must record my gratitude to Janet Easterling. She never complained at my endless updating of footnotes, as fresh information came to light. Without her hard work, good humour and professional approach, this project would never have got off the ground.

Gavin Roynon,
Wargrave, August 2004

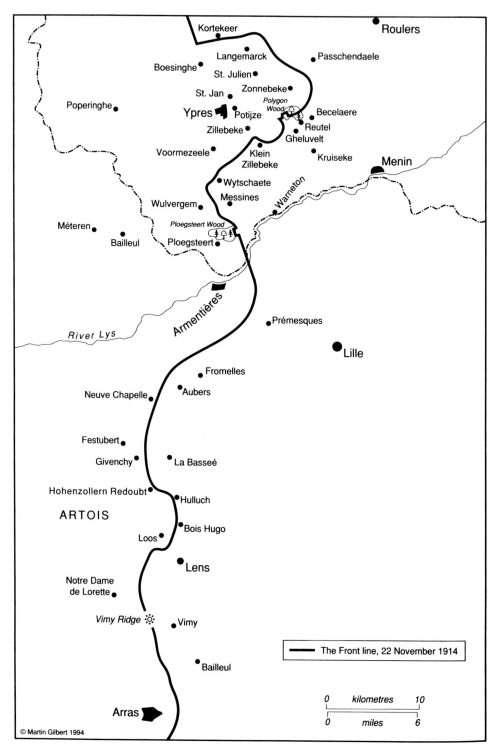

The Western Front, 1914–15. (*First World War, Martin Gilbert*)

The Eastern Front, 1914–16. (*First World War, Martin Gilbert*)

YPRES
THEN AND NOW

Editor's Note

'I should like us to acquire the whole of the ruins of Ypres . . . A more sacred place for the British race does not exist in the world.'

Winston Churchill, addressing the Imperial War Graves Commission
London, 21 January 1919

Churchill was back in the Government as Secretary of State for War in Lloyd George's peacetime Coalition. In the highly emotional atmosphere of the early months after the Armistice, there was a strong British and Canadian lobby for the centre of Ypres to be kept in ruins *en permanence*, as holy ground and a 'zone of silence'. Happily, by the end of 1919 Churchill was putting his weight firmly behind the construction of the Menin Gate by Sir Reginald Blomfield. This would be dedicated to the huge sacrifices made by the British and Commonwealth Armies, and be the finest Memorial to the Missing.

The atmosphere is still emotional. No visitor can fail to be moved by the poignancy of the ceremony at the Menin Gate. Every evening at 8 p.m. the noisy traffic is diverted, 'the busy world is hushed' and silence falls. Eyes are riveted on the thousands of names carved into the walls of soldiers killed in the defence of Ypres between 8 August 1914 and 16 August 1917, who have no known grave. They number almost 55,000. (A further 35,000 British and New Zealand servicemen, who were killed after that date, are commemorated on the Memorial at Tyne Cot.) Then the Last Post is sounded, as it has been – except from 1940 to 1944 – every day since 1 May 1929.

On 31 October 2001, the Duke of Edinburgh and Princess Astrid, daughter of King Albert of the Belgians, attended the 25,000th Last Post,

followed by a special service in St Martin's Cathedral. In 2002, the 75th
anniversary of the unveiling of the Menin Gate Memorial by Field Marshal
Lord Plumer and the foundation of St George's Memorial Church, Ypres,
were commemorated. This church, in which so many families, regiments and
schools have presented memorial plaques, has become a British military
shrine. The Friends of St George's enjoy widespread support and make an
annual pilgrimage to the war graves, memorials and battlefields of the Salient.
The Chaplain told me that, in 2003, 170,000 people made a pilgrimage to his
church – a figure of which many cathedrals might be envious. The historic
ties which bind Ypres and Britain together are as strong as ever.

Yet, long before the defining events of the twentieth century, the
medieval city of Ypres had stamped itself on the pages of history and enjoyed
strong links with England. In the Middle Ages trade was the key to the
prosperity of Ypres. For centuries, sheep-farming in medieval Flanders had
produced the wool needed in the cloth industry. High-quality Flemish cloth
was in demand, and to meet the increasing demand for woollen garments,
wool was also imported from England. Thus, the earliest visitors from these
shores were neither soldiers nor tourists, but wool merchants. Ypres
prospered. Her population rose so rapidly that by 1260 she had 40,000
inhabitants – about ten times that of contemporary Oxford.

In the same year, construction began on the Lakenhalle or Cloth Hall.
Reputedly completed in 1304, the massive, but elegant, building, where the
wool-trading took place, was a symbol of the wealth and influence of
contemporary Ypres. One of the Gothic glories of Europe, 125m long and
boasting a superb belfry 70m high, the Cloth Hall stood for more than six
centuries. It was to be totally destroyed by incendiary shells on 22 November
1914. Sir Morgan Crofton, who had arrived the previous week at the Front,
reports the catastrophe in his diary. He took some photographs of what
resembled one of El Greco's more hellish scenes and gives an eyewitness
account of the carnage.

Happily, the medieval builders and craftsmen had no premonition of the
horrors which would ultimately destroy St Martin's Cathedral as well as the
Cloth Hall. The Hundred Years' War was approaching. In 1383, English
soldiers were attacking Ypres and experienced the mud of Flanders for the
first time. The German nation did not yet exist and Richard II's foes were
the French. The besieging armies, led by the Bishop of Norwich, took the
outlying areas, but not the city.

But Ypres suffered in the long term. The Hundred Years' War caused the
import of English wool to cease and the weaving industry declined. Flemish
weavers crossed the Channel to find work in East Anglia and Ypres ceased to

be the commercial capital of Flanders. Spanish rule was established in 1555, and the province became part of the Spanish Netherlands. Sectarian religious wars were rife. Not for the last time, Ypres saw a massacre of the innocents when zealous Protestant 'reformers' slaughtered Roman Catholics – and vice versa.

Spanish control yielded to French, and Louis XIV instructed his great military engineer Vauban to build a ring of defensive walls around Ypres, with bastions for the artillery. Centuries later, the British soldier found these walls an invaluable backdrop as he sheltered behind them in his dugout. The core of Vauban's defensive works, including the Lille Gate, survived the four years of battering they received from German shells. Today, visitors should doff their hats to him as they enjoy the fine ramparts walk overlooking the canal.

Only in 1830 did Belgium become independent, and a kingdom in 1831. Aware that Belgium would make an admirable springboard for the invasion of England, the British Government negotiated the Treaty of London, which guaranteed Belgium's neutral status. Signed in 1839 by the major European powers, no treaty has cost Britain more dearly. It was to honour this famous – or infamous – 'scrap of paper' that Great Britain, under Asquith's premiership, declared war on Germany on 4 August 1914.

Before the First World War Ypres had enjoyed relative obscurity, but now it leapt into undesirable prominence. By the end of the third week of August, Brussels had fallen, the British Expeditionary Force was falling back alongside her French Allies, and German troops reached the little town of Meaux, about 20 miles from Paris. Von Moltke faltered, and, following the crucial Allied victory at the Marne, both sides sent troops rapidly northwards in an attempt to outflank each other. They clashed in Flanders, and the First Battle of Ypres, fought from 19 October to 22 November, reaped a terrible harvest of casualties. The war of movement was over.

It is during this battle that Capt Sir Morgan Crofton arrives at Ypres to join his regiment, the 2nd Life Guards. Pitchforked at once into the trenches, he jots down his experiences in standard-issue Army notebooks and provides the reader with a personal and powerful account of his experiences. From the six handwritten volumes of his 'Anglo-German War Diary', we gain a clear insight not only into the grim privations men suffered, but also the camaraderie and close friendships formed. 'Bored in billets, terrified in trenches.'

Nor does Crofton hesitate to be controversial. 'Poor little Belgium', the Christmas Truce ('this is WAR, Bloody War, not a mothers' meeting'), the state in which the French 'always' leave their trenches, the breakthrough at Neuve Chapelle that proved such a damp squib but cost 'nearly double the loss of the British contingent at Waterloo', Churchill's demotion in the Cabinet, the dire British shortage of shells – all are exposed by Crofton's pen.

But it is the decision after the Second Battle of Ypres to hold on to the Ypres Salient at all costs which most arouses the diarist's ire. Years later, in his *History of the First World War*, Liddell Hart regrets that Haig did not 'fulfil his idea of withdrawing to the straighter and stronger line along the canal through Ypres. It would have saved cost and simplified defence.'

Long before the historians had their say – and before the war is even one year old – Crofton, who is on the scene, cuts starkly to the heart of the matter:

> The Salient at Ypres is simply an inferno. It is not war, but murder pure and simple. The massacre which has been going on here since April 22 is not realised at home. From May 1–16, we were losing men at the rate of 1,000 a night. Why we don't give it up now, God alone knows. As a strategic or tactical point Ypres is worthless. . . . The town is a mere heap of rubble, cinders and rubbish. . . . We cannot conceive why the Salient is not straightened and given up. Hence why keep Ypres to impress people?

These words were written on 5 June 1915. When Crofton confided this blistering attack on the Higher Command to his diary he did not know there would be a Third Battle of Ypres (Passchendaele). Nor could he have predicted that, by the end of the war, more than 200,000 British and Imperial troops would lie dead in 170 different military cemeteries, all contained within the few muddy square miles of 'the Immortal Salient'.

'For your tomorrow, we gave our today.' When we look – through Sir Morgan Crofton's eyes as well as through our own – at the plethora of names on the Menin Gate, we are left with the sickening conviction that thousands of them need never have been there.

Gavin Roynon

AFTERNOTE

In May 2003, Edward Crofton and I visited Ypres and many of the surrounding villages where Sir Morgan Crofton had billeted the troops of the 2nd Life Guards from 1914 to 1915.

During our visit, in a moving little ceremony, Edward officially returned to the Dean, Jaak Houwen, the fine leaded fragment of the East Window and the key of the West Door of the Cathedral, which his father had saved from the rubble eighty-eight years earlier (see diary entry for 8 February 1915, p. 144).

Biographical Note on Lieutenant Colonel Sir Morgan Crofton, Bt DSO

As Sir Martin Gilbert so ably describes in his Foreword, we are a military family. Our forebears and descendants have served the forces of the Crown for over two hundred years. In addition to those of my ancestors to whom Sir Martin specifically refers, my father's father and his two brothers were also commissioned, and this military tradition has continued into the twenty-first century.

My father did not have a particularly auspicious start in life. Born the younger son of the youngest son of the previous generation, his father died when he was three years old, leaving him and his elder brother to be brought up by their mother. Times were difficult and the two boys spent their early years commuting between their maternal grandfather in Colchester Garrison, and their paternal grandmother (the widow of Colonel Hugh Crofton) at Marchwood in the New Forest. While his brother attended Eton, my father followed members of his mother's family to Rugby. His two surviving Crofton uncles had also both died early, and so when his brother died aged twenty-four he was on his own.

In 1897 he was appointed Second Lieutenant in the Militia Forces, and in 1898 he was successful as an Infantry candidate at the literary examination for entry to RMC Sandhurst.* The following year he was awarded a Commission in the Army.

From the outset of his military career he pursued a particular interest in military history, and his knowledge of the subject over ensuing years was profound. He became a notable contributor to military journals, and was an

* The Royal Military College Sandhurst at Camberley, Surrey. In 1938 the decision had been taken to amalgamate with the Royal Military Academy Woolwich. However, the advent of war in 1939 caused the decision to be shelved until 1946, when planning for the new Academy recommenced. The Royal Military Academy Sandhurst was officially opened in the following year and remains in this form to the present day.

acknowledged authority on Napoleon and the Waterloo Campaign. The publication in 1912 of his booklet on the role of the Household Cavalry Brigade at Waterloo earned him many plaudits. This was followed in the same year by an article on *The Relative Values of Certain Present Time European Agreements* which was reviewed as being remarkable for its political insight and accurate diagnosis of the European situation. He rightly underlined the dangers of a Europe in which the five great empires were polarised into two armed camps by the Triple Alliance and the Triple Entente. This insight may explain the commentaries on Central European and Near Eastern campaigns, which he includes in his diaries.

My father enjoyed a distinguished career after the Armistice. Following retirement from the Regular Army in 1919, he served in 1922 as Commandant of the Schools and Depot of the Ulster Special Constabulary. Throughout this period, he continued his military writing and developed his skills as a cartographer. He compiled the highly detailed and intricate campaign maps for *Liaison 1914*, written by his old friend Sir Edward Spears. He was High Sheriff of Hampshire, the county in which he lived, in 1925/6 and a Gold Staff Officer at the Coronation of His Majesty King George VI. For a time in the 1930s he was a 'Blue Button'* with a firm of stockbrokers in the City of London. In 1942 he was appointed Commanding Officer of the 28th (Bay) Battalion of the Hampshire Home Guard, remaining in command until the Home Guard was disbanded in December 1944. He died in 1958, ten days after his seventy-ninth birthday.

Divorce had necessitated his retirement from the Army in 1914, and so it was perhaps fortuitous that events unfolded as they did later on that year, enabling him to return to the Colours. Thus his diaries were born, and they represent a vivid and candid account of his daily experiences on the Western Front in the early months of the First World War. As with others of his generation who were fortunate enough to survive, the horrors of this conflict left an indelible impression on him. He never held back from saying what he thought and, as the reader will soon discover, political correctness was not in his make-up. I therefore believe that the genuine and heartfelt opinions which he expresses accurately portray the acute sense of frustration and despair which became so prevalent on the Western Front during those four terrible years.

Edward Crofton

---

* The term 'Blue Button' enabled the individual to obtain share prices from jobbers on the floor of the Stock Exchange. However, it did not authorise trading in shares. Holders wore a blue button to denote the practice, which ceased in 1986 with the advent of the 'Big Bang' in the City of London.

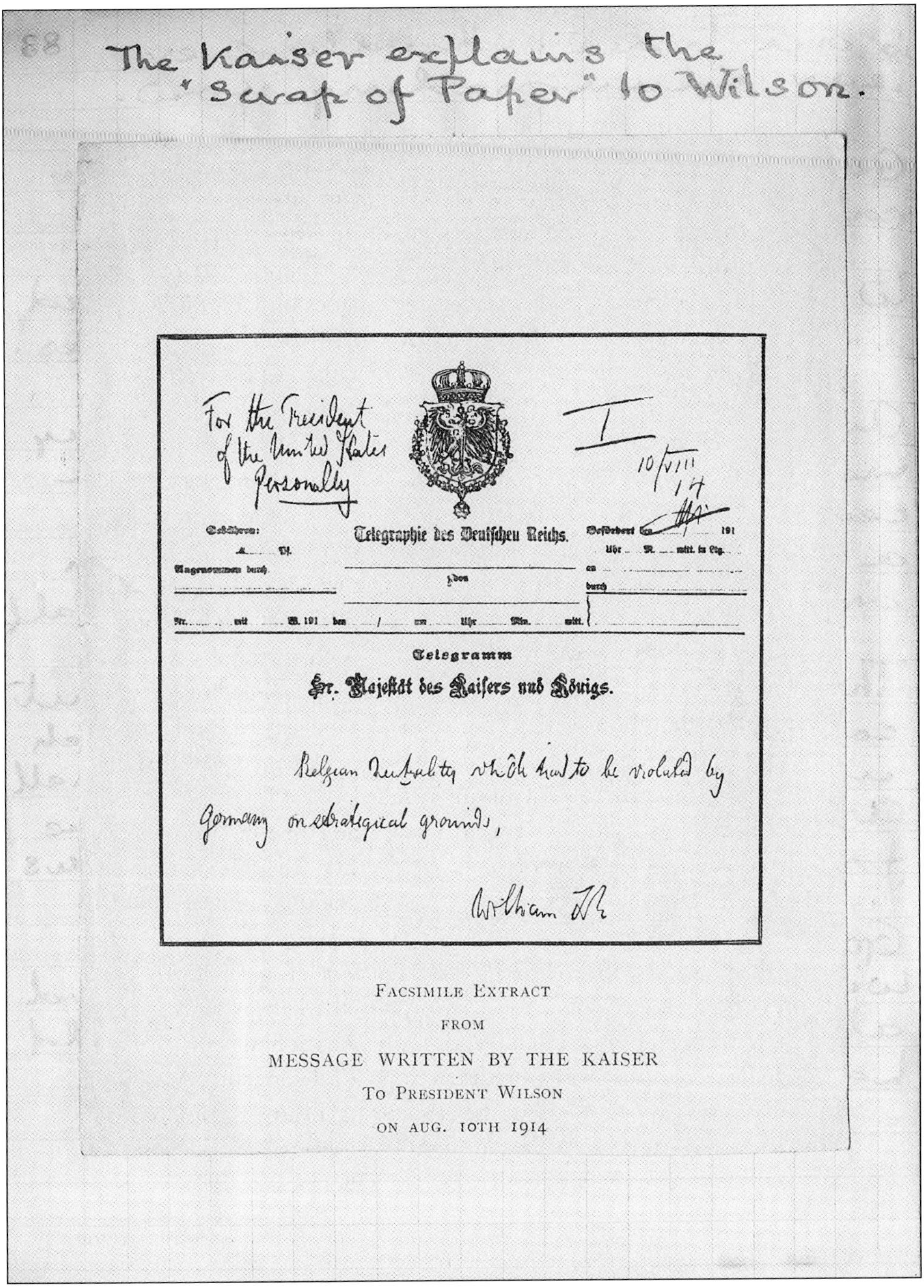

The Kaiser explains the
"Scrap of Paper" to Wilson.

For the President
of the United States
Personally

I
10/VIII
14

Telegraphie des Deutschen Reichs.

Telegramm
Sr. Majestät des Kaisers und Königs.

Belgian Neutrality which had to be violated by
Germany on stratigical grounds,

William I R

FACSIMILE EXTRACT

FROM

MESSAGE WRITTEN BY THE KAISER

TO PRESIDENT WILSON

ON AUG. 10TH 1914

The Kaiser's 'Explanation'.

VOLUME I

OCTOBER 27–DECEMBER 3, 1914

TUESDAY OCTOBER 27

Captain Sir Morgan Crofton, Bt
2nd Life Guards

Herewith a copy of telegram received from War Office. Please arrange to hand over your duties as Area Staff Officer, South Eastern Area, as soon as possible to Captain F.W. Ramsden (late Coldstream Guards) 5, Upper Brook Street, W. (Telephone Mayfair 3717).

As soon as you have handed over, please report to this office and then proceed to Windsor to join Depot 2nd Life Guards.

Horse Guards,   G.Windsor Clive
Whitehall,   Major
S.W.   General Staff, London District
27 October 1914

I returned to my flat from the Marlborough Club, where I had gone after finishing my daily round in the South Eastern area, reaching home about 6.30 pm, and then found the above communication from the London District Office enclosing a War Office wire, directing me to rejoin my Regiment at Windsor for duty.

This was because of the heavy losses in officers which the 2nd Life Guards were sustaining in the desperate attempts of the Germans to reach the sea at Calais which had resolved themselves into a series of terrific struggles round Ypres. This memo was very welcome, for it had for a long time been very irksome to be at home in a comfortable staff billet, when the Regiment was going through such strenuous times in Flanders.

The Regiment had left Ludgershall Camp on October 6th, being railed to Southampton for Ostend and Zeebrugge, where it disembarked early on

October 8th, and came under the orders of General Sir Henry Rawlinson*
commanding the newly formed IV Corps.

The Regiment in conjunction with the 1st Life Guards and the Blues**
forms the 7th Cavalry Brigade under Brigadier General Kavanagh. This
Brigade, and the 6th Brigade consisting of 10th Hussars, Royal Dragoons and
3rd Dragoon Guards, forms the 3rd Cavalry Division, and is under the
command of Major General Byng.†

I was thankful to give up the Area Staff job, although it had been useful
and very essential. I had to survey, and lay down the Defence plan for every
vulnerable point in the South Eastern Area of London. These included
power stations, gas works, bonded stoves, purifying stations, sewage works,
the Charing Cross railway bridge (a ticklish job, with trains coming from
every direction, every few minutes), and the Penge and Chislehurst Tunnels.

I had a good liaison with every police station in my area. These jobs keep
me very occupied every day of the week from 9 am to dark. The tunnels were
tricky to inspect, as were also the Vickers Works at Erith. However, this was
now finished and I could now return to my Regiment on service. I therefore
got onto Ramsden and arranged with him to hand over all maps, plans, notes
and details of all sorts connected with the South Eastern Area at 10 o'clock
the following day.

WEDNESDAY OCTOBER 28

Handed over to Ramsden as arranged, and reported (11 am) myself to GOC
London District, Sir Francis Lloyd, who was very kind and friendly, and
thanked me for my work.

Packed and left for Windsor by the 3.40 pm train from Paddington.

Reported at 5 pm to the OC 2nd Life Guards Reserve Regiment, Colonel
Oswald Ames. (The tallest man in the British Army,†† a dear man but not

---

* Rawlinson led IV Corps throughout 1915 and was then promoted to command the
newly formed Fourth Army for the Somme Offensive. A strong advocate of beginning the
Battle of the Somme with limited attacks, he was overruled by Haig. After the Armistice,
he served in Northern Russia and then became Commander-in-Chief, India in 1920. He
died in 1925.
** Royal Horse Guards.
† Later FM Viscount Byng of Vimy. He was the inspired commander of the Canadian Corps,
who captured Vimy Ridge in April 1917. His special link with the Canadians was recognised
by his appointment as Governor-General of Canada in 1921. A fine portrait by Philip de
Laszlo hangs in the National Portrait Gallery, London.
†† Probably true, as his height was 6ft 8½in! Ames had retired in 1906, but rejoined the
2nd Life Guards in August 1914.

very quick or enterprising.) Trooper Hosegood told off to me as Batman, for the time being.

THURSDAY OCTOBER 29

Went to London after lunch to buy kit and get ready for the Front. Got 2 pairs of ankle boots, a British Warm and a pack saddle trunk. Wired Fuller, my groom at Woodside, to bring up my charger and saddlery to Windsor. Returned to Windsor 6 pm.

There were a lot of strange faces amongst the officers at Windsor. Some had been there weeks, and did not seem to me to be particularly anxious to leave the comparative peace and security of the Cavalry Barracks.* Ames did not have enough 'Ginger', he was too kind and friendly to push some of these people out. I suppose this sort of thing always happens in war. All the Regular officers were abroad, either with the Regiment or on Staff Duties, and a stream of individuals arrived from all sources, of all kinds, some ex-officers retired from various Regiments. Some Planters, many Civilians from every Profession.

Most of these were quite excellent, keen, brave and most anxious to get out and do a job of fighting. Some had come hurrying home from South America, Canada, East and South Africa. The real offenders, who should have known better, were nearly all retired ex-officers who had been called up from obscurity and soft lives.

However, it wasn't my affair. It was Ames's funeral. I made it quite clear that I insisted on going out with the next reinforcements.

FRIDAY OCTOBER 30

To London again to finish my kit buying.

FRIDAY OCTOBER 31

Finished equipping myself. Was inoculated against enteric** at 9.30 pm.

---

* Renamed Combermere Barracks by the 1st Life Guards in 1900 after Lord Combermere (Colonel of 1st LG until 1865). But the 2nd Life Guards and the Blues refused to use the new name! It is still the home of the Household Cavalry in Windsor. The original barracks, completed in 1804, were built on a plot of land given by Eton College. In earlier centuries, the site housed a leper hospital.
** Enteric fever or typhoid.

Fuller and Horse arrived from Marchwood, with all kit, so I am now ready for all eventualities.

SUNDAY NOVEMBER 1

Stayed in all day and wrote letters. Inoculation began to work, felt very cheap!

MONDAY NOVEMBER 2

Got a day's leave to go to Woodside* to settle up matters there. Arranged to close the house for the 'Duration'. Returned to London at 7 pm. Reached Windsor at 8.

TUESDAY NOVEMBER 3

Went to London to try on my British Warm, make a few 11th hour purchases. Got hair cut!

WEDNESDAY NOVEMBER 4

Went to London to see my Lawyer. Had tea with my Mother at Buckingham Gate. Returned Windsor 7 pm.

It struck me in London that there was a profound air everywhere of anxiety as to the Battle for the Channel Ports.** Now approaching its climax before Ypres. I felt more and more restless at not being in it. The casualties seem very very heavy.† From what we hear the Regiment seems to be in the thick of it day and night, and we are expecting that substantial reinforcements will soon be called for.

The Composite Regiment has been disbanded, and its component parts have been drafted to the 3 Regiments in the 7th Cavalry Brigade, which will help to fill the depleted Cadres. Anyhow we shall soon hear something definite.

---

* His home at Marchwood near Southampton in the New Forest. It was destroyed by a bomb in December 1940.
** The British Expeditionary Force relied on the Channel ports of Boulogne, Calais and Dunkirk for reinforcements of men and munitions. The fall of Ypres would have left the route to the coast wide open.
† This was true. See 15 November.

About 8.30 during Dinner the Orderly Room Corporal appeared with an Order, just received, from GOC London District that 5 officers were to proceed as soon as possible to the Front, 2 to the Blues, 2 to the 1st Life Guards and 1 to the 2nd. This is my chance!! A few words with Ames clinched it.

THURSDAY NOVEMBER 5

Sent for to the Orderly Room at 8.30. Told to pack instantly and leave for the Front that evening. Ward-Price* (the brother of the *Daily Mail* Special Correspondent) and I were ordered to join the Blues. Packed and left Windsor by the 12.05 train.

Reported to Colonel Holford, 1st Life Guards, at Knightsbridge Barracks at 2.30. We arranged to leave for Southampton at 9.50 pm.

Wrote letters until 3 o'clock. Sent some wires and said goodbye all round. Went to my Mother's flat and stayed with her until 9.15 pm, when I left for Waterloo to catch the train, picking up my luggage at the Marlborough Club en route. At the station I met Mathey (an ex-diamond expert) and Goodliffe, late 17th Lancers, both of whom were joining the 1st Life Guards.** Holford came to see us off, and Lady Holford gave me some letters for her son, Stewart Menzies, the Adjutant of the 2nd Life Guards.

We reached Southampton Docks at midnight – an exciting day.

FRIDAY NOVEMBER 6

Midnight. Having arrived at Southampton Docks Station, we then had a long walk in the dark to where our ship was berthed. We received our tickets and warrants from the Transport office, and went to board the *Lydia* about 1.15 am. Berths were allotted to us. Mine was 155, but as all four were put into it we objected and succeeded in getting a larger one into which Ward-Price and I went. Slept well until 9 am.† Cabin like a monkey house.

---

* Severely wounded on 13 May 1915, 2/Lt L.S. Ward-Price was later transferred to the 2nd Life Guards. He volunteered for the Royal Flying Corps, but was killed in an aerial action over France in January 1918. His fate was discovered from a report in a German newspaper.

** Capt H.W.P. Mathey and Capt H.M.S. Goodliffe.

† Other ranks had a rougher passage. Tpr George Frend, aged nineteen, and his brother Will crossed to Le Havre on the same night in a small ship used for transporting horses. 'We dossed down in the cattle pens almost in darkness, but before we got down to it, Will and I, we saw a notice about our heads – "This Scupper may be used as a Urinal only". From a document lent by Col Nigel Frend.

Had a bad and expensive breakfast at 9.30. Beautiful fine hot day, the sea like glass. Humorous Canadians issued us tins of Bully Beef and a loaf of Bread at 1 pm to each of us as rations for 2 days! Nowhere to carry this simple food so made it up into a parcel, which on landing fell into the sea.

Reached Le Havre at 2, and after threading through Minefields came alongside the quay at 2.45.

Several very large steamers came in with us, with the 8th Infantry Division on board. Landed about 3.15, and after considerable difficulty secured a cab, and having piled in our kit and luggage drove off into the town to report our arrival.

Reached the office of the Base Commandant about 4 pm. Found a mob there of recently landed officers milling round an unfortunate staff officer of the Gordon Highlanders* who was half suffocated. Joined the mob and helped the process! His piteous appeals of 'It's getting too hot here, gentlemen, please stand back' produced little effect. Room finally cleared of all but myself.

Received orders to leave for Rouen by the 5.50 train. Went off and got lunch with Ward-Price, who got very muddled over 2 glasses of Chablis.

Greatly struck by the number of women in the streets in deep mourning.** Watched the 1st Battalion Hertfordshire Regiment march through the town en route for the Rest Camp outside. Very strong and fine Battalion – grand fellows.

At 5.15 we drove to the station after picking up Goodliffe and Mathey. Given a Chrysanthemum by a small girl in the street, and shook hands with several unknown persons in various stages of cleanliness! Put our luggage consisting of 4 valises, 4 boxes, 8 saddles and 6 various into a first class compartment, and got into the next one ourselves. We were told that we should reach Rouen in 3 hours. As a matter of fact it took 6, arriving there at midnight.

Reported our arrival to the Station Staff Officer, a seedy individual with a hacking cough. Told to go into the Town for the night, and report at the Remount Depot at 8.45 in the morning.

---

* The 2nd Gordon Highlanders had suffered severely at Zandvoorde on 30 October. Along with the 1st Grenadier Guards, 2nd Scots Guards and 2nd Border Regiment, they formed part of the 7th Division, described by Cyril Falls as 'In infantry, possibly the best division in the British Army.' See his *Life of a Regiment – The Gordon Highlanders in the First War*, 1958, p. 13.
** Belgian and French women bereaved as a result of the war wore deep black: 'widows' weeds' were a common sight in France up to and including the 1950s.

We collected our kits and stepped over several officers' valises which were spread out on the platform, in which their Batmen were soundly sleeping. We then sallied out into the town to find a Hotel, followed by half the population of the place!

SATURDAY NOVEMBER 7

12.30 am. Found Hôtel de Paris near River Quay. Hall crowded with various officers more or less all in varying stages of alcoholism. Rum looking lot! Our arrival hailed with considerable levity. The Patron, an individual of villainous aspect, introduced himself to us. We decided to stay here pending Orders. To Bed, after a supper of Beer, Omelettes and semi-raw Beef, at 2.

8.45 am. We taxi to the Remount Depot which was 3½ miles away, out near the Race Course, and report ourselves. We were told to 'Stand By' and to report every day at 8.45 and 3 until we get Orders to move.*

Decide to live in Camp so as to be near Orders. Return to the Hôtel de Paris at 12 to collect kit. Lunch at a Restaurant near the Cathedral, and return to Camp at 3.30. No tents, but are allowed to use the Mess Marquee to sleep in. Return to dine in Rouen at the Hôtel de la Poste, where we got a bath. Back to our Marquee and bed at 11.30.

SUNDAY NOVEMBER 8

Damp, cold and misty day. Got tent and put it up. Ward-Price and I in one, Goodliffe and Mathey in the other. Also got servants. Ward from 17th Lancers as Batman, Young, 2nd Life Guards, as Groom.

No orders. Told that they may be expected any day.

Lunched and dined at Hôtel de la Poste, where I bumped into a certain MacCaw, 3rd Hussars, with whom I had once been on a course at Aldershot. He was now acting as DAAG,** and as such was responsible for the posting of Officers as they joined the Depot. I explained quite definitely that I did not want to go to the RHG but to my own Regiment, 2nd Life Guards. He said that he would see what he could do. So I pushed in at once for Transfer.

---

* . . . and until they could collect their horses. The role of the Remount Depot was to supply mounted units with horses, ideally after they had been trained in the UK. But nothing could have prepared either horses or men for the chaos which ensued two days later. See 9 November.

** Deputy Assistant Adjutant General. Capt G.H. MacCaw was also a qualified first-class interpreter.

After dinner, sort out kit and repack valise, etc. for the Front. Return to tent, very damp, to bed at 11.

MONDAY NOVEMBER 9

The battle for Ypres had been raging since 19 October. It was vital to get the horses to the troops in Flanders as soon as possible. Many horses were frantic after the sea crossing and liable to lash out. Here Crofton skates fairly lightly over the 'strenuous efforts' needed to choose and equip his horses.

Trooper George Frend was at the same Remount Depot outside Rouen and witnessed the pandemonium. 'Thousands of horses had recently arrived from Canada, Australia and the Argentine. There was no kit to groom them with; there were no bridles to put on them, but they had to be taken to water two miles away twice a day; each man riding one and leading two with nothing but head collars and ropes. Horses and men went spare all over the country and to my knowledge, at least two men were killed.'

Getting the horses to the right station and on to the right train was the next hazard. Crofton's horses get lost en route, but despite being hauled over the coals by a choleric general, he keeps his cool . . .

Awakened at 6.30 by an excited Orderly who ordered us all to pack at once, collect Horses and Saddlery, and get to the Station. Scene of great confusion followed. Got packed and succeeded in choosing hurriedly from line of 500 Horses, 2 Chargers and a Pack Horse. The Saddles fitted badly, and we couldn't get Bridles on. However, after strenuous efforts we succeeded in getting ready around 10.30.

Start off for Train. Baggage waggon late, so leave Servant to pack on it and follow at once. Groom rides 2nd Charger and loads Pack Horse. All now start off riding to the Station. Great difficulty in finding Station as there are four in Rouen, and we are not told which one to go to.

On the way we pass a Brigadier General with a purple face, whom I recognise as Tyndale-Biscoe,* late (very late) of the 11th Hussars,**

---

* Fondly remembered as the CO of the 11th Hussars before the war, who insisted that 'all ranks should be skilled oarsmen'. He personally drilled all ranks in these skills. After a long and colourful military career, Maj Gen J.D. Tyndale-Biscoe died in 1960 at the age of ninety-three.

** From 1911, the 11th Hussars had the surprising distinction of having Crown Prince Wilhelm of Prussia as their Colonel-in-Chief. His appointment was hastily terminated in 1914. See Peter Upton, *The Cherrypickers*, BAS Printers, 1997.

who bellows from the window of his Car 'Advise you hurry up. You are very late!'

Finally we reach the right station at 12 o'clock. Several Trains waiting and Details of 12 Cavalry Regiments are entraining.

Am put in charge of Train, and handed a bundle of documents, and then asked to sign a Form that I have received 250 Horses. But remembering that I shall probably have to pay for them in the future I politely decline. No one seems to mind. Neither our Servants, Baggage nor Spare Horses arrive. Find afterwards that they went to the wrong station, also that my 2nd Charger went through a Shop Window!

Everybody fusses, and the choleric General demands in a voice of thunder when we shall be ready! I tell him I think about the New Year. He says 'Things very badly arranged'. I agree! He says that we must wait behind as he can't keep the Train. At 12.45 the Train goes off, leaving us four and our Servants who now begin to arrive.

After long search finally collect all Horses, kits, etc. and proceed back to Hôtel de Paris, but return the Horses and Servants back to Camp, where we eventually proceed to report. Told to continue to report at 8.45 and 3. Lunch and dine at Hôtel de la Poste. No further Orders. Change Charger which went through shop window for nice Bay.

I saw a poor man badly kicked at the Remount Depot, and superintended his removal to Hospital. Make final arrangements and draw more Blankets for Horses. All ready now to start, so return to Rouen. Town full of Infantry as British Base at St Nazaire now moved to Rouen. No news from the Front. Am greatly struck by the *total* absence of any Birds, even of the commonest species.

TUESDAY NOVEMBER 10

Went to camp at 8.45. I am told that we are under Orders and may go at any moment. I realise what a Fire Engine Horse must feel like when standing ready for eventual call, which sometimes comes, and sometimes doesn't! Return to Rouen 11.30, do some shopping, and all lunch at the Café de la Cathédrale. More shopping in afternoon. Return to Camp at 3.30. No Orders! Dine at Hôtel de la Poste.

See the Adjutant of the Remount Depot there who tells me that my transfer to the 2nd LG from RHG has been sanctioned. He seems most affable, and says that only one officer need report at the Depot in future. He also tells me that his Wife is sick at the Hotel and that he is looking after her. I deeply sympathise with him. He then says that in future no one need come up to the Depot to report, but that he will telephone us any Orders which may come in. *Civilitas Civilitatum omnia Civilitas!**

Just heard news of the destruction of the Emden.**

WEDNESDAY NOVEMBER 11

No Orders up to 11.30. Send Mathey and Goodliffe up to Camp to see our Horses, and warn our Servants to be ready. At 12 o'clock we went round the Town† to see the places of interest. The Cathedral is beautiful, but very finicky, the tall spire, 500 feet high of wrought iron, was added to the building in 1842. The Glass in the Windows is old and very good, and the Organ is magnificent. The Interior of the Building itself is not unlike Salisbury. The Doors are poor. The Best Church was Saint Maclou, the carving and stone work being very fine, but the Interior decoration is rather tawdry. There is however a beautiful Louis XV wood carving over the Altar.

All the Churches and the Cathedral here date from the 14th–15th Centuries. We next taxied to see where Jeanne d'Arc was burnt. This spot is now occupied by the Halles which are not unlike the Covent Garden Market on a very small scale.

There is a simple stone let into the pavement which says

Jeanne d'Arc
30 Mai 1431

and on the wall above a tablet which says

Here stood the Stake at which Jeanne d'Arc was burnt

It adds the information that her ashes were thrown into the Seine.†† This being the case, we did not search for her Tomb which we had otherwise

---

* *Civilitas* (Courtesy) was a quality expected of a Roman citizen. This Latin oddity seems to be a parody of Ecclesiastes 1:2 'Vanity of Vanities, all is Vanity' for which the Vulgate gives *Vanitas Vanitatum Omnia Vanitas*. I am indebted to my former colleague, David Simpson, for this insight.

** The fast German light cruiser *Emden* had been dispatched to wreak havoc with British shipping in the Indian Ocean. She sank fifteen unarmed merchant vessels, a Russian cruiser and a French destroyer. Her exploits ended when she was sunk by an Australian light cruiser, the *Sydney*, off the Cocos Islands, on 9 November.

† Rouen.

†† Joan of Arc had been condemned to death for witchcraft and heresy, following her inspired leadership of the French in the Hundred Years' War. In 1920 she was canonised by Pope Benedict XV.

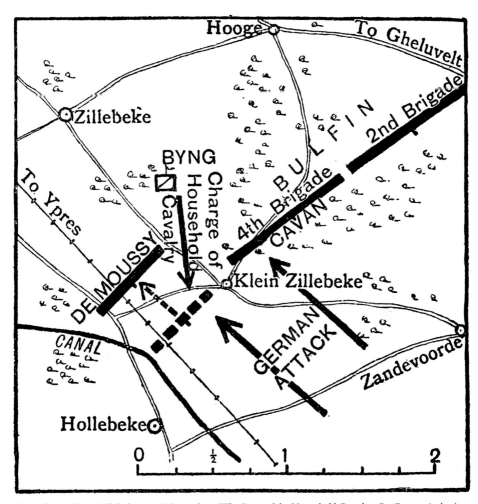

The Fight at Klein Zillebeke on 6 November. (*The Story of the Household Cavalry, Sir George Arthur*)

decided to do. Returned to Hotel and lunched at 1.30 at the Restaurant de la Cathédrale.

At 3.30 went up to the Camp and found Goodliffe's Servant in the Guard Tent drunk. Got him another Groom. Blofeld and Townsend turned up at the Hotel en route to join the Composite Regiment,* which had just been broken up and its Members returned to the three Regiments in the 7th Cavalry Brigade.

---

* At the outbreak of war, each Regiment of Household Cavalry provided one squadron to form the Composite Regiment, which embarked for France in August 1914. The 'Composites' were envied by those left behind, since the Campaign was going to be 'sharp and short', said the pundits. But Kitchener disagreed and predicted the war would last at least three years. John Pollock, *Kitchener*, p. 375.

Saw the account in the *Daily Mail* of Dawnay's and Arthur O'Neill's deaths.* They were killed in the counter attack at Zillebeke on Nov 6th when the Regiment was brought up to fill a gap in the line. We had several Casualties that day. Dawnay had only just returned from the staff to take command as we had had so many losses. A very fine soldier and a delightful man. Arthur O'Neill returned to the Regiment on the outbreak of War from being a Member of Parliament.**

At 6.30 we were told that we should probably go up to the front by the 9.15 Train tomorrow. Dined at the Hôtel de la Poste. Very wet returning to our Hotel.

I fear that I shall find many of my friends missing from the Regiment when I get to it. It has had a very gruelling month's fighting, and the situation at Ypres is still very shaky. However, we shall soon see now.

THURSDAY NOVEMBER 12

Called at 6.30. Immediately got on to the Telephone to find out when we were to start. Hear that Parade is at 11.30 for the Train, so imagine we shall get off about 1.30 pm. A beautiful bright sunny morning. What a pleasant change it makes. 9.30 went out to shop. Had my Razors ground, bought some Tinder, etc.

Saw a Motor Car (4 seater) standing outside a house in the rue d'Elboeuf which was riddled by Shrapnel. Spoke to Chauffeur, who said that the car belonged to the Headquarters of 7th Division, and was now employed in the Supply Service, and that, while standing outside the Staff Office at Ypres, a shell had pitched 20 yards off, and hit the car in 40 or 50 places. The aluminium body was pierced and the mudguards and door handles also knocked to pieces, but no one was hurt.

At 12.30 went to the Station to see if I could get any information respecting our departure. After interviewing several officials, who indicated several different departure points, we at last discovered the right platform, and found that the Train would leave Rouen about 2. Great confusion, as on the former occasion, seemed to exist as to which Station the Train left from.

---

* Maj the Hon. Hugh Dawnay was a close friend of Winston Churchill, with whom he had served at Omdurman. He took command of the 2nd Life Guards on 26 October, but he only commanded the Regiment for twelve days.
** Capt the Hon. Arthur O'Neill had been Unionist MP for Mid-Antrim from 1910. He was the first MP to be killed in action in the war.

Opinions were equally divided as to whether the Station was on the Left or the Right Bank of the River Seine.

As usual the Servants went to the wrong Station with the Horses, but they were fortunately met and stopped. I waited at the station and Goodliffe and Mathey returned to the Hotel for our Baggage. Was very pleased to leave the Hôtel de Paris, a dirtier or more squalid hotel I have never been in. After considerable trouble and loss of temper, the Horses were finally boxed and the luggage piled in an empty Third Class Compartment.

At 2.45 the Train left. As it got dark about 5 we decided to have Tea, and we made an excellent meal off Bully Beef, Bread and Butter, Foie gras, Jam, etc., washed down with Chablis. As the Carriage was only lighted by an old obsolete Oil lamp, from now onwards we were in a condition of semi-darkness.

At 7.30 we stopped at a place called Abancourt, 'Not in the Cromwell Road', as my Servant explained, and here we got out our Rugs and Sleeping Bags.

About 8.30 pm we had a Supper very similar to our Tea, and then we settled down to spend a very uncomfortable night. Must have fallen asleep about 10.30, and slept fairly decently except for a few breaks when we stopped at stations during the night.

FRIDAY NOVEMBER 13

Woke about 7.30 and found ourselves at Calais, where however we did not stop, the Train going slowly on to St Omer, which we reached about 8.30. Here we were told the Train would stay 10 minutes. Rushed round the Station and bought a Paper full of news 2 days old, and tried unsuccessfully to get some Coffee. The Train stayed much longer than we thought it would, and so we got a bucket of hot water and washed on the line! We also got some hot water from the Engine Driver and made a can of quite decent Tea.

We left St Omer about 9.15, the Train moving very slowly, stopping every mile or so. The country round reminded us very much of England, and on all sides the Peasants can be seen cultivating their fields apparently oblivious to a War going on. There seemed to be more Birds in this Area, as we saw the first ones today that we had seen since we arrived in the country.

Train continually stops, and at each stop Men climb out on the Line. There is plenty of evidence from the empty Bully Beef Tins all along the Line, that many Troop Trains have passed along here. Our Train is a heavy one with 2 Engines and 42 Carriages and Trucks. From time to time we see small groups of Belgian Soldiers. As we approach Hazebrouck,[*] which is one of the Railheads, the Trains stop more frequently and ahead of us we see 6 Trains and 5 are behind us. An Armoured Train carrying a 4 Inch Gun passed us going to Calais, with 2 of its Trucks showing bad shell marks.

We did not reach the Station at Hazebrouck until 1.15 when all Trains ahead of us had been dealt with. There is a quantity of Belgian rolling stock here. Several Trains of French Troops passed us going towards Calais. These made frantic efforts to cheer and shouted *Vivent les Anglais* and *Vive L'Angleterre* very heartily. My Sergeant appeared with some very welcome slices of hot Bacon, cooked in a Mess Tin in his Carriage on some hot cinders which he had borrowed from a French engine. Still very wet and cold.

We found a Staff Officer at Hazebrouck who told us that our Railhead was at Steenbecque, a station 6 miles off to the South. He thought we should get there in an hour, but he doubted it. He said that we should detrain there, and find our Regiments. We asked him how things were going. He said all right, but he believed that the French had lost some ground yesterday, and were now trying to capture Messines. He said that Ypres was being badly shelled, and a lot of wounded had gone through in the morning, who were cheerful and sitting up.

At 2 o'clock we left Hazebrouck and reached Steenbecque at 2.30. Here we were ordered by the Station Staff Officer, Denny, 19th Hussars, to leave our kits at the Station, and the Train was sent on 4 miles to detrain the Horses. I sent my Servant on to bring mine back, and got out myself, with my kit. Got Orders to proceed tomorrow to the Château 1 mile SW of Ypres to report to the GOC 3rd Cavalry Division. In the meantime we were to billet for the night at Morbecque about 1 mile away. With great difficulty in heavy rain we collected all our kits into an empty Motor Lorry and set off for the village. This we reached about 3.30 and at once set about getting a billet.

The village was crammed with Motor Transport. I counted over 200 Lorries there, the Drivers being mostly London Bus Drivers. About 4 pm we found a house with two large empty rooms into which we put a quantity of straw with our Valises on top. We were all four in one room. Wandered round the Village and found a Café at which we each drank 4 glasses of

---

[*] This French town, near the Belgian border, provided a vital rail link between the Channel ports and the Ypres Salient.

excellent coffee and felt better. Four Motor drivers in a corner of the room were playing some Card Game with the air of four old gentlemen in a London Club.

Servants arrive with our Horses at 6.30. Pouring wet. Have to picket out the unfortunate animals in the Rain. Men wet through. My Servant turns out to be an excellent Cook. Arrange for dinner at 7.30 and return to our house to have a Bath, Shave, etc. We all Bathed in the Bedroom of the Uncle of the Landlady. Feel much cleaner. We collected some food and prepared to have a Banquet. Discover some excellent slices of bacon in my Servant's kit, also Bread, Jam, Bully Beef and some Tabloids of Turtle Soup from my Valise.

Dinner a great success. Turtle Soup like a Guildhall Banquet. Excellent Coffee. Room full of Motor Drivers who seem most amusing characters. Returned at 9.30 to Bed. Put a lot of Straw under my Valise and made it like a 'Heal's'* Bed. Slept like a Log.

SATURDAY NOVEMBER 14

Awakened early by the continual hoarse crowing of a Cock, found that outside our window was a large and smelly Farmyard. All washed in Uncle's Bedroom and dried on his sheets! Had an excellent Breakfast at 8 am of Tea and Bacon which we had scrounged from a Sergeant of the Supply Column. A beautiful fine crisp morning. Out in the main street a column of 65 large Motor Lorries, full of Supplies for the various Divisions, was loading up. The Village is a funny straggling one on one long street. Many Houses have quaint old Sundials as their fronts.

We *meant* to start at 9, but, as usual, the Horses were late and we did not finally get off until 9.30. As the Others were still fussing about I rode off alone, with my Groom bringing on my two other Horses. Set out for Hazebrouck, which was about 4 miles off. The Roads are all paved with Granite or stone setts in the centre, which makes it very good going for Motor traffic, but bad for hacking. The vehicles must keep to the centre of the road, and that makes it a terrible nuisance for people riding, as the sides which are unpaved become mere bogs in places. These paved roads are the saving grace of this Campaign, without them it would be impossible to run these lengthy Supply Columns at all.

---

* Founded in 1820, Heal's in Tottenham Court Road produced the finest-quality handmade beds in the land.

About 2 miles out I passed an empty column of 65 Motor Buses[*] returning to the Railhead to refill. They have all been painted a grey colour, and many have facetious inscriptions chalked on them such as 'Grove Park to Berlin' etc. Every one had a Name and it was curious that with the exception of one which was called 'John Bull' all the rest had Ladies' names. Possibly the 'Girl Friend' of the Driver. I counted 10 Gladys and 7 Lotties and nearly every English name was well represented.

Hazebrouck was full of Waggon and Motor Parks. I took the Road to Bailleul which was about 9 miles off and left Hazebrouck about 11. The Bailleul road runs through cultivation very like that of English fields.

About 2 miles out of Bailleul I began to hear the first sounds of considerable cannonading. To the right and left the sullen roar continued almost continually. Reached Bailleul at 12.30 and found the Headquarters there of the 5th Infantry Division.[**] The Central Square was crammed with Transport, and everywhere the Engineers were putting up Air Lines.[†] I stopped at the Hôtel du Falcon for lunch and to water and feed the Horses. Tried to buy a pair of Woollen Gloves but couldn't find any in the Town. Had some very hot Coffee at the Pub, and dried my leather gloves as best I could. Set out again at 2 for Dickebusch, which was about 6 miles off.

The Cannonade got louder and louder. When about three miles past the Town, a German shell pitched into a Farm house about 30 yards off. Horse didn't care about it much, nor did Groom! I thought I had better push rapidly on. The Sun came out, and all the Clouds cleared away, and away to the Right, very high in a bright blue sky I saw a plane slowly sailing up and down, being followed, always behind and much lower, by little tufts of Cotton Wool which were the bursting of German Shrapnel[††] trying to bring it down.

---

[*] One of these has been retrieved and may be seen on display in the Imperial War Museum, London. Thirty vehicles were allocated to each brigade. One soldier noted that the bus taking him to Ypres was the same one, with the same driver who had taken him to work each morning before the war! David Lomas, *First Ypres*, p. 37.
[**] The British Expeditionary Force (BEF) had gone to war in August with one cavalry division and four infantry divisions, the 1st, 2nd, 3rd and 5th. By contrast, France had seventy-two divisions. The total ration strength of the BEF was approximately 110,000. E.L. Spears, *Liaison 1914*, p. 474.
[†] They were rigging up telephone wires.
[††] Named after Henry Shrapnel, a British officer who invented this air-bomb shell during the Napoleonic Wars. The shell contained lead balls about the size of a fingernail. The term was also used for fragments of the shell casing – lethal debris which scattered while the shell was in flight.

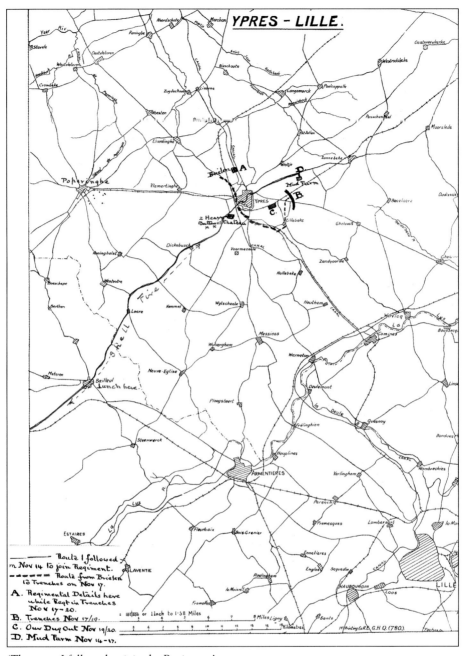

Route I followed
m Nov 14 to join Regiment.
Route from Brielen
to Trenches on Nov 17.
A. Regimental Details here
   while Regt in Trenches
   Nov 17-20.
B. Trenches Nov 17/19.
C. Our Dug Out Nov 19/20.
D. Mud Farm Nov 14-17.

'The route I followed to join the Regiment.'

Passing a Convoy of six waggons on the way to Dickebusch, trotting hard to get out of the shelling zone, I reached the village about 3.30, and found it packed with French Infantry. On going through the street half a dozen or so shells flew over and pitched beyond the villages to my left. No one seemed to bother at all. In the field where the shells pitched a man was lungeing a young horse,* and he continued to do so. Children were playing in the street, and women were sitting at the Doors knitting. More shells came over, so I trotted on to reach the Château near Ypres, where the Headquarters of the 3rd Cavalry Division were located.

Near the Road leading to the Château were 2 French Heavy Batteries, which fired at regular intervals, apparently taking their ranging and observation from the small aeroplane which still continued to sail up and down slowly along the sky. The Guns were about 4 Inch, and each one was most cunningly concealed with branches of Trees. Their Wheels had flat plates fixed on the rims to enable them to go over rough ground. The Horses at first did not like the continuous firing, but finally they got used to it! I found the Château about 4, where also I discovered two of our party who had come a different way.

The Château was a typical French one, still with its hanging Chandeliers and Pictures, but most of the furniture had been cleared out. The Conservatory housed the office with its Orderlies and Clerks. We had Tea in what was the Drawing Room, where we got our Instructions as to how to rejoin our Regiments. Our orders were given to us by Colonel Davey, late 18th Hussars. The rest of our party arrived during Tea. While we were all talking Dosie Brinton,** late of my Regiment, came in. He had some small job on the Divisional staff. I rather think Camp Commandant. I also saw in the distance our ex Vet, Barry.

Outside the Château we found our Servants and kits which had been dumped there by the Convoy Lorry. We had great difficulty in finding another, finally we persuaded a Belgian one, into which it was all packed with the Servants, and started off for Popjke where we believed that our Regiments were to be found. Left the Château at 5.15 in pitch darkness, with full Instructions as to where to find our Billets, which lay 2 miles beyond Ypres. The road to Ypres was full of French Troops, and very difficult to move on. We carefully rode ahead in single file, the Leader carrying an electric Torch.

We reached Ypres finally after many halts, and filed through its dark and deserted streets. The Town had been well shelled for some little time, and

---

* This was exercising the horse with a long rope (a lunge), while training it to canter in a circle.
** Lt Col John Brinton had been severely wounded at Khartoum in 1898. He then served on the Staff of Sir John French in South Africa and again with him in Flanders. He was author of *This Realm, This England*, writing under the nom de plume of Don Dosio. Garrison Library Printing Office, Gibraltar, *c.* 1955.

from the fitful flashes of our Torch we could see gaunt walls and debris, the result of this shelling. There was something very eerie in our procession along the pavé streets, which re-echoed to our horses feet. Not a soul appeared. It was indeed a City of the Dead. Not a light, no sign of any living existence. Finally we arrived in the Square in which were some troops of French Cavalry, and the light of our Torch shone on their Cuirasses.*

There were several English Ambulances in this Square, and the NCO in charge said that they were waiting there to take away German Wounded. On the East side of the Square was a large Building in which a few lights flickered. It was a hospital of sorts, and we heard that there were many Germans lying in it dying of gangrene, since there was no one to look after them. Guns were going off on all sides, and from time to time the French fired Star Shells which lit up the night very brightly for a minute or so.

We left Ypres by the Menin Gate,** and embarked on the long road leading to the Trenches. As we emerged from the Gate and Ramparts away to our left we saw a village in flames which lit up our road. A mile outside Ypres we ran into a tremendous Traffic block, caused mostly by vehicles from the Front trying to pass those going forward. We passed Mouse Tomkinson, Royal Dragoons, and Howard, 16th Lancers,† directing the traffic to the best of their ability with Torches in their hands, and without their efforts we would never have got through. Further on two upset waggons further increased the block.

Firing was heavy on both sides of us and from time to time a shell sailed over the road, and burst with a resounding explosion in an adjacent field.

After many delays and much unpleasant riding on the edges of the road, where every few yards was a deep hole full of water, since the metal crown of the road was one stupendous procession of lorries and guns and waggons, we finally reached the lane which led to the Farms where our Regiments were billeted.

At the first farm we found the Headquarters of the 1st Life Guards and the 7th Cavalry Brigade Staff. Newry, 1st LG and Potter and Meade, late 10th

---

* Armoured breastplates and backplates, which French Cavalrymen wore with panache over their uniforms. According to Sir Edward Spears, 'The cuirassier regiments, magnificent to look at in their armour, seemed accoutred to take on the bowmen of Agincourt'. *Liaison 1914*, p. 97.
** Now an imposing memorial, recording the names of 54,896 officers and men with no known grave. They are remembered every evening at 8 p.m., when the buglers of the Ypres Fire Brigade sound the Last Post. See 'Ypres Then and Now', Editor's Note.
† Maj H.A.R. Tomkinson and Col Cecil Howard. The latter was ADC to King George V from 1933 to 1934 and later Colonel of his Regiment, the 16/5 Lancers, from 1943 until his death in 1950.

Hussars, Staff Captain and ADC to Kavanagh the Brigadier.* The Farm was knee deep in mud. The mud is awful. I remembered Napoleon's saying *J'ai trouvé en Pologne un cinquième élément. C'est la Boue.*** How that would apply to Belgium too! Newry very pleased to see us and lent us an NCO to direct us to the 2nd LG farm. We left Goodliffe and Mathey with the 1st Life Guards, while the rest of us struggled over two fields to our Billets. We reached the Farm containing the Regiment at 9 pm. It is a small farm house of 3 Rooms, 2 of which are filled with Men, Kits and Cooking arrangements.

The third room is the combined Messing and Sleeping room for the Officers. Am delighted to find Dinner going on. Find there Stewart Menzies[†] the Adjutant, Hidden the Quartermaster, Jack Speed,[††] and Walker the Vet. I introduce Townsend and Blofeld.[‡] All the rest of the Regiment were in the Trenches.

Bed down in the Loft after dinner with about 14 others. Our kit turned up just as we got to bed. Very cold night. Incessant shelling, especially from 2 British batteries of heavy guns which are in a field near us. Shells occasionally hum over us. We are apparently shelled from both sides, as Ypres lies in the apex of a triangle which forms the German line thus:

Very tired. Get to sleep about 10. Shelling continues all night. Wake at intervals to hear shells hum over. Everyone in loft snores!

SUNDAY NOVEMBER 15

Woke at 6.30. Very cold, snowing outside. Breakfast at 7. Feel much better! Orders came which were cancelled afterwards to say that our Brigade was to be relieved and to go back some miles to refit and rest. Snow turned to driving sleet about 10.30. Bitterly cold wind cuts like a knife. The heavy

---

* On the outbreak of war, Brig Gen Sir Charles Kavanagh had been appointed to command the 7th Cavalry Brigade. Promoted Major General in 1915, he later commanded the reconstituted Cavalry Corps in the tank offensive on the Somme.
** 'In Poland, I found a fifth element. Mud.'
† Later Head of the Secret Intelligence Service in the Second World War. Sir Stewart Menzies supervised the Government Code and Cipher School at Bletchley Park. Its crucial achievement was the breaking of the German 'Enigma' code.
†† At the outbreak of the Second World War, Lt Col Jack Speed was CO of the Household Cavalry Composite Regiment (still unmotorised in 1939). See Humphrey Wyndham, *The Household Cavalry at War*, p. 10.
‡ Crofton became a close friend of these two officers, with whom he travelled out to the Front. He was immensely saddened when both 2/Lt F.D'A. Blofeld and 2/Lt S.G. Townsend were killed in action at Frezenberg Ridge. See 13 and 15 May 1915.

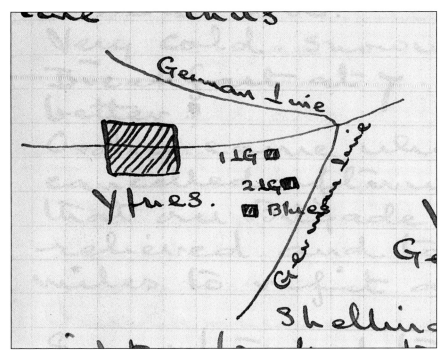

Triangle formed by the British Forces holding the Ypres Salient. The line which passes through Ypres represents the Menin Road.

Guns fire incessantly, working over the ground in squares on a Map. Whole house rocks with it. So far no German shells have come over today. Orders came in about 11.30 to say that our move to the rear had been postponed for the day owing to lack of Billets further back, and that the Regiment was to stay in the Trenches for another night. Lunch at 1. Good Bully Beef Stew, cooked with Curry powder, and Coffee.

Hear all about the last fortnight's fighting. The Second (LG) took it heavily. Dawnay, O'Neill and Peterson* killed. Vandeleur, Hoare, Anstruther, Graham** and Todd missing.† Smith-Cuninghame and Sandys wounded in addition to ones who were with me at Windsor viz Lyons,

* 2/Lt W.S. Peterson was killed at Klein Zillebeke on 6 November. His grave is in the Churchyard. See 20 November.
** 2/Lt M.W. Graham survived to win distinction in the Second World War as Maj Gen Sir Miles Graham. He was FM Viscount Montgomery's Chief Administrative Officer from 1942 to 1946, and died in 1976 at the age of eighty.
† Capt A.M. Vandeleur, Capt J.F. Todd and Lt J.A. St C. Anstruther were all killed at Zandvoorde on 30 October. See 15 December.

Fenwick-Palmer,* Wallace, Victor Montgomerie and Ferguson, the CO wounded. Pemberton and Robin Duff** killed. Sam Ashton, Murray-Smith and Palmer† missing. Bethell and Archie Carlton home with sprains and Bronchitis. So of the Composite Squadron Officers who left for the Front on Aug 14, only Jack Speed, Archie Sinclair and Frank Penn are left out here, and of the Regiment which left Ludgershall on October 4, Stewart Menzies, the Adjutant, and his brother Keith alone are left.

I saw today a Communiqué from Sir Douglas Haig, Commanding 1st Army Corps. He stated that the German attack which was defeated and driven back on Nov 11th was composed of 15 Battalions of the German Guard Corps, which had been specially brought up to smash through to Ypres and capture the Channel Ports. To assist these Battalions the 23rd and 27th Reserve Corps†† and the 13th Active Corps were added. This attack was badly defeated.

Went out about 3 o'clock to have a look at the country round the Farm, which now has been dignified by the name of 'Mud Farm'. I must say it lives up to its name, a more filthy place I have never seen! Our Guns going like mad. The Horses stand about all over the place looking miserable. They have had no hay for a month and they gnaw everything that they can get hold of. There is not a Tree which has not had its bark gnawed off as high as a horse can reach, and a Waggon stands just outside our door which is half eaten by them, one side entirely and half the other. Cartloads of Bricks from destroyed Houses are being shot into the large holes by the side of the pavéed part of the road. The Roads all round are being mended by parties of the Belgian Household Cavalry, still in their crimson trousers and sky blue stable jackets. I fear that they are better at this sort of thing than fighting.

---

* Though wounded, Lt R. Fenwick-Palmer survived to rejoin the colours in the Second World War, when he commanded both the 8th and 31st Battalions of the Royal Welch Fusiliers.
** Capt E.P.C. Pemberton was killed on 19 October at Hooglede. Lt Sir Robin Duff, one of the earliest casualties at 1st Ypres, was killed at Westrobeeke on 16 October.
† Both Capt Sam Aston and Lt Kenneth Palmer had been taken prisoner on 19 October. Lt Murray-Smith 'was left in a trench near Warneton on 20 October in the hands of the Saxons who are known to be gentlemen. He was taken to hospital in Lille, but died a few days later, when about to be moved to a private house.' From the diary of Surgeon Maj R.M. Cowie, 1st Life Guards.
†† Said to contain the flower of German youth, many of these fresh reserve troops were volunteers from the educated middle classes, imbued with patriotic fervour. Hence the expression *Kindermord* (Massacre of the Innocents), the origin of which goes back to King Herod. See 16 December.

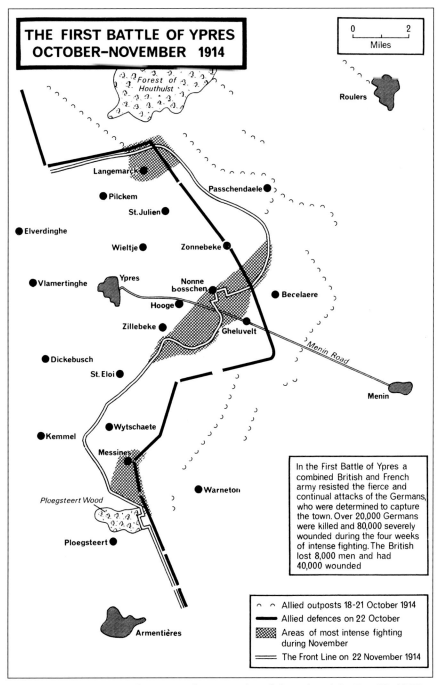

First Battle of Ypres, October–November 1914. (*Routledge Atlas of the First World War*, *Martin Gilbert*)

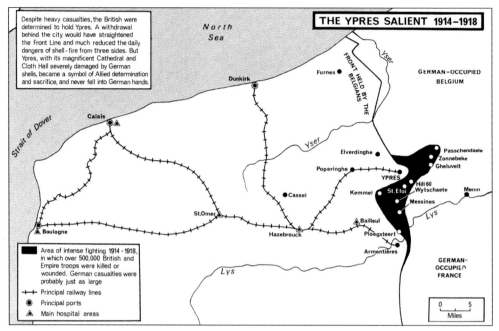

The Ypres Salient, 1914–18. (*Routledge Atlas of the First World War, Martin Gilbert*)

Heard news today of Lord Roberts'* death. He was on a visit to the C in C at St Omer, and got a cold which turned to pneumonia. A Gallant old Man, who died as he would have wished to – at the Front!

A Woman and a small Girl of about 4 years old, apparently live somewhere in this dilapidated Farm, but I don't know where. Three Sheep and two Pigs also live there, at the foot of the ladder leading to the Loft. I think the Woman and child live there too!

No Orders to move, so settle down for the night. The Regiment returned from the Trenches about 9 o'clock. A great meeting with Archie Sinclair, the Nib and the Pill.** The present CO is a chap named Torrie,† who has

---

* Earl Roberts of Kandahar, Pretoria and Waterford. He died aged eighty-two. After the Boer War he lived at Englemere, Ascot. In this large mansion, built with funds provided by a grateful nation, the Field Marshal set up a South African War defensive *laager*, complete with weaponry. The most unexpected gift he received was presented by a maharajah from his India days, who appeared at his house one day with two elephants. Information given in a letter from Maj Douglas Goddard to the editor.

** Capt F. Penn and Surgeon Capt E. Luxmoore, RAMC.

† Lt-Col T.G.J. Torrie, formerly 2nd Madras Lancers, had taken over command of the 2nd Life Guards on 7 November from Hugh Dawnay, who had been killed the previous day. Clearly Torrie made a very favourable impression on his fellow officers. He was moved to Gen Rawlinson's HQ, Fourth Army, on 13 June 1916, but was killed later during the Somme Offensive.

latterly come to us from an Indian Cavalry Regiment. He seems a nice fellow, and friendly. We have a variety of people now transferred or attached from other Regiments. Our heavy casualties made such gaps, and it is better to fill up with people who have had experience of this warfare, rather than from the Depot at Windsor. Heavy shell fire most of the night. 10 Horses killed, but nothing hit our Farm.

MONDAY NOVEMBER 16

Ready to move off at 7 but no Orders. Watched Germans shelling 4 Inch Battery about a mile from here. Three 'Jack Johnsons'* dropped near a windmill to our Left, and one or two in front. We watched these tall black greasy mushrooms rising into the sky for some time, sometimes accompanied by a pinkish mist of pulverised bricks whenever a house was hit. Fine and warmer, with occasional showers. No further Orders.

Torrie asked me today to act as Second in Command, and take over the Machine Gun Section as well, as the other Machine Gunners were Casualties and there was no one else trained for this work.

Could not help feeling terribly sorry for the wretched existence that our Horses were living.** On mobilisation we had 400 or so requisitioned horses sent to us, which had come from every kind of home. Many were 100 Guinea Hunters and Coach Horses belonging to people like Vanderbilt and other rich men, and these animals had lived in well warmed stables, with masses of good food and straw for their bedding. For weeks now they were always in the open, tied up all day and night to trees and hedges, and owing to every man being required in the Trenches, only a few could be spared to look after 20 or 30 each.

The dependence of the BEF on huge numbers of horses is often overlooked. This did not just apply to the cavalry regiments. Each infantry division required 6,000 to 7,000 horses and mules to bring up the wagons bearing crucial loads of food and

---

* Type of German shell, which burst emitting black smoke. It was named after the champion boxer who was the first black winner of the World Heavyweight title, in 1908.
** In his essay 'The Last Hurrah – Cavalry on the Western Front, August–September 1914' Richard Holmes quotes Pte Nobby Clarke of the Bays who remembered: 'We were often hungry and so were the mules and horses – and how those poor creatures suffered. . . . Innocent victims of man-made madness. They broke your heart, especially when you passed the injured ones, left to die, in agony and screaming with pain and terror.' (*Clarke Papers, Liddle Collection*).

munitions. Within twelve days of the outbreak of war, 165,000 horses of mixed pedigree were requisitioned. But this was not nearly enough to solve the horse supply question. Hundreds of thousands of horses were imported to the UK, principally from Canada and the USA.

In his monumental History of the British Cavalry, *vol. 8, the Marquess of Anglesey writes: 'Without the horse, not even the infantry, let alone the artillery – a six-horse team was necessary for drawing every 18-pounder – the engineers, the medical services and above all the vast supply organisations could have operated at all.'*

The contrast between the use of horse power and mechanised transport in the First World War is stark. The British Army boasted only 643 motor vehicles in August 1914, of which 116 were motorcycles and none were motor-ambulances. Even by the end of the war, the replacement of animal traction by motorised transport was on a limited scale. Crofton goes on to show his deep distress at the suffering of the horses in his Regiment.

There were no Horse rugs because of the transport and they were out in all weathers, with hardly any oats, since that too took up too much Transport which was required for more vital stuff. These wretched horses existed on anything they could get at to eat. Hardly any grooming and often standing for days up to their hocks in mud. Their coats were starving and the splendid condition which they were all in when they came to Belgium had now completely gone, and as long as we had to use every man we could get to man the Trenches, this sort of thing had to go on. But it was very saddening.

To bed at 9 in our Odoriferous Loft!

TUESDAY NOVEMBER 17

Woke 6.30. Very cold. Went out to watch the Germans trying to find our 4 Inch Guns with 'Jack Johnsons'. At 11 o'clock Orders were received to saddle up and prepare to make off at once. Shells falling all over the Billeting area. Germans apparently found out our existence. Very good to move. At 12 we marched off towards Ypres by the Menin Road, and on reaching the Town turn off by a road to the West, bypassing the Town itself, to avoid the shelling. It begins to rain heavily.

We take the road to Brielen, a village about 2 miles to the NW of Ypres. We reach there at 2 pm. En route we pass the Leicester Yeomanry and I see Noel Newton, who had been in the Second about 3 years ago. We also pass K Battery RHA first by the Canal then on the Brielen road. Called by the

Troops 'Tattenham Corner'. Here I see Geoffrey White[*] and Reggie Maitland, a neighbour of mine in the New Forest. They were both standing in a doorway having elevenses! We were all very cold and wet when we arrived at Brielen, and the Horses were picketed out in a field. Here we got the orders to spend 48 hours in the Trenches. We fall in at 3.30 to march back to the Trenches. Fearful traffic blocks on road from baggage columns and the led horses of the 18th Hussars.

We reach Ypres about 4.15 when it is getting quite dark. Arriving at the West entrance of Ypres we turn sharp right and march along the Railway line, the Horses stumbling over the sleepers, and sticking the rails with their feet. Ypres Station is an absolute wreck from shelling, as the Germans continually shell it to try and catch our Armoured Train, which annoys them very much. The whole of the permanent way is ploughed up, with frequent shell holes in which you could bury a Motor Bus. Whole lengths of lines and sleepers have been torn up by explosions and flung onto the surrounding fields. Most of the holes are full of water so progress is very slow and dangerous. Towards 5 pm we are clear of Ypres and it is now nearly pitch dark.

We now dismount to continue the march on foot, and hand over the Horses to one of our No. 3s[**] who will return to Brielen under Prescott's command. I remove my spurs and prepare for a muddy wet filthy walk. It is now dark as pitch and we stumble along a lane until we reach a partially destroyed village called Zillebeke. Not a light nor a living soul appears. Silhouettes of ruined houses mark our dismal journey through the rain and mist.

On entering the village we suddenly come under Machine Gunfire and a stream of bullets whiz over us. We rush to the battered wall to take cover for a short time while it lasts, and we proceed crouching along the ruins until it ceases. These shots came apparently from the direction of our Support line, at which the Germans are firing like mad. We stumble on, my Machine Gunners alongside me carrying the Guns and tripods on their shoulders, with others behind with the Belts and Ammunition Boxes. A terrific musketry fire is going on all round, and every now and then the big Guns join in, so the noise is considerable. After about 10 minutes it dies away as suddenly as it began. When the musketry has more or less ceased we move on.

---

[*] Maj Geoffrey White commanded K Battery, attached to 7th Cavalry Brigade. He was promoted Major General in 1918 and was Colonel Commandant of the Royal Artillery 1934–40.

[**] These were the horse-holders, a nucleus of grooms and farriers, who took over the horses while Crofton and his fellow Life Guards were on duty in the trenches. See 17 December.

We climb a Bank and over into a muddy field, down a slope we go, the mud over our ankles, over a small muddy stream, then up a slope, at the top of which 200 yards away is our Line of Trenches which we are to occupy just below the crest. By now the night has become fine and frosty and it is about 6 pm. There has been a considerable fight during the afternoon and we have to wait at the sloppy muddy mouth of the entrance to the Trench while the Casualties are being removed.

The North Somerset Yeomanry and the 3rd Dragoon Guards had held the Trenches into which we were to go, against several ineffective German attacks. The North Somersets seem very rattled, they had lost several killed and 33 wounded.* They came down their Communication Trench in threes and fours when they were relieved, and doubling themselves up, so as to make as small a target of themselves as possible, they were off down the muddy slope like scalded cats. They had had quite enough of it. I didn't see any 3rd Dragoon Guards. I think they came out of the next Communication Trench to the Right. After a long wait, half frozen in the mud, we filed down the narrow trench which led to our front line.

A group of 10 dead Somersets were laid in a line next to the Ration Dump which was going to be issued to us. We stumbled down the Trench making slow progress, as it was very narrow and half way up was blocked by a dead man, over whom we slipped and fell in the darkness. At the end of about 50 yards of Trench we came to our Front line of Trenches which stretched away to the Left and Right of the Communications Trench up which we had come. A man lay across the front Trench very badly wounded, I think in the Lungs, for he moaned a lot, and as he breathed he hissed like a punctured tyre. He was removed after a great deal of difficulty and delay, for the Trenches were very narrow and made of sandy soil thrown up both sides, and about 5 feet deep.

As our Men filed away to the Right they found it blocked by 2 dead men, who had been left behind by the Somersets. They finally were removed with great difficulty and exertion, as again the Trench was only about a yard wide, and a line of Men filing along didn't leave much room. It was horrible, for the Corpses were dragged and pushed along like sacks of Potatoes, anyhow, to get them clear of the Trench, the oncoming Men

* But before being relieved the North Somersets had repulsed the Prussian Guard, who had got within 20 yards, but were driven back three times. They were congratulated by Sir John French on their fine work in the trenches which had cost heavy casualties. See *A Short Report on the North Somerset Yeomanry during the European War*, by A.S. Flower, Bath.

cursing and falling over them. By 8.30 we had fully occupied the Trench, and removed the Casualties.

I fixed up my Machine Guns on niches on the parapet which was the best I could do, and I had no idea of what the ground in front was like. The German trenches were about 50–100 yards off. The night was bitterly cold, but very clear, and the stars shone like electric lamps. We settled down for a most uncomfortable night, huddling together in heaps, and eating cold Bully Beef and Chocolate. About 20 yards out beyond our Trenches we heard wounded Germans, the result of ineffective attacks in the afternoon, calling out in a plaintive and mournful manner. They were like Banshees.* Then one by one the cries ceased presumably as the men died. We slept for intervals of half an hour or so during the night. Every now and again I had a walk along to see that the sentries were on the look out.

Towards 11 o'clock, the French who occupied the Trenches on our Right started a terrific rifle fire, for they seemed terribly jumpy. After a time, as usual, the big guns joined in, and the place was like an inferno. We stood to Arms, but did not join in the silly racket. A few German shots came over, but not many. After 10 minutes it died away as suddenly as it had started and silence came down again on us. The French are awful at wasting ammunition. How lucky it is that they have not got a Magazine Rifle, pumping out lead, which they would use like the garden hose – as they would fire away a week's supply in a few minutes.

About 11.30 a French Chasseur Alpin** clambered into our right trenches and crawled towards us saying that his Friend had been killed, and if we would lend him a man to help him carry him out, he would bury him outside below the back parapet of our Trench. We of course did so, as usually the French bury their casualties in the Trench, so that the next Regiment occupying that part of the Trench generally dig them up when they are improving their cover, or cleaning up the filthy mess which the French always leave their trenches in.

WEDNESDAY NOVEMBER 18

Bitter!! Slept in snatches of a few minutes each until 4.30, when we stood to our Arms. No signs of a German attack. At 5 it got much lighter, enough

---

* A Banshee is a phenomenon more familiar to Irish and Scottish households. It is a spirit whose wail portends death in a house.
** The Chasseurs Alpins were an infantry corps trained to fight in the mountains – but there was no Alpine campaign until Italy entered the war.

anyhow to see a bit of where we were and the general layout in front of us: a beautiful fine frosty morning, very clear, we were all covered with a thick white frost rime. Our caps were white plates with a small circle of Khaki about the size of half a crown in the centre where the tops of heads touched the inside of the cap top and the warmth melted off the white frost.

We looked out over the front line through a peephole and could see about 40 German bodies lying about in front of our section of the Trench. Some were hanging on the barbed wire entanglements where they had been shot down. The nearest were about 20 yards in front of my Machine Gun post. Some lay like heaps of old clothes, others were on their knees with their heads resting on the ground on their foreheads, as if they were trying to stand on their heads. A Sapper Officer in my section of the Trench who had witnessed the attack yesterday afternoon said that it was very halfhearted and that they ran forward as if expecting to be killed. Many of them didn't seem to know what to do if they had been successful. Some of them had reached a small wire fence of one strand of barbed wire, which had hurriedly been put up the day before, and were all killed.

The morning was extremely cold, and word had passed down the Trench that an issue of Rum was going to be served out. About 6.30 Trooper Boyce,[*] an extremely good and reliable youth who had been in my C Squadron at Windsor, came along with 2 jars of Rum, carrying one in his hand, and one on his Shoulder. As he passed us I took the jar from his hand, to serve it out to my Machine Gun detachments and others who were posted near me. Boyce was a very lighthearted individual, with a supreme contempt for the Germans.

A few yards outside our Section was the partial ruin of an Estaminet,[**] of which some of the walls remained, which were enough to support the timbers of the roof, with a few tiles still on it. In these Rafters there lurked a Sniper, who could get a short view of a break in the Trenches parapet, so that anyone passing could be seen for about 5 seconds while he passed the four foot opening. This Sniper had been annoying us since Daybreak by firing at anyone who showed over the Trench, or in the parapet gap. He was given the name of 'Dick Deadeye' by us in the Trench. He fired with deadly accuracy from a top window whenever he got a chance.

We warned Boyce of this man, when he went on to the other end of the Trench with the Rum Jar on his shoulder, to bob down higher up the Trench as it was very exposed. He however didn't think it worthwhile to do so, and he hadn't passed us 20 Seconds when we heard a 'phut' followed by a thud,

[*] Tpr Herbert George Boyce, of Beeston Hill, Nottingham.
[**] A small café.

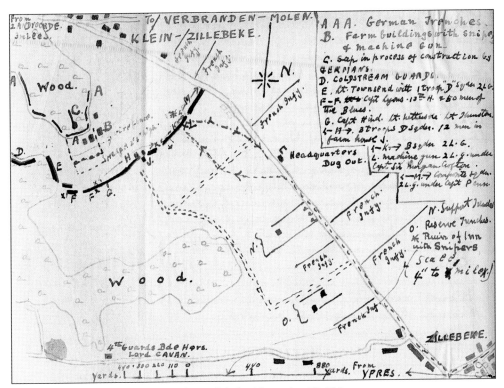

'Our position in the trenches near Klein Zillebeke, November 17–19.'

and a white face looked round the corner of our dugout, and said 'They've got him, Boyce is hit'. We crawled up to him. He was making terrible noises, but we found that nothing could be done. He had been shot clean through the chest, and he died in about five minutes. The Rum jar however was rescued and passed on. Boyce's Body lay where he fell all day until nightfall, when it was pulled out and buried outside near the North Somersets of last night.

At 7 o'clock we made a Breakfast of Rum and Bully Beef. The day got warmer later on and was very clear and bright. About 10 o'clock the first shells fell over our Trench. These increased in number very shortly until about 10.30 when a perfect inferno was raging over the whole of our line of the Trench. They were chiefly of the Black Maria* and Lyddite Types. It was all very shaky. We lay prone on the bottom of the Trench, but from time to time looked out from the peephole to see if there were any signs of a German attack. The shells pitched very close in front, the Germans obviously had

---

* Nickname for the explosion of the German shell, from the smoke it emitted.

the correct range, and tore in the Parapet, thus causing the sandy sides of the Trench to silt in. We were half stunned, choked with sand and half-buried in the debris. The explosions deafened us.

About 11 I saw 3 Black Marias and 1 Lyddite burst in a line a yard apart, about 10 yards from me. I was hit in the eye by a piece of mud and nearly smothered by bits of turf, stones, mud and sand. The force of the explosion went through my ears like a knife, making me perfectly deaf. Wounded men with panicstricken faces now began to drag themselves painfully along the crowded and narrow way. Some were hit in the head, some in the stomach, and one or two in the leg, all by splinters.

With a terrific crash several shells seemed to fall in Archie Sinclair's section of the Trench which was on our right front. I thought that they must all be wiped out, and as a matter of fact 11 out of 20 were wounded. The noise was frightful and to make matters worse a German Machine Gun played up and down all over our Trench which effectively stopped anyone showing himself.

About 11.30 Keith Menzies crawled past and said, 'Archie Sinclair's Trench is blown in, and they have nearly all been knocked out, but Archie is all right'. I then crawled down the Trench towards the Communication Trench, the mouth of which I found filled with wounded. Penn was lying there half insensible from the effects of a high explosive shell. He was semi-conscious for half an hour. The plight of the Wounded was bad. We had no Doctor, and we could do very little for them. About 12.30, to our great relief the shelling died down, as our big Guns got onto the German Batteries, and until Dark, about 5, only an occasional shell came over.

We were all rather shaken, and did not at all look forward to a repetition on the following day. A note was sent towards the evening to Kavanagh, the Brigadier, saying that we had had a pretty good dusting and many casualties, and that it would be difficult to stand another such day, and asking that we could be relieved by the Regiment in Reserve.

About 7 when all thoughts of being relieved had gone, the Blues suddenly appeared and said that they were relieving us. The welcome news spread very rapidly down the Trenches and was received with the greatest enthusiasm. However, in my case it was somewhat damped by the further intelligence that I and the Machine Guns were to remain for another night with the Blues, as they had no Guns and no Machine Gun Officer.[*]

---

[*] So they had to 'share'. Clearly, machine guns were already in short supply. Only in May 1915, when Lloyd George became Minister of Munitions and began to galvanise production on the Home Front, did the situation begin to improve.

By 7.30 the relief had been carried out, and the same difficulty occurred in getting Trooper Boyce's body, and that of Corporal Dean, who had been killed by the same sniper about 6, being hit in the centre of the forehead as he looked out over the parapet of the front line Trench. Their bodies were buried at last on the reverse slope of the field just outside the entrance to the Communication Trench. The Blues then filed in and took over and occupied our places, but the crowding was greater than with us, as their numbers were larger. At 9 o'clock some Sappers arrived and proceeded to rebuild with sandbags the Trenches on our Right, which had been so damaged during the morning's shelling. Their work was completed by Midnight. I also succeeded in persuading the Sapper Officer in charge to spend some time in similarly improving my Gun Emplacements.

My feelings on seeing my Regiment march off were akin to those of a man on a sinking ship who sees the last boat row away! Very cold night. Had the usual snatches of 5 minutes sleep. A very pleasant day, I don't think!

THURSDAY NOVEMBER 19

Same old breakfast (Rum and Bully Beef) at about 6.30. The day was very dull and cold and about 3 o'clock it began to snow.

My Gun emplacements were much better, but the falling in of most of the adjacent trench walls made them wider and offered less protection to the Gun Team. Desultory shelling started about 8.30 up to 9.30, when it greatly increased, and I feared that we were in for another dose like yesterday.

Several bursts quite close which covered us all with mud and sand. The German Machine Guns were playing all over the parapets and the Snipers were very busy.

The shelling seemed to get less about 11 o'clock. The Blues Squadron Leaders set about improving their parapets and dugouts by ordering all their men to dig like mad. At first they called for 'Volunteers', but the response did not square with their desires, so all hands were ordered to the pick and shovel.

George Meyrick, a 7th Hussar who was attached to the Blues as his Regiment was in India,* was in command of their Squadron on my left. He lives in the New Forest and I used to often see him out hunting. His Father being the large Landowner at Hinton Admiral.

---

* Posted to Bangalore in 1911, the 7th Hussars were fated for most of the war to 'kick their heels in semi-idleness, while Europe was rent by the bloodiest war in history'. See J.M. Brereton, *The 7th Queen's Own Hussars*, p. 151.

The French and English Batteries, were hard at it in counter battery work and they seemed to have obtained superiority of fire towards midday as we weren't bothered a quarter as much as we had been yesterday. Our shell fire was terrific and must have done considerable damage. It was good to hear our shells scream over our Trenches and going the other way!

The German Snipers however bothered us again a good deal. 'Dick Deadeye' was at it again. About 1 pm they hit one Blue through the left eye, and out of the back of his head. He was led past me bleeding very much. The cold was beastly and my feet were like ice. The bottom of the Trench was very wet, so I had no chance to keep my Boots dry. They were soaking and I hadn't had them off for over 48 hours. I walked along and had a long talk with George Meyrick. He told me that he thought the two subalterns which he had were 'Bats' and not much good to him. As we were talking a shell knocked in the side of the trench and nearly buried us. The Snow came down more and more and by 4 o'clock the country was under a thick white cover.

About 4.15 the Sniper from the ruined emplacement hit another Blue bang through the forehead. The Body was dragged past me with great difficulty as it was very heavy. Dead Household Cavalrymen are not easy to get out of a narrow trench. His friend covered his head with a macintosh sheet, but as he was being pulled along it fell off, and I have never seen such a look of surprised horror as the poor dead man's face had as he passed me. While talking to Meyrick I stood up, and had just moved when phut a bullet went into the sandbag behind my head. The Sniper nearly had me.

Several Humorists in The Blues entertained themselves in putting their Caps on the end of their Rifles and holding them up in the Air, where they were at once hit by the watchful Sniper. This at first caused some hilarity but it became very unpopular, since the bullet after piercing the Cap often went ricocheting down some other trench some distance off, causing some dismay amongst those who were not taking part in the game. So eventually an order was passed down 'that this practice will cease forthwith'!

Earlier in the morning several individuals conceived a plan to thoroughly annoy the Germans. In places their trenches were only 20 yards or so from ours and we could in the clear frosty atmosphere hear them talking and singing. About Breakfast time we could see rising above their Trenches thin columns of smoke every few yards which showed where they were cooking their food. 4 or 5 men then opened up with rapid fire which made the bullets strike the parapets of the German trenches just where the smoke was rising.

This threw mud and sand over the fire burning below, and over the cooking pot or frying pan and so their contents received a very liberal contribution of filth and slime, to the utmost annoyance of those who were waiting for their cooked breakfast. A volume of curses and oaths used then to arise into the still air, which we could very plainly hear, which showed us the success of our 'fun'. And we used to cheer and yell back which gave us great content.

As the Sniper's toll was getting heavy, we managed to contact a British supporting Battery who finally located the Building very accurately, and then sent a stream of shells into the wretched Building, completing its destruction and saying 'Finis' to the Sniper. Bricks, rafters, tiles flew into the air and Dick Deadeye discontinued his hobby.

From 5 onwards we sat waiting for the relief. It seemed as if it would never get dark. It had been arranged that the French were to take over our Section of the Line, but about 5.30 we heard that Foch had objected and refused to take over our Trenches, as he did not consider that he had sufficient reinforcements to do so. The French always require four men to do what one of ours does.

However, at 6 o'clock we heard that we were being relieved by the 1st Life Guards from the Support Line. At 7 o'clock they began to arrive, and as soon as I had handed over my emplacements and given the incoming Officer all the information and tips which I possessed including a warning of Dick Deadeye, I dismantled my Guns, and with my Gun Teams was away down the Communication Trench, and out over the snowy slopes like greased lightning.

The night seemed very light and the dark columns of the relieving Troops stood out very clearly on the snow. The Germans could easily see us, and there were a lot of bullets flying over us, but harmlessly. The cold and the mud made the going very difficult, and the shell holes were now nearly full of water. We kept slipping into them. So instead of continuing down the slope and across the little stream, I struck out left handed so as to join the Road at once near the Brigade dugout. The CO Torrie met us on the road, and I was delighted to see him. He said that he had never seen a group of men move as fast as we had!

Near Zillebeke we rejoined the rest of the Regiment, and orders were received to spend the night in some dugouts which had been cut in the bank of a deep railway cutting, at a point about 1 mile out of Ypres. The roads were very wet, and a frost was just starting. We reached our dugouts on the railway line about 8.30. They were rather ingeniously cut out of the sloping side of the cutting, and covered over with corrugated iron and doors taken from ruined houses. On the floor was about a foot of rather dirty straw, but that did not disturb us after the Trenches. We bedded down for the night about 9 o'clock after a scratch meal.

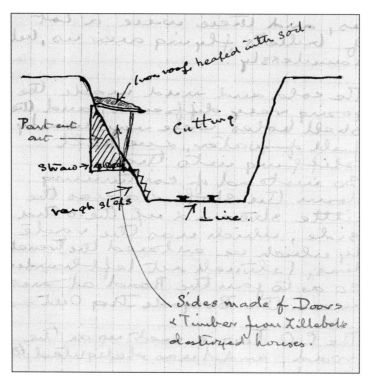

Iron roof heated with sod

Part cut out —

Cutting

Straw →

rough slats

↑Line.

Sides made of Doors & Timber from Zillebeke destroyed houses.

'Our dugout in the railway cutting, near Zillebeke.'

On the whole the dugouts were very comfortable. They consisted of 6 sheds, made chiefly out of salvaged material from Zillebeke. Luxmoore (the Pill),[*] Stewart Menzies, the Adjutant, Torrie and I huddled together under Pill's mackintosh.

Torrie's Servant made a fire on the line outside and made us some coffee, which we well laced with Rum. This improved our snack, which chiefly consisted of Potted Meat on Biscuits.

Slept at intervals, as usual, during the night, which was infernally noisy, since the Germans shelled Ypres tremendously all through the night, and several shells dropped near us.

The Brigade Staff was in the next dugout to us on our right and C Squadron of the Regiment on our Left. The other two Squadrons were away about half a mile to our Right down the Line. The Germans seem now to be setting about the destruction of Ypres systematically. Perhaps they now

[*] After serving in India with the 17th Lancers, 'Pill' Luxmoore became Medical Officer for the 2nd Life Guards in 1911. He was awarded the Military Cross in 1917 'for many gallant actions'. Brig Speed, in his fine tribute (*Household Brigade Magazine*, Autumn 1955), writes 'He knew every man, woman and child in the Regiment and was trusted and adored by them all'.

recognise that, with the defeat of their heavy attacks on November 11th when the Guards suffered crushing casualties, all their chances of occupying Ypres and reaching the Channel Ports have vanished, for the time being at any rate, into thin air. So they are now pulverising what they are unable to enjoy or make use of.

What a lot has happened since I left Windsor a fortnight ago today!

FRIDAY NOVEMBER 20

Woke at Daybreak. Bitterly cold. Felt like nothing on earth! About 6.30 we had Breakfast of Rum, Coffee and Bacon cooked outside on the railway line. A very hard frost outside, everything like Iron, but pleasant change from the everlasting mud! The day turned into a brilliant one with a cloudless blue sky.

After Breakfast felt much better and I went out with the Pill to have a look at the effect of the German shelling. We decided to walk back to Zillebeke* which was about a mile off to see what the damage there was like in the daylight. We got there about 10, and found a fearful state of wreckage. Every house had been hit, whole fronts were torn away. The steeple had been knocked off the Church which was filled with Bricks and rubbish. The Altar had been hit and was covered with rubble under which the Altar cloth could be seen torn and stained. All the Candelabra, Pictures, Statues, etc. were lying on the floor, broken and torn off the walls. In one corner a cupboard had been broken open, and the gold embroidered vestments were lying about on the floor covered with Bricks and Mortar. All the windows were broken but the Organ was untouched.

Outside in the Churchyard,** marked by rough wooden crosses were the newly made graves of Lord Bernard Gordon-Lennox, Lord Congleton and Symes-Thompson, all of the Grenadier Guards,† also Lt Peterson of my Regiment, and about 20 others all of whom had been killed in the attack of Nov 6th when Dawnay and O'Neill were also killed.

---

* Beeks (bekes) or becks are streams. Most in this area flow north-east to the River Lys. 'Beke' is a common suffix for local place names in Flanders, i.e. Zillebeke, Zonnebeke, Hollebeke, etc.
** Nowadays, this churchyard (beautifully renovated) is referred to by battlefield guides as the Aristocrats' Cemetery.
† The 2nd Battalion of the Grenadier Guards had dug themselves in on the Zonnebeke–Langemarck road on 20 October. Eight of their fourteen officers were killed. See Sir Frederick Ponsonby, The Grenadier Guards in the Great War, p. 171.

The Aristocrats' Cemetery at Zillebeke church today. (*Author's Collection*)

Every house had its windows broken and in some cases the whole façade had fallen down and lay in a heap below, making the house rather like a Childs Doll's House with all its floors showing, and all their contents. Books, Bedding, furniture and clothes lay all over the street.

I believe that the French had looted many of the damaged houses. I counted 15 shell holes in the Street each large enough to bury a good-sized cart. I felt so glad that it wasn't an English village.

All the time that we were in the village, wounded were coming in from the front line Trenches, amongst them 20 of the 1st Life Guards, who had relieved us last night. As a few shells were now beginning to fall in the village, we decided to walk back to dugouts on the Line.

About 2 o'clock Kavanagh, our Brigadier, walked up and told Torrie that the whole British Army was going back to refit and that the 2nd LG were to return to Brielen, which we had left on Tuesday afternoon. Tomorrow we were to march back 16 miles, to an area where we were to be billeted and would refit.

While waiting to get our Order to fall in, I sat on a small iron bridge spanning the Cutting in which was our dugout, and watched the Germans punch shell after shell into a Farm about a mile away which was situated on the road we followed when we went up to the Trenches. It was a pretty depressing act to watch. The fall of the shell was followed by a bright flash and then a tall column of black smoke mushroomed upwards and a pinkish mist rose from the pulverised bricks. This went on at intervals of about five minutes, each shell seeming to fall exactly in the Farm buildings. The Germans seemed to have the range to an inch.

At 5 o'clock we fell in and started our march back to Brielen. The roads were packed with French Artillery and Transport moving up to the Line. We bypassed Ypres by the same route that we used on Tuesday last, as some Crashers were falling from time to time in Ypres, and much of the Town was on Fire.

Reached Billets at Brielen about 7 o'clock. Had dinner in a Billet with Archie Sinclair and the Pill and was much relieved to remove my Boots which I had had on since 6.30 last Tuesday morning.

Had a gorgeous sleep in my Valise.* Was told by Torrie to act as Billeting Officer tomorrow.

SATURDAY NOVEMBER 21

Reported at 7 am at Brigade Headquarters, and joined the Billeting party of 1st Life Guards and Blues. It was a clear frosty morning and the road was very hard and slippery. The Sun was like a red Ball. Had to walk most of the way owing to the awful state of the roads.

Arrived at Caestre at 12, but could find no big Farms. Roads blocked with 150 French Berliet motor Transport waggons.

I decide to billet all the Regiment in Eecke for the night, as I hadn't time now to get over the area before dark, as the roads were so slippery. Returned to Caestre at 3.30 to await the Regiment. It arrived at 4.30 and I led it up to Eecke, where we succeeded in getting all the men under cover, but the Horses had to be tied up again in the fields. Got a bed in the house of the local Brewer. I fixed on an Establishment called *Au Grand Saint Georges* as our Mess room. Had a very cheery dinner and slept like a top.

SUNDAY NOVEMBER 22

Got up very late and had Breakfast at 9. Fried eggs and Bacon. Wot ho! Spent the morning finding new billets for the Machine Gun detachment.

---

* Large waterproof case for an officer's bedding and spare clothing.

Billeting lines at Eecke, where C Squadron was based until 14 December.

Found three good Farms, and decided to move into these. Farmer very angry at first, but got more amiable later. The Natives are beginning to get fed up with putting up Troops. Have had too many billeted on them.

Went round the village, a nice little place with a funny old church like three houses side by side. Inside rather tawdry. It was dated 1782. Penn wants to stable his Horses inside the Church while the service is going on! I tell him that it can't be done. He says that it used to be done in Napoleon's Wars. So we left it at that!

Torrie has taken my Bedroom so I move into a house kept by an Agent for 'Sun Assurance'. Bed not bad, but not so good as the one Torrie has taken. We find Estaminet *Au Grand Saint Georges* too noisy, so leave it and set up our Mess in the Brewery. The men are being re-clothed so look cleaner, and more like Soldiers. Has been a beautiful fine day – very frosty. Am invited by small Boys to slide, but consider my dignity wouldn't stand it. Walked round Billets with Torrie. C Squadron are in Eecke. B and D Squadrons in nice farms about 2 miles away.

MONDAY NOVEMBER 23

Had a Bath, the first for a fortnight. Dislike my room of last night, so decide to move elsewhere. I join Hidden, the Quartermaster, Luxmoore, the Pill,

Capt Hugh Hidden, the Quartermaster, and Lt Keith Menzies at Eecke.

the Vet and the Interpreter in the Girls' School by the Church! Very snug large room with stove in the middle and desks all round. We put straw and Mattresses under our Valises. There are good Maps on the Wall, and a cupboard of 'Relics', which I must investigate. Some previous Individual who had occupied this Billet had chalked the following verse on the wall:

Adieu, charmant pays de France
Que je dois tant chérir
Berceau de mon heureuse enfance
Adieu, te quitter c'est mourir.

I understand that the last occupants were Zouaves.*

Am writing my Diary on desks made for little Girls of 10, and therefore am a bit cramped.

Penn, Jack Speed and Keith Menzies go home today on three days' leave. They are naturally very excited over it all. The Owner of our Mess room at the Brewery tells me that the real owner is a Prisoner of War in Germany, and that she is looking after the establishment for him. The house is filled with the most trashy objets d'art and vertus.** The pictures on the Wall are of the most diabolical looking children!

TUESDAY NOVEMBER 24

Our Room like a Monkey house, what with four of us and the stove. Thaw set in during the night, very muggy outside, and the eternal mud once more. Torrie came today to look at my Machine Gun Billets, he seemed to approve.

A Court Martial is sitting today on various Absentees, etc. Pill went into Hazebrouck today to get some Serum for second Typhoid Inoculation. It is a great relief being out of Shell range. Also I am thankful that the eternal roar of Gunfire which has deafened our ears for the past fortnight has sunk to an occasional distant rumble.

The old Lady who is looking after our Messing room appeared with a Bottle of 40 year old Claret. We drank it at dinner but it was very thin and sour.

The old Cloth Hall at Ypres, dating from the 13th century, was destroyed by shellfire last Sunday night.

WEDNESDAY NOVEMBER 25

Spent morning with my Guns, looking at the Horses, and getting men re-equipped. The Pill succeeded in getting the Inoculation stuff, and so gave me my second dose of it at 4.30. Was inoculated in the public room of the Inn. This was full of people, who were much interested!

* Algerian infantry, belonging to a corps founded in 1831.
** Curios or knick-knacks.

The Cloth Hall and St Martin's Cathedral, Ypres, 9 April 1912. (*Antony of Ypres*)

The tower of the Cloth Hall ablaze, 22 November 1914. (*Antony of Ypres*)

Destruction complete, later the same day. The wooden scaffolding, in place before the war, added fuel to the flames. (*Antony of Ypres*)

After lunch went walking round the Billets with Torrie and discussed possibility of Ferguson's return. We received Orders to consider ourselves a Reserve for the next 48 hours. Horses to be saddled up, and everybody ready to move out if required, in a few minutes. However, don't suppose that we shall actually be wanted. After dinner orders came in that the area

Haverskerque – St Venant – Aire was to be reconnoitred. Torrie asked me to do it.

My arm begins to hurt very definitely after the inoculation but I look forward to the reconnaissance which is a job which amuses me. Torrie is such a nice fellow that it is a pleasure to do anything he asks for.

THURSDAY NOVEMBER 26

Felt damned awful when I got up from the effects of the inoculation but felt better after I had been up a short time, and had a decent Breakfast. Started off at 10.30 with Humphreys of the Inniskilling Dragoons, who was attached to us. A cold dull day. We rode to Hazebrouck, and then on 13 kilometres to Haverskerque, passing en route the village of Morbecque in which I had spent the night of Nov 13 when en route to rejoin the Regiment.

We got to Haverskerque at 12.30. Had lunch, an Omelette and Coffee, at the local hotel. Found an Ammunition Column of 65 Lorries stationed there. Started again at 1.30 for Aire via St Venant. A flat open country, the fields are bordered by ditches but there are no hedges. There are dozens of well built prosperous looking Farms, which seemed ideal for Billets.

We rode to Aire along the Canal Bank. The Barges on the Canal were enormous, 50 yards long and 10 feet high, and there were many of them. We reached Aire about 4, left our Horses near the Cathedral, and went to look for Billets. We met General Rimington* in the Street who directed us to the Mairie. He was waiting at Aire for his Cavalry Division which was coming from India, consisting of 4 Brigades which were concentrating at Orléans.

Aire is a delightful Town, with a beautiful little Cathedral dated 1772. It is surrounded by Trees, which in the summer must greatly hide its beauties, which is a pity. After some time we found the Mairie and obtained Billets. With great difficulty found the addresses given us, and even more difficult was persuading the Owners to take us in. Finally I got a bed in one House and Humphreys went a few doors off. Felt infernally seedy so went to bed at once. Slept moderato during the night, had a Temperature.

---

* Enlightened in some ways – he was an early supporter of armoured cars – Lt Gen Mike Rimington took command of the Indian Cavalry Corps in France in 1915. A gallant officer, but not noted for his tact, he did not endear himself to the Indian element (about two-thirds) of his Corps by describing them as 'only fit to feed pigs and so forth'. Quoted by Lt (later Maj Gen) Roland Dening in *A History of the British Cavalry*, by the Marquess of Anglesey, p. 223.

FRIDAY NOVEMBER 27

My 35th Birthday!

Woke at 7.30 feeling much better, Glorious sunny day. The Lady of the house gave me some nice hot coffee well laced with Brandy! Went off at 8.15 to Breakfast at a Hotel called 'La Clef d'Or', filthy hole. The key may have been golden but it was more than the Breakfast was.

Rode out at 9 with Humphreys. Warm and bright, altogether a delightful ride. Made our Reconnaissance and returned to Haverskerque for lunch at 1.30 – usual Omelette and Coffee! Country looked well. Saw 2 Magpies. Lucky! Started for Eecke at 2.30. Reached Hazebrouck at 3.30. Clouded over and began to rain. Reached Eecke about 4.30. Found Letters and parcel containing my Rubber Waders.

Heard very good news about the Russians,* but not much detail. A Birthday dinner with the Boys.

SATURDAY NOVEMBER 28

Court Martial Parade at 10.30. 3 Prisoners. One sentenced to be shot. Two to Penal Servitude for 5 years. Death sentence afterwards commuted to 5 years. The other two reduced to 2 years from 5. All for absenting themselves from the trenches. Sentences had great effect. I thought that the man sentenced to death would die of fright.

Spent the day writing out my reconnaissance report and doing a sketch. Am writing some letters for Pill to take to England when he goes there tomorrow for 3 days' leave. 6 pm Handed over my Report and sketch to Torrie. 8.30 Torrie and Stewart Menzies very pleased with my reconnaissance report.

SUNDAY NOVEMBER 29

The Parson came to lunch, and held a Service afterwards in the Mission Hall. The Hall is in a great mess owing to most of B Squadron sleeping in it. Had all the straw cleared out. The Altar was made of a Table covered with a Blanket over it, with a Union Jack on top. Service at 2.30. Good Address by Parson. Hall crowded. Communion after. 20 stayed for it.

At 3.30 Torrie, the Pill, and Archie Sinclair left on their 3 days' leave. I have asked Archie to bring me back a set of Safety (Gillette) Razors in lieu of the old Seven Days Set which hitherto I have always used.

---

* Though the campaign in East Prussia had been disastrous, in the south-west four Russian armies had overrun Austrian territory in Galicia to a depth of 150 miles.

MONDAY NOVEMBER 30

Spent the morning with my Guns. Rode into Hazebrouck at 2 o'clock with Stewart Menzies and Jack Speed to have a haircut. Cold and inclined to rain. Couldn't find a decent Barber's shop, all filthy, so didn't have it done.

Walked up the Town to the Headquarters 3rd Cavalry Division, where I found an old friend, Colonel Gage, 5th Dragoon Guards, who gave us a great Tea! Not much news. Heard that The King is at Boulogne for a few days, visiting Troops. Returned to Eecke about 5.

German fire almost entirely ceased on our Front. Hardly ever hear cannonading now. Gale blowing and heavy rain started at 10 o'clock.

War is a funny game. Bored in Billets. Terrified in Trenches!

Am studying the early enemy movements in this War. A certain number of facts, and a good deal of information on this subject is now available. The German turning movement* completely diddled the French with a result that our Small Army suddenly received the full force of the hammer blows. God knows how we escaped. Without Smith-Dorrien's stand at Le Cateau,** we would never have done so.

TUESDAY DECEMBER 1

Cold but fine, not much news.

Dosie Brinton, late of my Regiment, came up at 12.30 from the Divisional Staff at Hazebrouck with the news that Stewart Menzies had got the DSO, also Alastair Innes-Ker† in the Blues, and Algy Stanley and Methuselah Wyndham in the 1st Life Guards.

Also that we were to go to Hazebrouck by 9 am tomorrow morning to be reviewed by The King. Orders to parade at 6.30 am tomorrow, and go to Hazebrouck to be looked over by His Majesty. Rest of today spent in spit and polish, and general gingering up.

---

* This was the sudden change of direction by von Kluck, Commander of the 1st German Army. On 28 August he wheeled his army south-eastwards, thus abandoning the original wide sweep intended to circle Paris.

** This stand, made by Gen Smith-Dorrien against his superior's wish, was a prime factor in checking the rapid advance of the German right wing. But the battle cost II British Corps 8,000 killed, wounded and missing.

† Capt Lord A.R. Innes-Ker had shown conspicuous courage on 26 October when, 'the Blues by bold and rapid movement across the front of two German Cavalry Regiments were able to extricate the 20th Infantry Brigade from Kruiseecke'. This tribute was paid by FM Earl Haig when he unveiled the Memorial to the Household Cavalry at Zandvoorde on 4 May 1924. It stands on the spot where Lord Worsley's body was found and marks the centre of the position held on 30 October 1914. See 15 December.

WEDNESDAY DECEMBER 2

We all got up at 5.30. Breakfast at 6. A brilliant Moon outside illuminated the rather twisting lanes leading to Hazebrouck, when we marched off at 6.30. Got very light and turned into a beautiful day about 7.15. Reached Hazebrouck about 7.30. The 1st Life Guards joined us en route.

Marched through the town and out onto the Hazebrouck–Lille road, where we halted two miles out and lined both sides of the road. Very cold standing about, and as we were in 'Drill Order', could not wear our mufflers and warm coats. The sun however came out brilliantly, which made things better, and we felt more congenial. At 10 o'clock The King came past, walking with General Allenby,* and General Sir Julian Byng commanding our Cavalry Division followed by the Prince of Wales and a very large Staff. Everyone who could possibly do so seemed to have joined it. We gave The King three cheers and waved our swords. He seemed pleased to see us, but I thought looked thin and worried. He was followed by 10 empty Motor Cars, all flying the Union Jack. Aeroplanes hovered overhead, but no Germans put in an appearance anywhere near. The King passed rapidly down the line, and we then marched back to Hazebrouck, which was very much decorated with flags and the streets crowded with people to see us go by.

We were followed by K Battery RHA, at the head of which I saw Reggie Maitland. The King went off to a large Château which is the Headquarters of Sir Douglas Haig, Commanding the First Army Corps, where he presented 4 DSOs, about 20 Distinguished Conduct Medals and 1 Légion d'Honneur.

Stewart Menzies, who went there to receive his DSO, said that the King seemed full of beans and most cheery, which I must say he did *not* look when he passed us. Stewart also said that Stamfordham** told him that General French was very pleased with the situation, and that it was possible for the time being that the German offensive in France was over.† Personally I think that the Germans will make one more attempt to get through here.

---

* Commander of the Cavalry Corps 1914–15, Allenby was promoted Field Marshal and created a Viscount in 1919. He was fêted as one of the great victors of the war, not least because of his inspiring capture of Jerusalem in December 1917. Cyril Falls, *DNB 1931–40*, p. 10.

** Lord Stamfordham, formerly Sir Arthur Bigge, was Private Secretary to King George V for twenty-one years until his death in 1931. Previously he had served Queen Victoria in the same capacity from 1895 until her death in 1901. Sir John Wheeler-Bennett, *King George VI, His Life and Reign*, p. 819.

† Sir John French was still optimistic about an early end to the war. As early as 6 September he had told the King he 'practically regarded the Germans beaten'. Sir George Arthur, *The Story of the Household Cavalry*, p. 95.

I am still convinced that they would never have destroyed the best part of Ypres, with its beautiful old 13th century Cloth Hall, if they had thought that they *had* a chance of getting the Town, which is the last Belgian Town left in our hands. We hear that the Kaiser had intended proclaiming the annexation of Belgium from the old Cloth Hall, and that was why he had the Prussian Guard* nearly annihilated in their very brave, but quite futile, effort to break through on November 11.

How deluded those unfortunate German Soldiers were may be gathered from the fact that the Name Boards on the Ostend Station were changed to ones bearing the name of Calais. This led the German Troops who passed through in the Train to suppose that the much advertised objective had been attained.

Poincaré** was at St Omer today and Marshal Joffre† went through Caestre, one mile from here, yesterday with his staff in eight cars probably to see The King. Sir John French was not at the Inspection today, nor was Sir Douglas Haig. Too busy I suppose.

The New Range Finder (Barr and Stroud) for my Machine Guns arrived today. Must make myself and the teams acquainted with it as soon as possible. It is generally decided that the Battle of Ypres – Armentières ended when we withdrew last week. The Germans have been very quiet ever since, and their march on Calais is now effectively barred. Our casualties have certainly been very very heavy. So far it has been the biggest Battle of the War, but the result is magnificent. The world sees now that for 3 weeks from Oct 11 it was touch and go.

If the 3rd Cavalry Division and the 7th Infantry Division had not held the gap round Ypres, between Dixmude and the left of the 6th French Army at Arras, whilst our Troops were coming up from Soissons, the Germans would have occupied Calais, and all the French Coast which is nearest England. The British Army has covered itself with the greatest glory. The German losses for this Battle cannot have been less than 200,000, and are probably more.††

Today a Roll of Snipers was called for. We ought to get a lot of volunteers, and so pay these blighters back in their own coin.

---

* Said to be among the finest troops in the German Army.
** Raymond Poincaré, President of France, 1913–20.
† Commander-in-Chief of the French Army, 1914–16, Joffre was unflappable. He insisted on regular and well-cooked meals and forbade his staff to disturb his night's rest.
†† An over-estimate, according to Martin Gilbert. He reports 20,000 Germans killed and 80,000 severely wounded. The British lost 8,000 men and had 40,000 wounded. See *The Routledge Atlas of the First World War*, 1994, p. 20.

We issued today Boots, new corduroy breeches and sheepskin coats to the troops. We shall probably start a new offensive soon, but I don't think that the Cavalry will be required, for the moment anyhow, for the Trenches again. We expect to be used as a mobile Reserve. Another month of what we have recently been doing would render our cavalry non-existent.

TUESDAY DECEMBER 3

The III Corps (Pulteney)* reports that 2 hostile guns were put out of action yesterday near Messines. The French also gained some ground North of Wytschaete, and a machine gun was captured at Langemarck. Reports have come in that the Germans are using captured French Guns, and their ammunition is faulty.

There is a distinct flow of Troops noticeable in both directions, but the movement to the East is now greater than that to the West. The Germans seem to be using very old shell. A cast iron shell, dated 1883, in which shrapnel bullets are held together by melted resins, has been found at Maubeuge. Guns firing shells of 1891 and 1896 have been directed against Armentières and Houplines.

Spent the morning getting the Machine Guns pack saddlery right. General Kavanagh, our Brigadier, sent up to say that he would inspect the Guns tomorrow at 9 am. Stewart Menzies and Walker the Vet go home today on 3 days' leave. Torrie, Archie Sinclair and Luxmoore return. Our 48 hours standing to ends at 7 pm tonight.

Intelligence reports state that the Austrian casualties amount to about one and three quarter million men. Their official accounts state that they have lost 38,438 killed by the Serbs alone. As the Austrian Army is estimated at about 3½ millions, it will be seen how heavily it has been hit. At least one sixth of the Austrian Army consists of Poles and Slavs who are Pro-Russian at heart, so that this sixth actively desires the defeat of the Armies in which they are compelled to serve!!**

* Lt Gen Sir William Pulteney had been appointed Commander of III British Corps on 31 August.
** These groups intended to gain their independence from the Habsburg Empire as a result of the war – and they succeeded. For instance, Czechoslovakia and Yugoslavia were created at the Treaty of Versailles in 1919. Also, the Polish Republic was restored. It had not existed as a separate state since 1795, when Poland had been partitioned between Russia, Prussia and Austria.

VOLUME II

DECEMBER 4, 1914 – JANUARY 5, 1915

FRIDAY DECEMBER 4

General Kavanagh came at 9 this morning to look at our squadrons and the machine gun. He seemed very satisfied, and asked a good many questions about the new Barr and Stroud range finder. At 10 o'clock we had a lecture on it from the Armourer Sergeant. It seems very simple and is most exact. The error is only 4 feet in 10,000 yards. We tried it on various subjects and could see the time with it on a clock in a tower 7,500 yards off. The chief advantage is that one man can work it. We must be very careful not to knock it as it is a very expensive instrument being worth, I believe, about £70.

Archie Sinclair returned off leave with my new safety razor, and a portable bath which will be most useful. Torrie asked me this morning if I would like to go to the Headquarter Staff as Assistant Narrative Writer. He thought that it would be an excellent thing to do. He suggested that I should go home on 3 days' leave and discuss it with George Arthur.[*]

Yesterday South of the La Bassée Canal the French captured the Château of Vermelles. An Agent (i.e. spy) reports that 15 rafts towed by small boats were observed moving from Spermalie towards Schoorbakke; apparently the Germans are bringing rafting material up to the Nieuport-Dixmude front.[**]

We hear that Austria is now employing 500,000 troops against Serbia, also that they have finally succeeded in taking Belgrade. Will be worth about the same amount to the Austrians that Brussels is to the Germans.

---

[*] Sir George Arthur first met Kitchener on the Gordon Relief Expedition of 1885, and became a close friend. A popular figure in London, with the right contacts in high places, Arthur was chosen by Kitchener to be his Personal Private Secretary when war broke out, and served him as such until the latter departed on his fateful journey to Russia on 5 June 1916. John Pollock, *Kitchener*, pp. 380–1.

[**] This material was needed because King Albert I of the Belgians had ordered the flooding of the 10 miles of territory between these two towns on 27 October. John Keegan, *The First World War*, p. 140.

Yesterday the French improved their position about Wytschaete and captured a machine gun west of Langemarck. French Intelligence states that the disposition of the German forces by divisions is:

	Active	Reserve/Ersatz	Total
Western Front	21	26¾	47¾
Eastern Front	4	18	22
			69¾

More reports show that there is a substantial movement both from this front and St Quentin through Charleroi eastwards. Heard news today of the capture of the renegade scoundrel de Wet.*

At 1 o'clock a Gunner Major arrived for lunch, and took us out afterwards into the fields, and made observations regarding the siting of trenches. He told us the sort of trench the artillery liked shelling, and how to avoid making trenches that make good targets. He returned for tea and was very interesting in his remarks on artillery work. He belonged to K Battery RHA which had come from Christchurch, Hants, when the 3rd Cavalry Division had mobilised. He told us that, to equip the original Expeditionary Force, all batteries which did not actually belong to it were broken up. The result was that a few days after the outbreak of war K Battery was denuded of everything except its guns, waggons and about two NCOs.

But when the 3rd Cavalry Division was formed late in September, it became necessary to resuscitate this battery, so that it is now entirely composed of reservists. He said that the co-operation of the German arms is wonderful and their system of telephones enables their gunners to fire at any target and constantly change. He said that the French field gun** is the best in Europe, and although it looks flimsy, in reality the worth of it lies in its slow recoil which does not shake the gun off its target. He said that a glass of water standing on the breech of a French gun wouldn't be upset.

The mechanism of the French gun recoil is a secret. It is supposed to be an air buffer, but no nation with the exception of the French has ever succeeded in inventing a valve or gland which can contain air to such an extent. The

* Boer Commander-in-Chief of the Orange Free State, Christian de Wet, was well known for his daring exploits. In March 1900, one of his coups nearly resulted in the capture of Kitchener. In 1914, he was still anti-British and led a rebellion against Botha, which foundered with his capture.
** 75mm, known as the Soixante Quinze. The French first produced this highly effective field gun in 1897 and had 4,000 in service at the outbreak of war. The rate of fire could exceed twenty rounds a minute, and by the Armistice 40,000 had been produced.

German field gun is an old one (1896) converted by a new carriage into a semi-quick firer.

Our gun, though only issued in 1906, is obsolete. Previous to the war, the War Office had plans for a complete re-armament. The French and English systems of fire are totally different and in this campaign the former has secured better results. The English system is to score hits and to fire slowly and deliberately hitting every time. The French system is to plaster a certain area as quickly as possible with hundreds of shells. Certainly to watch their *rafales** and volleys of shells is most instructive.

The only guns which really do us much damage are the 5 inch howitzers and 8 inch guns (Jack Johnsons). The Major considered our 5 inch guns must make the Germans sit up. Our explosive Lyddite is more powerful than the German one. It is numbers alone that up to now have kept us back. This is essentially an Artillery War. If it had not been for the German guns the war would now either be over, or we should be approaching Berlin. The verdict of the British Artillery on the German field gun is that its shrapnel shells are 'mere squibs'. It is the big stuff that causes us damage.

Our Artillery casualties are not so heavy as has been supposed. Since K Battery came out on Oct 4, and after nearly a month of continuous fighting, it has lost 10 men killed and 20 wounded. The Gunner told us that yesterday he had met a Field Battery which had been out the whole time, and had had its first man killed a week ago by a stray bullet.

He believed that we were now getting out a new 9 inch gun. The German cavalry is beneath contempt. They overload their saddles so much, both fore and aft, that they can neither dismount when mounted, nor mount when dismounted. They have by now disappeared, none have been seen anywhere for ages. It is difficult to call their infantry contemptible** for they come on blindly and hopelessly to certain death. They seem to expect it and they certainly get it, but there is not a soldier in this army that does not count himself as worth 4 Germans. The German attack forms a target that up to now has been the Gunner's Dream. The fullest advantage has been taken of it. A French field officer only last week said to a member of this Regiment 'we reckon that your men are worth 3 of ours and 5 Germans'.

---

* Sudden bursts: compare *une rafale de balles* – a hail of bullets.
** A gibe at the Kaiser, who on 19 August was said to have dismissed the British Expeditionary Force as 'General French's contemptible little army'. Thereafter the soldiers called themselves 'The Old Contemptibles'.

SATURDAY DECEMBER 5

Been at Eecke a fortnight today. Woke at 7, pouring and sleeting outside. Route march postponed from 10.30 to 2 pm. Had a rifle inspection at 11. At 11.15 day cleared up completely into one of brilliant sunshine. Decide not to go home yet as I shouldn't get home later when I really want to go; so write my views to George Arthur.

An engineer officer is coming on Monday to instruct us in the art of building an 'ideal trench'. Instruction that is badly needed. If the trenches at Zillebeke had been properly constructed,* how many useful lives would have been saved.

Heard today that Corporal Backhouse died. He was hit near me in the trench on the 17th by splinters of a shell. He crawled along the communication trench to some dugouts behind and lay there, people doing what they could for him. After he had been there about an hour another shell burst near his dugout and covered everyone with mud and sand. His wounds filled with sand and filth. This caused his death, as it was impossible for several hours to cleanse the wound.**

The sun coming out at 11.15 deluded Torrie into supposing that the day was going to be fine, and he ordered the Regiment to parade for the much talked-of route march at 12 o'clock. We had no sooner mounted and ridden down the main street when a fine driving rain began. We were however committed to this outing and personally being equipped with mackintosh and india rubber boots, I didn't care twopence if it rained red ink. We fetched a compass of about 3 miles, and trotting all the way returned to our billets very wet *outside* at 1 o'clock.

The report that de Wet had surrendered to Colonel Brits at a farm west of Mafeking is today confirmed. He was surrounded and surrendered with about 50 deluded rebels without firing a shot. He is now securely lodged in a fort in Pretoria.† What a wretched fiasco, after his performances in the Boer War, although had the British possessed but one aeroplane in that war, he would have been located in a week. His waggon tilts would have given him away, and the long weary treks of thousands of mounted men for months would have been entirely avoided.

---

* These trenches are described as 'shallow and unconnected' in the report held by the Household Cavalry Museum. Later (7 December) Crofton refers to the Zillebeke trenches as 'death-traps'.
** Cpl Alfred Backhouse, a clerk from Whitchurch, Hampshire, died two days later. He is buried in Poperinghe Old Military Cemetery.
† Sentenced to six years' imprisonment for treason, de Wet was released after one year.

Wireless too would have severely cramped his style. The Boer War, fought with our present appliances of aeroplanes, wireless, and motor transport and motor cyclists for scouting and dispatch riding would not have lasted a year.

The Russians have reached to within 7 miles of Cracow. This is the last obstacle to the flooding of Silesia with Russians. The investment should begin this week, and we have no reason to suppose that the resistance of this fortress will be any more effective than that of Liège, Namur, and Maubeuge. The day of the fortress is over. High explosive shells filled with a ton or more of devastating material dropping like a bolt from the blue, will pulverise any fortifications yet devised by the wit of man. This is the *first* great lesson of this war.

Torrie told us that, when he returned off leave three days before, he had seen a pack of hounds being entrained at Boulogne for the Front. They have been variously reported as belonging either to the Duke of Westminster or Bouch.* This pack is evidently following the precedent created by the Duke of Wellington in the Peninsula.

Archie Sinclair got a note from Winston Churchill who is now at Bailleul asking him to go over and see him. Churchill told Sinclair, when he was here on leave last week, that the aviator Briggs** who threw the bomb on Friedrichshafen last week had entirely destroyed the hydrogen plant there, and also the framework of a new Zeppelin.† He also said that the bombs thrown on Düsseldorf had caused £200,000 worth of damage.

A proposal has been made to use harpoons fired from harpoon guns which are to fix themselves in the enemy's wire entanglements. Then by hauling on a rope attached to the harpoon, the latter are to be destroyed.

There is a report that one of our airmen has succeeded in dropping a bomb on Krupp's works at Essen. Pourpre, the famous French flier who was the first to fly to Khartoum, has been killed by a fall from his machine.

---

* A prominent figure in the hunting world, Thomas Bouch was Master of the Belvoir, 1912–24. At this time he was a major attached to Cavalry Corps HQ.
** Three Avro pilots of the Royal Naval Air Service, led by Sqn Ldr E.F. Briggs, flew from Belfort on 21 November to Friedrichshafen on Lake Constance, where they achieved the first long-distance bombing raid of the war by literally throwing bombs out of their machines. Air Ministry Reports on the Destruction of German Airships, Imperial War Museum Archives, ref. 44990.
† Named after Graf von Zeppelin, the first notable builder of these slow lighter-than-air airships. Described by one historian as 'the H-Bomb of its day', the Zeppelin gave civilians their first taste of air raids, but was susceptible to gales and fog. See R.L. Rimell, *Zeppelin! A Battle for Air Supremacy in World War I*, p. 31.

SUNDAY DECEMBER 6

About 9 o'clock this morning a German aeroplane sailed over Hazebrouck and dropped several bombs. One of these fell into the station and killed 5, and wounded 15 men of the Loyal North Lancashire Regiment.* A great firing began both with guns and rifles but the aeroplane was too far off and did not get hit. We saw the infernal thing returning home over us. The German Taube is easily distinguished by its wings.**

It was a fine light morning but rather cold. At 12 o'clock we again had a service in the Mission Hall, and it was followed by Holy Communion to which about 15 stayed. The service was very effective and short, both services lasting three quarters of an hour. It was rendered more realistic by the muddy boots and gaiters which the parson had on, under a still muddier cassock. The Altar again was formed of a table on which was spread the Union Jack. At the back of it the Cross stood on a miniature platform made out of a bully beef tin with a napkin spread on it.

During the afternoon we received copies of The King's speech to the Army. It is rather reminiscent of General French's effort. Perhaps the same man wrote both. The King returned today to London.

Archie Sinclair came to dine and we had (with Torrie) a great discussion on the future of the Cavalry which is at present uncertain, like that of Horse Artillery. Nobody, however, can deny that this arm has rendered the most important services during this war. The retreat from Mons, August 22–September 3, was only rendered possible because of the screen of cavalry which enveloped the rear of the retreating II Corps.

When we remember the storm which arose ten years ago in England when it was first proposed that cavalry should be armed with the rifle, we cannot help feeling thankful that this arming was carried out, although in the teeth of the fiercest opposition.† The possession of this weapon has conferred very great power on the cavalry. It was owing to this power that we were able to screen the sorely stricken infantry, and keep the hostile masses at the proper distance. I hope that this example in favour of cavalry will not be overlooked when the day comes to decide our future.

---

* Thirteen battalions of the Loyals were involved in France and Flanders at various times. Overall the Regiment lost 357 officers and 7,232 other ranks.
** It is ironic that this type of aircraft is known as a Taube, i.e. a dove. The dove is traditionally considered a messenger of peace, not a harbinger of death. But given the role of the dove sent out by Noah after the flood – to make a reconnaissance – perhaps the name is not so inappropriate.
† Despite this, by the end of 1905 all cavalry regiments had been equipped with the same rifle as the infantryman, the .303 Short Magazine Lee Enfield.

A second example. When it was decided to draw away our forces round Soissons towards the end of the battle of the Aisne, and push our allied line up towards the North Sea, it became apparent that the Germans were doing exactly the same thing. The movement developed into a race for the coast. The German forces were sent corps by corps to extend their right and we had to extend our left to meet their menace by withdrawing our troops from the centre. The five brigades of cavalry were then dispatched (about October 5) to fill the gap in Belgium which existed between the left of the French (our extreme left) and the right of the 7th Infantry Division and the 3rd Cavalry Division, whose forces were coming down to join our Allied Forces. They had landed at Zeebrugge on October 8.

The line from the coast to Dixmude was held by the Belgian Army, so the gap practically had for its centre the town of Ypres. It was round this town that the desperate series of battles raged from about October 19 to November 22.* How the furious German attacks were driven back and the Prussian Guard almost decimated is now a matter of history, and the part taken by the seven cavalry brigades is one which should stand strongly in favour of the retention of our present amount of cavalry. But for the cavalry, the Germans would have broken through to Calais during the early days of November, for it was impossible to get the Infantry up in time. Again the possession of rifles enabled us to display the holding power of infantry when our increased mobility had brought us up in time to save Ypres.

It remains to be seen what future opportunities we shall have. The French have been disappointing and have brought off no very startling coups. Both cavalries are armed still with carbines which have no more effect than pop guns would. The whole of the 1915 class of French conscripts, which number about 200,000 men, are to be sent this year into the infantry, not one conscript goes to their cavalry. This shows the opinion of the French General Staff with regard to the role of cavalry in this war.

We hear too that no more yeomanry will be sent out, in fact the antithesis of the South African War. Dismounted men only are now required.

With Russia however the war is different. Cavalry is to Russia, what the British fleet is to England. The steppes of Poland and the sandy wastes of Eastern Prussia furnish the required terrain. The Russians possess 20 divisions of regular Cavalry, and nearly 500,000 Cossacks.

What will happen after the war to our Horse Artillery? Up to now it has been found that they are neither one thing nor the other. The gun is very

---

* Generally now known as 1st Ypres, to avoid confusion with 2nd Ypres (April–May 1915) and 3rd Ypres, or Passchendaele (July–November 1917).

heavy and the batteries cannot really move any faster than field batteries and at the same time they can only throw a shell of 13lb as compared with the Field Artillery one of 18lb.

On the very rare occasions when cavalry will meet cavalry in shock tactics, the only possibility of a battery being able to accompany a charge would be if that battery consisted of very light guns, which would be useless at any other time. The effect of these light guns being so doubtful, it is difficult to see how a Horse Battery can in the future justify its existence.

The true effectiveness of cavalry varies so much with the theatre in which it operates; for instance, great things happened with the Southern Cavalry in the American Civil War, mainly because this cavalry operated in a district where all the inhabitants were friendly and in sympathy with their cause. The opposite happened with the German Cavalry in 1870, which did little because it operated in territories notoriously hostile to it. Our position in South Africa was in reality the worst of any, for our cavalry operated in an area which should have been friendly, but which in reality was bitterly hostile!

In this war, the work of reconnaissance, which is one of cavalry's chief roles, has largely been done by aeroplanes and motor cycles. Our aviators have acquired the command of the air, but the French aviator is disappointing. All their flying is devoted to tricks, flying upside down, looping loops, etc., which are amusing to watch, but useless for military purposes.* They have no idea whatever of reporting or obtaining information, every scrap of which is nearly always secured by our fliers.**

MONDAY DECEMBER 7

About 11 o'clock I was sent for by Torrie who told me that he had orders to send a billeting party on to the General's house at once, as the Regiment was to move. He asked me to do the billeting and go off to General Kavanagh at once. I left Eecke at 11.30 accompanied by the Interpreter and four orderlies. I reached the General's house at 12.30 at Hondeghem. He gave me orders to take up a new billeting area west of the railway line Hazebrouck–Cassel. He

---

* After watching an aerobatics display in 1913, Gen Foch reached a similar verdict; 'Comme sport, magnifique, comme intérêt militaire, zéro'. Philip Warner, Field Marshal Earl Haig, p. 110.
** Perhaps a touch of bias here! 'In the years immediately preceding August 1914, Britain had lagged alarmingly behind the other European powers – and particularly France – in military aviation.' Ralph Barker, The Royal Flying Corps in France – From Mons to the Somme, p. 9.

said that he regretted having to move us, but that large numbers of French troops were coming up, and that they wanted our area so there was nothing for us but to go back.

I left the General's house about 1 pm to take over our area, which was the triangle Les Ciseaux–Maison Blanche–Staple. Staple being the centre of our area and a fairly decent village. I at once allotted it to the Regimental Headquarters and the Machine Gun. I reached Staple about 1.30 and after sending for the Maire proceeded to find billets for 200 men and horses. All the French farms and villages that I have seen are very deceptive. To look at them, one would think that a great many horses could be put up in them, but one invariably finds that a farm that looks as if it could house 25 horses, can only put up 5 or 6. The French fill their barns with straw and hay and have a small space only for threshing in the middle, and that is the only space in which horses can be put.

The Maire was very ancient and incoherent, and looked like the Ancient Mariner.* He spat a good deal but didn't do much else. I rapidly trotted round the farms and village and by 3 o'clock had allotted all the billets. As usual I fixed on the school as the sleeping abode of the Headquarters, so thither we directed our steps accompanied by the Maire, and by this time most of the village.

A class of little boys was being held at the school. The master appeared and was informed that the schools would be required at once for the troops, and so the little boys were to be *en vacances* as long as we were here. The Master seemed to bear up very well, and there was the greatest enthusiasm amongst the pupils who cheered and shouted like mad.

We next went off to commandeer the Girls' school for the sick horses. Here the Mistress gave way even before she was asked, and luckily approved an apparently unlimited holiday. On being told that the seizure of the school would necessitate a holiday, she replied that 'there was nothing that she would like better'. When I added that the visit of British soldiers would be a pleasant remembrance she said that it was quite true, and that it would serve as a history lesson in future.

The village clusters as usual round the little church which is dated 1737. The inside is rather meretricious and tawdry but large for so small a village. The system of teaching children in the French schools I have seen is distinctly good. There is always a compass painted on the ceiling

---

* A reference to the famous poem by Samuel Taylor Coleridge (1772–1834). It has been interpreted as a symbolic portrayal of the poet's own unhappy wanderings.

'1. My bed, 2. Simpson's bed, 3. Luxmoore's bed, in the Girls' School at Staple.'

and the words Nord, Sud, Ouest, Est, written on the four walls. The walls are covered with pictures showing plains, plateaux, mountains, etc., and very amusing prints showing virtue always winning, and vice getting a very bad time.

There are also dozens of precepts dotted about the room. Over the door was the excellent advice that 'Greybeards are to be saluted whenever youth meets them'. This possibly accounts for the reverence with which our interpreter is treated in the various villages in which we stay. Although in reality fairly youthful, he has the appearance of premature senile decay.

They seem to have an awful down on alcohol in France. In this school there are 15 tracts which deal with this subtle temptation and here are a few of them:

> Alcohol paralyses the brain.
> Alcohol does not help the digestion.
> Alcohol is not nourishing.
> Alcohol doesn't give any strength.
> Alcohol doesn't warm you up. **(It does.)**
> Alcohol causes you to lose your will.
> Alcohol doesn't quench your thirst.
> To buy Alcohol is to buy Death.

The door of the Tavern leads to the Hospital. I couldn't help writing under all these Oscar Wilde's mot.*

Nothing succeeds like excess.

If the children will only absorb half these maxims, future France should indeed be an Utopia. The *chef d'oeuvre* is a large picture over the desk which shows two nice little girls handing over a watch to a very doubtful-looking policeman and under which is written

To keep what one finds is to steal.

Archie Sinclair returned today from his two days visit to Winston Churchill at Headquarters.** He said that a net was being spread for the capture of the five German battleships in the Pacific and that a battle was expected any day.

Churchill said that the German ships were concentrating and that he understood that the *von der Tann*† had got out of Kiel and joined them. He also said that the Germans did not realise what a large Naval force there was against them in the Pacific, that a large Japanese squadron had come up, and also the Australian squadron, and reinforcements from England to replace the *Good Hope* and the *Monmouth*.††

Archie Sinclair said that it was quite true that our battleship *Audacious* had been sunk two months ago by a German mine off the NW Coast of Ireland. She had struck the mine while at battle practice and had steamed at 18 knots for land. She had got in sight of it when she sank. Her crew with the exception of one man had been taken off by the liner *Olympic* which was

---

* From Act I of *A Woman of No Importance*. Lord Illingworth has just declared 'Moderation is a fatal thing, Lady Hunstanton . . .'.

** Sir Archibald Sinclair, later Viscount Thurso, was a close friend of Churchill before the war. Both men had American mothers, both had a cavalry officer's training, both enjoyed polo. After the 'disgrace' of Gallipoli, Churchill took over command of the 6th Royal Scots Fusiliers and Sinclair served as his second-in-command. Close political allegiance followed and in the Second World War, Sinclair was Secretary of State for Air from 1940 to 1945 in Churchill's wartime Coalition Government.

† The first German battle-cruiser to be built, the *von der Tann* was equipped with eight 11in guns and fired shells weighing 305kg. At Jutland she blew up the *Indefatigable* in the first fifteen minutes of the battle.

†† These two armoured cruisers had been sunk by Admiral von Spee's Pacific Squadron at the Battle of Coronel off the coast of Chile on 1 November. 1,440 British sailors were drowned – there were no German dead.

Capt Sir George Prescott (left) and Lt Sir Archibald Sinclair.

standing by on her way from America. The passengers of the *Olympic* were sworn to secrecy and notices put up in the cabins asking the passengers not to mention what they had seen. These notices however were foolishly left up in the ship when she reached Liverpool, and were seen by the dozens of men who come on board when a ship arrives at a port.

Notwithstanding this, the secret was well kept and it took the Germans six weeks to find out that it had sunk.* Even now they don't know what is happening about her, for the Admiralty has spread a rumour that it is being got up, although there is really no hope of that.

Sinclair had been out with Seely** and Churchill the day before to visit the trenches near La Bassée which are held by the 16th Infantry Brigade. They seemed very different from the death traps of Zillebeke. They were dug in clumps large enough to hold 3 men each, each of these clumps were connected by a short communication trench to a long lateral trench which ran behind. This in turn was connected at intervals by trenches leading to dugouts where the men could rest when not actually using the front line. These dugouts were very comfortable, and lined with straw, and in the centre were braziers of coke or charcoal. The brigade had two regiments at a time in the trenches, and two in support in trenches further back. They spent a fortnight at a time in the trenches. All the trenches were connected up by telephones and the men received their food properly cooked and all their mail very frequently. The arrangements in rear of the trenches for lavatories were most elaborate.

The whole system is an example of what can be done by troops who understand digging. The men infinitely prefer being in the front trench for a fortnight to being in support for the same time. A system of mirrors rather like the periscope of a submarine allows the front to be watched without a man's head showing to be sniped at. The trenches were about 9 feet deep at the back, the front ones being about 6 feet deep, and possessing a step for a man to stand on when he wanted to fire. In the wall of the front of the trench, two foot above the floor, were scooped out ledges where the men on

---

* The Cabinet kept the news secret because – according to the diary of Margot Asquith – 'the news of the sinking, had it reached the Germans, would have cheered them up dangerously'. But the secret only lasted for two weeks. A passenger on the *Olympic* took a photograph of the *Audacious* sinking. This appeared in an American newspaper, the *Philadelphia Public Ledger*, on 14 November. See Martin Gilbert, *First World War*, p. 95.
** Secretary of State for War from 1911, John Seely was forced to resign in March 1914 as a result of his actions in the Curragh Mutiny. He commanded the Canadian Cavalry Brigade in France for most of the war, and was created 1st Baron Mottistone in 1933.

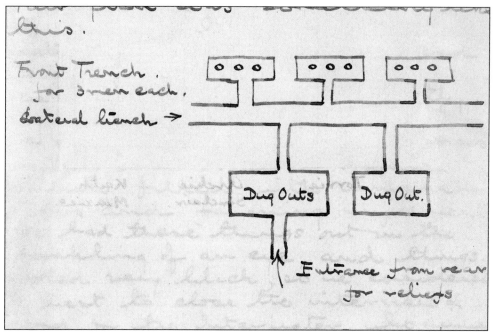

Diagram of trenches visited by Churchill and Seely at La Bassée.

duty could lie in comfort. The drainage was perfect, but early in their existence the Germans had succeeded in flooding them out (see plan above).

We went on duty as the Duty Division at 7 pm for 48 hours.

TUESDAY DECEMBER 8

A beautiful fine morning. Breakfasted at 8 and then went with Torrie and Speed in the motor to show them all the billets as it had been too dark the night before to see much. D and C Squadrons had been late in taking them up. All were satisfactory with the exception of the ones at the Château where I had placed the machine guns. Here the owner was evidently trying it on. He declined to allow the horses in his barns, which were merely filled with ramshackle traps and farming implements. We had these things out in the twinkling of an eye, and things looked very black, so we considered it best to close the interview and send for the Interpreter, who arrived breathless in a few moments.* Things were very soon arranged and we

---

* At the outset, interpreters had been in short supply. The War Office had telephoned Eton College on about 3 August. Three members of the Modern Languages Department volunteered – Charles Gladstone, Eric Powell and George Fletcher – all of whom were officers in the Eton Officers Training Corps. They sailed for France twenty-four hours later. (Letter from Sir William Gladstone to the editor.)

Lt Col T.G.J. Torrie (left), Lt Sir Archibald Sinclair and Lt Keith Menzies, off duty at Staple.

departed after being plied with red wine by the now thoroughly mollified proprietor. Torrie later in the day handed over to me D Squadron, as Hind, the squadron leader, had returned to his own Regiment, the 13th Hussars.

So I gave up the two guns, which had been of great interest and amusement for 3 weeks, and took up again, most willingly, the role of a squadron leader. I proposed moving down to my new command, which was billeted about half a mile off in three farms near Longue Croix, at once; Torrie however asked me to stay with the Headquarters until the next move.

During the morning I walked round and took some photos of the village, church, and the château where my late guns were lodged. About 1 o'clock the brilliant sun departed and a rainy mist set in.

People are awfully kind in sending out things to the men. We get tons of chocolate, tobacco, pipes, etc. and inside the parcels there is generally a card or letter from our unknown friends with very nice sentiments on it and the man who gets the packet writes a little note back. The letter from Mrs Russell is a typical one.

I wrote a very nice reply to this good lady.

We often have very interesting discussions on the war and on the undoubted progress that ourselves and our Allies have made in four months. One cannot help having a feeling of extreme thankfulness that this war has come when it did. It is clear now that Germany has been reduced to the

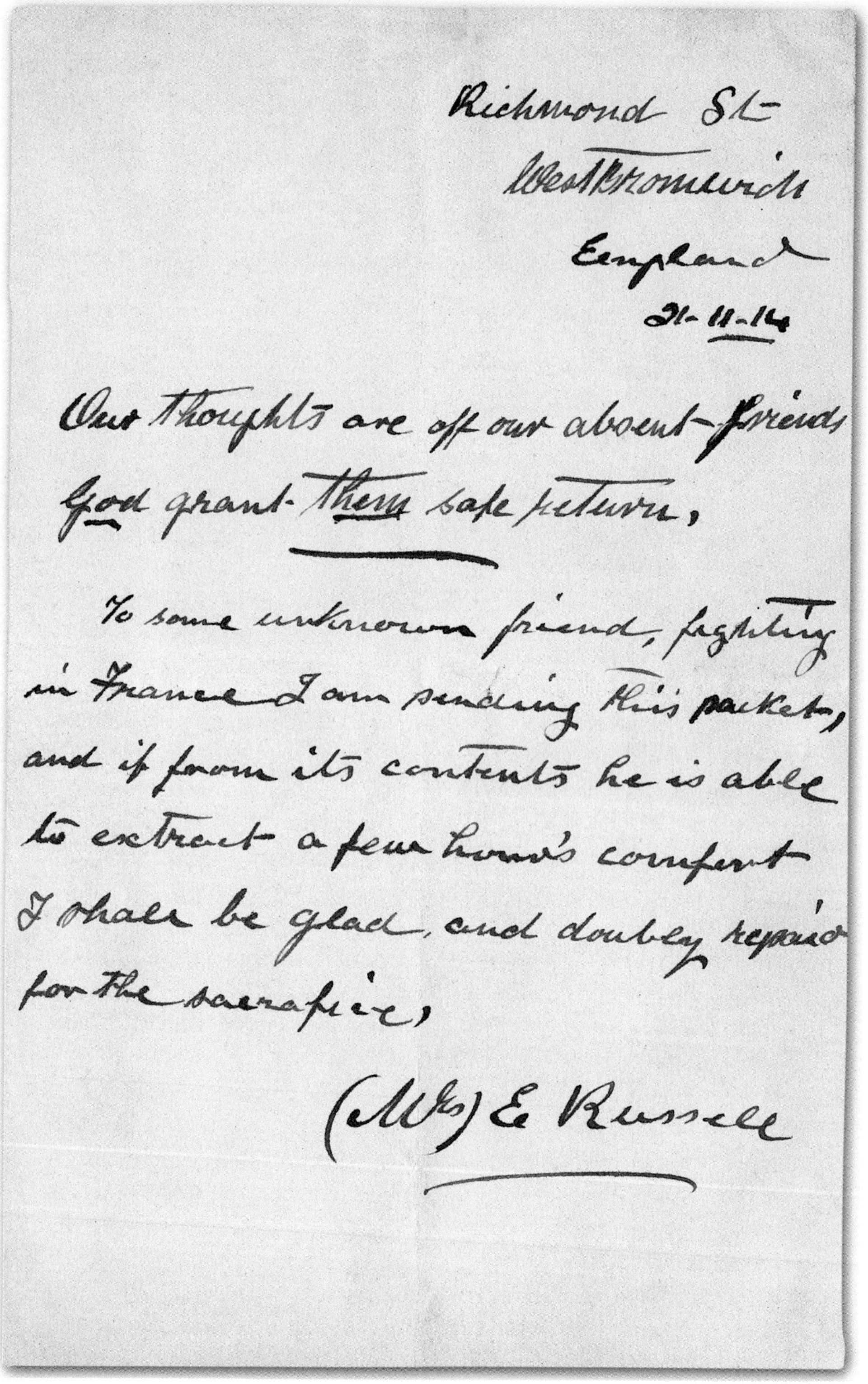

Richmond St
West Bromwich
England
21-11-14

Our thoughts are off our absent friends
God grant them safe return,

To some unknown friend, fighting
in France I am sending this packet,
and if from its contents he is able
to extract a few hour's comfort
I shall be glad, and doubly repaid
for the sacrifice,

(Mrs) E. Russell

'To some unknown friend . . .' from Mrs E. Russell of West Bromwich.

strategic defensive. As Lord Sydenham* says, 'In the West she is striving to retain occupied territory on the Bismarckian plan of *beati possidentes*.'**

The entire plan of campaign, of which time was a vital element, was shattered when the retreat to the Aisne began. In spite of immense efforts, the initial failure has not only not been redeemed, but the German strategists, once their carefully elaborated scheme for crushing France was foiled,† showed loss of military judgement and indecision. The master von Moltke would in this case have seen that it would have been easiest to retire to the Rhine, and throw every available man into the Eastern theatre.††

Instead of doing this, obsessed by the idea of reaching Calais, the German Staff expended the equivalent of more than five Army Corps, without any result except inflicting wholly disproportionate loss upon the Allies who are now stronger in numbers, positions and artillery than when the fighting in Flanders began.

The prestige of the German Army of 1870 has departed, never to return in this campaign. The economic pressure is becoming steadily more acute and after four months, the relative naval strength of Great Britain remains unimpaired.‡

WEDNESDAY DECEMBER 9

A wet drizzling day, which but for Rum, my mackintosh, and gum boots would be awful. As it is I don't mind if it snows red ink. Went down to my new Squadron. Inspected thoroughly the four farms in which they are billeted. Sanitary arrangements in all of them are practically nil. Lecture about 12 o'clock by Torrie on certain tactical points. All rumours point to a move very shortly.

The trains passing through Hazebrouck have been packed lately with the 1915 conscripts proceeding up somewhere near the front. Two of my subalterns went into Hazebrouck to get their hair cut, and returned with the

---

* Baron Sydenham of Dulverton, Somerset (1848–1933) had been raised to the peerage in 1913, when his controversial six-year term as Governor of Bombay ended. He was deeply disappointed not to be called upon by the British Government in 1914.
** 'Possession is nine-tenths of the law' would be a free translation.
† The Schlieffen Plan.
†† FM Helmut von Moltke, architect of the Prussian victories in 1866 and 1871. By contrast his namesake (and nephew) as Chief of General Staff presided over the failure of the Schlieffen Plan and was replaced in September 1914 by Falkenhayn.
‡ True of surface vessels on the High Seas, but the U-boat menace was still underestimated.

Capt Sir Morgan Crofton (left) and Lt N. Wilson in the Village Square at Staple.

tale that columns of French artillery consisting of every kind of gun, from a field gun to a 6 inch howitzer, have been passing through the town in the direction of La Bassée.

The Russian victory round Lodz seems to have now considerably watered down. Although the losses of the Germans have been colossal, yet there is a

The diarist (centre) in jovial mood is flanked by Surgeon Capt E.J. Luxmoore (left) and Lt Col T.G.J. Torrie.

chance that if the Russians have to retire on to the Vistula, they may also have temporarily to give up the investment of Cracow.* This of course would be a setback for us, and would materially alter the conduct of our campaign on this side.

At 6.30 Quartermaster Hidden came in and told us that we are all to pack up and move off at 9.30 tomorrow.

THURSDAY DECEMBER 10

At 7 o'clock we had breakfast and having packed up we started out, my squadron leading. We crossed the railway at Les Ciseaux and took the road to Hondeghem. As we passed through the village we saw General Kavanagh who inspected us as we passed him. We then found that the march was a surprise one, and we were ordered to march back to our old billets via Ste Marie-Cappelle. It was a ride round of about eight miles; the day was fine up to 12 when a drizzle set in. I saw several very large coveys of partridges, I counted one of 23 and another of 21. They are frightfully wild and would be

* 'The Battle of Lodz ended on 23 November neither as a Russian defeat, nor as a German victory.' J. Keegan, *The First World War*, p. 181.

very difficult to approach. We only possess one shot-gun and we should have to use the whole Regiment as beaters. The French are <u>most</u> dangerous. They loose off with their rifles at any hare or partridge that they see!

An important Serbian victory is announced today, and it is confirmed in Vienna.* The Serbians have been one of the surprises of the war, and their last victory, which took place when everyone imagined them to be moribund, will have great results in the Balkans. I fancy the Austrians must be using Hungarian troops against the Serbians.

It will be interesting after this war to know what workings have been going on between the British Government and the various Balkan Governments to ensure their participation in the war. The memory of the Treaty of Bucharest** is still fresh enough in Bulgaria's memory to make her very troublesome. Greece too is very exigent. 'You offer Bulgaria more for her neutrality, than you do us for participating in the war', said Venezuelos the Greek Premier to Sir Edward Grey.† The Germans last night attacked our 19th Brigade, but were not very successful and were easily repulsed.

Great rumours of Kaiser's illness.

FRIDAY DECEMBER 11

Another rainy day. Went down to my squadron at 8 o'clock and watched troop drill. A lot requires to be done. It takes weeks to shake off the effects of a few days in the trenches. It is the most extraordinary thing that 24 hours in the trenches make a man oblivious for weeks to his appearance or state of cleanliness.

We received the excellent news about midday that Admiral Sturdee has sunk the *Scharnhorst*, *Gneisenau*, *Leipzig* and *Nürnberg*, and that of the whole

---

* Belgrade had fallen to the Austrians on 2 December. But next day FM Putnik launched an offensive which, after several days of fighting, drove the enemy out of Serbia. See 16 December. Austrian efforts to conquer the Serbs were not renewed until the autumn of 1915.
** Signed on 10 August 1913, this treaty ended the second Balkan War in which Bulgaria had been defeated by the combined forces of Serbia, Greece and Romania. 'Bulgaria was compelled to accept the exaggerated claims of Serbia and Greece, who split most of the Turkish territory of Macedonia between them.' Ernst Helmreich, *The Diplomacy of the Balkan Wars*, Ch. 18.
† Nor did Grey, Foreign Secretary 1905–16, manage to keep Bulgaria out of the war. But his diplomacy with America over the naval blockade was more successful. Without it the USA might have put an embargo on the export of crucial munitions to Great Britain. Grey had been appointed Knight of the Garter in 1912, the first commoner to receive that honour since Castlereagh in 1814.

squadron only *Dresden* escaped. This is evidently the victory which Churchill expected when he was here last Monday.*

The Australian and New Zealand contingents have arrived in Egypt.** There must be nearly 70,000 of our troops there now. I do not believe that the Turks will have any success there. The desert which protects the frontier is no mean obstacle. Napoleon always placed deserts first, then rivers, and lastly mountains as obstacles.

The only two roads from Syria to the Suez Canal are effectually barred, one, which lies along the coast, by the British fleet, the other is closed by our capture of Akaba.† The capture of Basra and the whole of the country from the junction of the Tigris and Euphrates by our Indian Expeditionary force is a great step. The town of Basra is the centre of the Arabian fig and date trade, and is equivalent to Marseilles or Liverpool. It is in addition the terminus of the much advertised Berlin to Baghdad railway. Should this railway ever now be finished,†† it will simplify matters for us to have the terminus on the Persian Gulf in our hands.

SATURDAY DECEMBER 12

Went down to my Squadron at 8 o'clock for more troop drill. A misty morning which became a brilliant day at 9 o'clock. General Kavanagh turned up to look on and we discussed a few matters.

He repeatedly emphasised the need to get the Cavalry spirit back into the men, and pointed out the great value of discipline. He seemed very pleased on the whole. I told him that some of the men were very heavy‡ and severely

---

* The victory of the Battle of the Falklands on 8 December, which wiped out Adm von Spee's squadron, was largely due to the superior weight of British metal. Each broadside from the battle-cruisers *Invincible* and *Inflexible* weighed about 2,000lb more than each one from the German armoured cruisers. There were 1,800 German dead, but the Royal Navy lost only thirty sailors. Geoffrey Bennett, *Naval Battles of the First World War*, Ch. 6.
** Many of these Anzac troops would take part in the ill-starred Gallipoli landings in April 1915.
† Akaba was captured by a Royal Navy party on 2 November. Then the next day Turkish ports at the Dardanelles were also bombarded – and Turkey responded by declaring war on the Entente Powers. See Martin Gilbert, *First World War*, p. 105.
†† The last two sections of the Berlin to Baghdad Railway, on which work in Iraq had begun in 1902, were not opened until 25 October 1918. This was five days before the Armistice of Mudros was signed with Turkey.
‡ The average total weight for a trooper on horseback with all his gear was about 18 stone.

punished their horses and he said 'Yes, aren't they awful!' Had a horse parade at 11.30. Squadron had 120 riding horse and 25 transport.

The Duke of Lancaster's Own Yeomanry have 1½ couple of hounds and they propose running a drag line with them.

A lovely Turkey and a plum pudding arrived by the afternoon post, and are to be kept for Xmas day. They caused great enthusiasm.

Saw a doctor at lunch who had been a week with a Belgian hospital. He told us a story of a German officer who was lying badly wounded there. He asked if there was any chance of his living, and the doctor answering in the negative he said, 'Well then I will tell you two things. First, I was shot by my own men. Second we are done, and it's only a question of time now to finish us.'

I hear the Germans are very depressed about their ships being sunk last Tuesday. They formed the German Chinese squadron station at Tsingtao. The crews had been together for six years and so were very efficient. Admiral von Spee, the German Commander,* was a great admirer of Admiral Percy Scott,** and had copied all his gunnery tips, thus making these ships the best shooting ships in the German Navy.

We also hear that that scoundrel Beyers had been shot and drowned in South Africa. Far too good an end for him. Thus ends this burlesque fiasco. Lord Buxton† states that the rebellion in South Africa is practically at an end. 7,000 rebels have surrendered.

SUNDAY DECEMBER 13

Monty Pease came round at 8.30 to the school to say that he found that he had to return to England that morning, and that he proposed motoring to Boulogne at once. He suggested that I should come with him for the trip. I asked Archie Sinclair to come too, and at 9.30 we all started off. The morning was beautifully fine. Penn seized the opportunity to send back to

---

* Adm Maximilian von Spee was drowned in the battle. He went down with his flagship, the armoured cruiser *Scharnhorst*, which sank with all hands.
** Technically retired in 1913, Scott was recalled to the Admiralty to deal with the U-boat threat. Remarkably inventive, and a pioneer in the improvement of gun drill, he had established a record for marksmanship and rate of fire in his own ship, the *Scylla*, before the war. Scott's elder son was killed as a midshipman at the Battle of Jutland. V.W. Baddeley, *DNB*, p. 753.
† Lord Buxton, newly appointed Governor-General of the Union of South Africa, had arrived in Pretoria as war broke out. He worked harmoniously with Gen Louis Botha through the campaigns in German South-West Africa (now Namibia) and German East Africa (Tanzania).

England some German lances, helmets and swords which his squadron was carrying about in their waggons.

These articles were put in our motor and created the greatest impression everywhere we passed. En route to Boulogne we passed through St Omer, which now is the General British Headquarters. The road winds a good deal after passing St Omer, and is very pretty! The fields all round were being well looked after and cultivated by French Territorial Troops. These people wear their own clothes but a military cap. This gives them an odd appearance. This system really is a good one, for it ensures the harvest next year, and the great loss of labour entailed by the conscription of every able-bodied man up to 30 is not felt nearly so greatly as it would be otherwise.

Ten miles from Boulogne the road runs perfectly straight down to the sea, bordered on each side by the futile French trees which are planted to give shade but which being 100 feet high with a perfectly bare stem, and a small clump of brushwood at the top, always fail to do so.

Several miles away from Boulogne the Napoleon Monument can be seen. This column marks the place where the centre of Napoleon's army rested in 1806, when he was waiting for the command of the sea to be gained, so that he could invade England. 109 years later it marked the centre of the large Rest Camp which was pitched in August last for our Expeditionary Army, after its disembarkation, prior to its advance to Mons.

Several times on the road, notably at the entrance and exit of St Omer and at the entrance to Boulogne, we were stopped by barricades of carts drawn across the road behind which stood armed sentries, one English and one French.

Our pass however carried us through. It now began to rain very heavily. There is a very steep and dangerous hill which leads down into the town. We reached Boulogne at 12.15, and went straight to the fish market. After being deafened by the vociferations of the most unattractive fishwives we bought a lot of sole and mackerel, which we thought would be a pleasant change in the Mess, and which eventually were rendered uneatable by the Headquarters cook.

After setting ourselves up with fish we went to the Hôtel Crystal, which had been turned into a Red Cross hospital. Boulogne is full of hospitals and all the people in the streets are doctors and RAMC.

At the quay were four clean newly painted hospital ships.

On reaching the Hôtel Crystal we asked if Trotter was still there and finding that he was, we went up to see him.* He was looking dreadfully thin

---

* Lt Col Algernon Trotter, second-in-command of the Composite Regiment, had been severely wounded at Warneton on 20 October. In the South African War he had been ADC to Gen Sir Redvers Buller, VC.

and worn, and very feeble. He seemed very pleased to see Archie and I and we had a long chat and told him all the news, regimental and otherwise. He said that the piece of shrapnel was still in his left side. It had been located by the X-rays but couldn't be removed yet. He was hoping to get back to London in a few days.

While we were sitting with him, from the end of the room arose a series of cries for a Nurse. The word Nurse was uttered about 15 times in succession and then gradually died away, only to recommence again shortly! It had a most depressing effect on us, and Trotter said it was getting unbearable. It was a wretched boy who had been wounded in the head by a shrapnel bullet, and who had only arrived the night before. As we left Trotter, we looked at the boy. His father (I suppose) was sitting by him holding his hand, and the boy himself was very pale and lay with a fatuous smile on his face. He palpably had an injury to his brain.

We had a very moderate but expensive lunch at the Hôtel Folkestone, where I saw Mrs Sofer Whitelune, who looked very plump and flourishing. She said she was helping in a hospital at Le Touquet and supposed that there was a move on, as they had had orders to clear out all the wounded.

I had my hair cut and then we walked up and looked at the old citadel. Bought several London papers of the previous day, and left for Staple at 4 o'clock. We got to Staple at 7, having passed two large touring cars lying smashed up in a collision by the side of the road.

Saw Torrie on our arrival who told us that during the afternoon we had had orders to move tomorrow at 7 o'clock.

We eat the sole for dinner with chastened spirits, for moves are always a nuisance. But such is war, anyhow this war.

MONDAY DECEMBER 14

Called at 5 o'clock, pitch dark but a clear dark morning with lots of stars. Breakfast at 5.45. Stuffed myself with porridge and bacon. One never knows in war when the next meal will be.

Horse came round at 6.20 and I rode off to join my squadron. I was sorry to leave the little school. My servant had a most affecting farewell with all the school staff. Tommy Atkins is really the most extraordinary fellow. He manages to make himself understood in very few minutes in any country in the world. My servant couldn't talk a word of French, and the school people couldn't talk a word of English, but all the same they talked away like mad all day long, and he could make them understand anything. He persuaded them to darn my socks, and do my washing and produce hot water at all hours of the day and night.

The rest of the people of Staple were not so sorry to lose us as they ought to have been. The fact is, that after five months of it, they are getting sick of having soldiers billeted on them.

In some places, such as our last billet, Eecke, which had, earlier in the war, been invaded by the Germans, they are naturally pleased to see troops, and especially English ones. In Eecke, even after three months, the broken and tangled telegraph wires, which hang in untidy branches on every pole, still show evidence of the German occupation. But Staple was lucky enough to be just behind the high water mark of the German advance.

The nearest point to Staple which was touched by a German patrol was the railway crossing at Les Ciseaux, one mile from the village. About five or six days after the declaration of war, this patrol had turned up at the crossing, but had ridden off on the approach of a small French infantry piquet.

I reached my squadron at 6.30, or rather where it ought to have been, but owing to the idiotic behaviour of my Corporal Major, who did not pass on the orders the night before, the time for parade had not been notified. After a pyrotechnic display of language, the squadron managed to get to the starting point in time. The 1st Life Guards came up from a lane on our right and great cheering broke out from them. I at first took this demonstration of lightheartedness to be caused by libation the previous evening. But afterwards I found that it was caused by a rumour that the Kaiser had died.

We marched in the same order as in our route march of Thursday last and reached Hondeghem at 7.30. From there we marched east to Caestre, which was full of very young infantry, and thence to Berthen. The roads were simply awful, the mud lay a foot deep everywhere.

From Berthen we rode to Westoutre, which we reached about 11.30. Here we learnt that we were to move on about three miles to a spot near Locre and remain all day in support, returning to our billets at Berthen in the evening.

Most of the little towns and villages were full of artillery or our ammunition waggons. One could have counted 100 lorries full of 4.5 inch and howitzer shells. Westoutre had the Royal Scots infantry billeted there.

About 12.30 we arrived at the field in which we were to take up our position. We formed up in Squadrons and dismounted, and then fed and watered. Most of the officers retired to a small farm at the entrance to the field, climbed into the loft and lay on the straw.

About 2.30 Torrie and I went for a walk up to where the General was making his temporary headquarters. In front of us there were two or three very big English guns pounding away, but no German shells came back over us. Either we were out of range, or else the Germans are saving their ammunition. I notice a very great difference on our return to the fighting

Supplies for the 2nd Life Guards are delivered by horse and cart.

Cpl Birch, Master Cook, with his fan club, about to issue the rations.

area, in the German fire. They no longer plaster every road and farm with large shells.

A most interesting German book was picked up by the French last month in a house that had been occupied by German artillerymen. It was the new German Artillery Regulations, which superseded the ones in use at the beginning of the war. Most important was the admission that shells were very scarce,* and that in future they were not to be used, 'unless the object in view justified the expenditure'. Night firing was forbidden altogether. This is understandable, for it was ridiculous the manner in which the Germans wasted their ammunition on trivial objects. For instance, on one occasion two batteries shelled, for 5 hours, two broken limbers** which the French had left on the road.

The shortage of copper is already affecting the German artillery. Shut out by our Navy, its price in Germany has risen to £160 a ton, whereas its market price elsewhere is £55.† Our ships remove every particle of copper off every ship they see. A great deal of what they confiscate is dumped at Gibraltar. The mole there is piled sky high with this stuff. It is taken off every ship, neutral and otherwise, and in cases where a discussion arises over the seizure, the British Government pays for the confiscated cargo and on no account is the capture ever given back.

We sat in support until 2.30 when we were ordered to return to our billets at the village of Berthen. Although it was only 3 miles back, it took us 1½ hours owing to the terrible state of the roads, and the state of congestion due to ammunition and transport columns. Having finally reached the village we went into our billets, which were bad. The horses again had to stand out in the open, and the men of my squadron and those of B Squadron had to share one farm, which made their quarters most crowded. However, there was a roof.

I still lived with the Headquarters as it was so close to my squadron. We had a great meat tea at 4.30 which was very much appreciated, as we'd had nothing to eat since breakfast at 6 o'clock. I shared a small cupboard 10 feet square with O'Kelly the temporary doctor who is filling Luxmoore's place. However, with my dear old valise and two bundles of straw, I slept like a king, probably very much better.

About 8.30, just as we were off to bed, orders arrived which hinted at staying here a few days, and giving us leave to unsaddle our horses, but to be ready to turn out anytime at half an hour's notice.

---

* But the shell shortage was far more serious in the BEF. Philip Warner, in *Field Marshal Earl Haig*, writes: 'The British guns were not merely inferior in numbers to the Germans, but at that time (1914–15) were limited to four rounds *a day*'. Blaming outdated equipment and a lack of urgency in the workforce, he reveals that British production was 22,000 shells a day, while the French produced 100,000 and the Germans and Austrians 250,000.
** The detachable part of a gun carriage, pulled by horses.
† An indication that the naval blockade imposed on Germany was already biting. Ultimately, the blockade on all goods destined for German ports proved a crucial element in the victory of the Allies.

My fur-lined fleabag from Debenham and Freebody is of more use as a pillow, than for its proper use. Our small box was lit up during the whole night by the flashes of the large French guns which crown the hills away towards Dixmude; we couldn't hear them, but the flashes were practically continuous all night. We heard, late at night, that we had been supporting an attack 3 miles to our front near Messines, during which we had captured several German trenches and about 60 prisoners. These were mostly in a very defeated and exhausted condition, and several without boots. I believe the Gordon Highlanders and the Lincolns carried out the attack.

The French also succeeded in capturing the château at Hollebeke yesterday, thus finally expelling the Germans from the Yser Canal, and showing that they are crossing to the right bank.

TUESDAY DECEMBER 15

Called by my servant at 5.30. Breakfasted at 6 and sat waiting for the order to saddle up.

At 7.15 went off to my squadron and made arrangements for building straw lean-tos in case we stay here a few days. Rifle inspection at 8.30. Sick horses at 8.45.

About 9.30 orders arrived for us to send down to a farm nearby for straw for the lean-tos. We started building these along the south hedges of our field. The men really are very good at this and in two hours we had got capital shelters up. Three weeks ago they were useless at this sort of thing. Necessity teaches. I suspect very strongly that they prefer this to Troop Drill.

It has, as usual, been raining at intervals. The mud is simply awful. General Kavanagh came round about 11, and seemed to think that we might be here some time. Got another barn for the men of my squadron to sleep in, as they were too crowded last night. It was fortunate that last night was so mild, as otherwise our horses, after being in barns for 3 weeks, would have suffered greatly.

The old censor stamp has been cancelled, and the new one was issued today.

We have had no communiqué for two days. There has been an almost total cessation of firing today, which is a relief. We heard today that perhaps Major Pirie, late 21st Lancers, is to come to us as Second in Command. I can't help thinking how this Regiment has changed since July last. The first group which went out was the Composite Squadron, and a few of the staff of the Composite Regiment. They left on August 16 and are indicated by a star. The remaining officers listed left England on October 6.

Roll of officers in the Composite Squadron and the Regiment:

Lt Col A.F.H. Ferguson	Wounded, Zandvoorde, Oct 30
★Lt Col A.R. Trotter	Severely wounded, Warneton, Oct 20
Maj Prince Alexander of Teck*	Posted to King of Belgians, Nov 5**
★Maj Hon. H. Dawnay	Killed, Zillebeke, Nov 6
Capt Hon. A. O'Neill	Killed, Zillebeke, Nov 6
Capt H.S. Ashton	Prisoner at Moorslade, Oct 19
★Capt T.C. Gurney	Mentally collapsed – returned home, Nov 14
★Capt F. Penn	
Capt Lord Belper	Returned home, Oct 18
Capt V.R. Montgomerie	Wounded by shrapnel, Zonnebeke, Oct 20
Capt W. Smith-Cuninghame	Wounded by shrapnel, Oct 30
Capt E.P.C. Pemberton	Killed, Hooglede, Oct 19
Capt A.S. Hoare	Disappeared, Zandvoorde, Oct 30
Capt Hon. M. Bowes-Lyon	Wounded by shrapnel, Oct 18
Capt A.M. Vandeleur	Killed, Zandvoorde, Oct 30
Capt Sir George Prescott	
Capt J.F. Todd (attached)	Killed, Zandvoorde, Oct 30
★Lieut D.E. Wallace	Severely wounded knee, Warneton
★Lieut Sir A. Sinclair	
Lieut Stewart Menzies	
★Lieut A.G. Murray Smith	Machine Guns, Killed, Warneton, Oct 21
★Lieut E.J.L. Speed	
★Lieut W.A.V. Bethell	Went home, sprained knee, Oct 20
★Lieut R. Fenwick Palmer	Wounded by shrapnel, Warneton
Lieut Lord Carlton	Returned home, bronchitis, Oct 25
Lieut A.C. Hobson	Wounded, Zillebeke, Nov 6
2nd Lieut W.S. Peterson	Killed, Zillebeke, Nov 6
2nd Lieut J.A.St.C. Anstruther (attached)	Killed, Zandvoorde, Oct 30
2nd Lieut M.W. Graham	Wounded, Nov 6
2nd Lieut K.Palmer	Prisoner at Moorslade, Oct 1
Lieut Sir R.G.V. Duff	Killed, Westrobeek, Oct 16
Lieut C. Prescott (Interpreter)	Wounded, Zandvoorde, Oct 22
Lieut G. Sandys	Wounded, Zillebeke, Nov 6
Lieut Keith Menzies (Special Reserve)	
Surgeon Maj R.M. Power	Returned Home with bad knee, Nov 12
★Surgeon Capt E. Luxmoore, RAMC	
Vet Maj E. Barry	
Vet Capt J.B. Walker	

* Brother of Queen Mary. He became chairman of the British Mission to the Belgians, 1914–15, and was created Major General the 1st Earl of Athlone in 1917.
** King Albert I. He assumed personal leadership of the Belgian Army and bravely rejected the Kaiser's ultimatum of 2 August 1914, demanding free passage of German troops across Belgium.

Quartermaster H.L. Hidden
2nd Lieut S.G. Simpson (Interpreter)

	TOTAL	
40 Officers	Killed	9
	Wounded	11
	Missing	1
	Prisoners	2
	Returned UK ill	5
	Survived unhurt	12

Hoare's disappearance is a mystery. He was last seen in a fainting condition lying behind a haystack on Oct 30 at Zandvoorde; nothing further was ever seen or heard of him, but he has been variously reported as having been seen at Torquay and Prince's Restaurant within the last two weeks.

Crofton now gives a brief, but vivid, insight into the carnage at the end of October at Zandvoorde. This was a bloody and gruesome engagement and effectively punctures the myth that the Cavalry were spared the realities of serving in the front line. The Cavalry Corps held a 9-mile front, with Kavanagh's 7th Cavalry Brigade at the very centre. They were occupying primitive, shallow trenches on the forward slopes of the gentle hill east of Zandvoorde, in full sight of the enemy. At 6.45 am on October 30, General von Fabeck ordered a massive bombardment from his 250 heavy guns which lasted seventy-five minutes and blasted them out of their trenches. Then Fabeck sent forward five fresh infantry divisions. Overwhelmed by superior numbers, the Household Cavalrymen stood no chance. The slaughter resulted in the almost total annihilation of one squadron of 1st Life Guards under Capt Lord Grosvenor, another squadron of 2nd Life Guards (Capt A.M. Vandeleur) and Lord Worsley's Machine Gun Section of the Blues. But the village did not fall until 10 am.

After the war, Zandvoorde was aptly chosen as the site for the Household Cavalry Memorial. It overlooks the slope occupied by 7th Cavalry Brigade and is strikingly tall, to permit enough space for the hundreds of names carved on it of those who died on that 'sad, but glorious day for the Brigade, for though their losses were great, the line held'.

Vandeleur, Todd and Jack Anstruther were in the squadron that was in the trenches when they were rushed by the Germans on Oct 30 at Zandvoorde. These trenches were perfect death traps, the supports being a mile and a half away and out of sight behind a hill. Only one man ever returned and his tale was very incoherent. He remembers hearing Anstruther call out 'Good God they've got round us' and then seeing him run out with his revolver and fall. No further news has ever been heard of Vandeleur or Todd, nor of the 70 men who composed their squadron in the trench. It is feared that all were bayonetted. Graham was also with them, and he was supposed to be missing. Then one day about a month later his mother wrote to the War Office and said that her son had been at home with her for three weeks, wounded. He can give no account of what happened on that day.

One troop under Nethersole, who is now in my squadron, was left behind a ridge in reserve, and so escaped the disaster, but with the exception of this officer and about 25 men, the remainder of C Squadron had utterly disappeared. The squadron on 29th October was reduced to 1 officer, 25 men and 159 horses.*

At 7.30 orders arrived for us to march at 9 o'clock tomorrow back to our billets at Staple. Great enthusiasm. The attack yesterday was fairly successful, but it was only carried out locally.

The gunner in a battery in front of us told me today that the Germans had fired 300 Jack Johnsons at his battery and not one had burst. Their ammunition is certainly getting more and more defective, but to my mind there are quite enough that do burst.

A number of reports have come in which state that the Germans are preparing a strong defensive line on the right bank of the Scheldt from Ghent to Tournai.

WEDNESDAY DECEMBER 16

Paraded at 9 o'clock, and marched off in the same order that we arrived in on Monday. A very bright sunny day, with a cold wind. Roads as usual awful. Reached our old billets about 2 o'clock and very glad to get back. I found to my surprise that the people welcomed us back very warmly; everything was ready, the billets having been warned by Simpson, the interpreter, whom we had sent on ahead, like John the Baptist, to prepare the way. Fires were alight and smiles everywhere. The men smiled and seemed very pleased too.

It is wonderful how thoroughly both sides understand each other, although neither is able to speak a word of the language of the other. Most of the people both here and at Eecke speak Flemish.

We paid out late in the afternoon 20 francs a man. I shrewdly suspect that, as it will all be spent in this area, this is why they are so pleased to see us. Over

---

* Normally a squadron was about 120 strong. On dismounting, about 30 to 35 men remained behind as horse-holders. See 17 December.

8,900 francs will be disbursed (about £330) by Sunday next. A French Regiment spends nothing as the men only get about one franc a week as pay.[*]

Torrie is most anxious for me to leave my squadron and come as his second in command. Would much rather keep the squadron, but don't see how I can refuse. I expect I shall stay here some little time, anyhow until the New Year.

Slatin Pasha,[**] the man whom the British troops rescued from the Mahdi at Omdurman, and who had been made a Major General, and given several British decorations, has, on going back to Austria, renounced all his English honours.

An analysis of the casualties amongst British Officers since the beginning of the war up to this date shows the following:

	Killed	Wounded	Missing	Total
Generals	8	7	–	15
Colonels	29	66	13	108
Majors	103	183	36	322
Captains	356	619	148	1,123
Lieutenants	637	1,350	316	2,303
TOTALS	1,133	2,225	513	3,871

The Foot Guards have suffered very heavily – their figures are:

	Killed	Wounded	Missing	Total
Coldstream	21	66	10	97
Grenadiers	24	31	3	58
Scots	22	21	15	58
Irish	13	21	4	38
TOTALS	80	139	32	251

A German prisoner has described the fate of the XXVII Corps to which he belonged. It seems that this Corps was formed of men of the 1st and 2nd Battalion of the Landwehr,[†] of many volunteers aged 17 to 20 (probably quite untrained) and of a few from the Landsturm. It was trained hard for six weeks.

---

[*] This scanty pay in 1914 of one franc per week for a poilu had the purchasing power in 2001 of 17.86 francs – or 2.726 euros. Michèle Pierron, Musée de l'Armée, Paris.
[**] Freiherr Rudolf von Slatin had won fame in the service of England over nearly forty years in Sudan. Imprisoned by the Mahdi (nationalist revolutionaries), he escaped in 1895 and was made a Pasha (highest rank in the Egyptian Court) by the Khedive (Ottoman Viceroy of Egypt). He can hardly be criticised for his 'defection' to his native Austria.
[†] The Landwehr were reservists while the Landsturm comprised local militia groups, normally called up only in time of war, and mostly from a more senior age bracket.

It went into action at Gheluvelt alongside the XIX Corps, and on Oct 28 at Ypres lost 2,200 men out of 3,000 in one Regiment.* The writer calls the fight a 'hell-battle', and declares that only a handful escaped, deaf and distraught. Two-thirds of the division to which the Regiment belonged were lost. This is very much like what our Gunner Major told us at Eecke on Dec 4, with reference to the success of our shrapnel.

We hear that the Serbians have re-occupied Belgrade. The Serbian success has been a very pleasant surprise, even at General Headquarters. Here they were regarded as 'all out', and evidently Berlin and Vienna had thought the same. For some reason the Serbian campaign has not interested people very much in England. The last six weeks' fighting must have been very severe on the Serbian nation, exhausted as they have been by three campaigns during the last two years. At the end of November the situation changed, the Serbians having received ammunition from France. At the same time the casualties were made good by recruits of the 1914 class, and King Peter** went to the front to raise the morale of the troops.

Meanwhile, the Austrians sent back 2 Army Corps to co-operate with the Germans against the Russians. The Serbians at once resumed the offensive along the whole front, drove back the Austrians, re-occupied Belgrade and Pozega, and inflicted great losses, nearly 17,000 men and several big guns being captured. The Austrians seem exhausted and there are difficulties in the supply of food and ammunition. Their morale is said to be much lowered.

THURSDAY DECEMBER 17

Paraded my squadron at 8.30 and had squadron drill in a large field at the back of the farms where the troops are billeted.

On the whole it was very good. There is no doubt that the Reservist is a far better man than the recruit. The question of future employment of cavalry in this war bears on this fact. There cannot be a large supply of Reservists left in England now, and every succeeding draft is composed of more and more

---

* These huge losses of around 70 per cent are confirmed by one of the survivors – Adolf Hitler. Sent to Flanders a few days earlier, he writes to his Munich friend Joseph Popp that, after four days' fighting, his Regiment's fighting force had fallen from 3,600 to 611 men. Ian Kershaw suggests the slaughter was partly caused by 'friendly fire', 'as Württemberg and Saxon regiments mistook the Bavarians, in the gloom, for English soldiers'. Ian Kershaw, *Hitler*, p. 90.

** Though aged seventy in 1914, King Peter of Serbia insisted on taking part in the campaign to save his country. In 1919 he became king of the newly formed Yugoslavia.

immature and untrained youths. This cannot be wondered at, for it takes at least 2 years to make a cavalryman. If the Cavalry are to be used as infantry, or in trench work, it is being uselessly frittered away and as it is the most expensive arm, it is useless extravagance to waste it.

A squadron consists, roughly on service, of 120 men: on dismounting the No.3s are left as horse-holders. This means 25 per cent of the strength, or about 30–35 men. Thus a strong squadron can only supply from 75–80 rifles in the firing line. Thus a Regiment of 3 squadrons can supply from 220–240, which is only what one double company in the infantry can supply. Hence the entire brigade can only supply about 700 rifles at the maximum.

Thus our entire Cavalry *Brigade* can only supply about two-thirds the number of men in a firing line that one infantry *battalion* can. It is amusing to note that, very frequently, Staff Officers, who must be totally ignorant of the Cavalry, imagine that the paper strength of a Regiment means the number of rifles which are available for attack or defence. They overlook the fact that it takes a certain number of men to hold the horses which are left behind, and in cases where the men are away for 48 hours in the trenches, to water, feed and groom them.

We are glad to hear that one of our submarines, the B11, has succeeded in forcing the entrance to the Dardanelles by diving under 5 rows of mines. She then torpedoed the old Turkish battleship *Messudiyeh* which was guarding the mine field. She safely effected her escape.*

The Suffolk Regiment reports that as a result of the bombardment on Monday, about 20 dead Germans were found at the western end of Petit Bois. An officer of the Middlesex Regiment, who went out on a night reconnaissance last night, reports large numbers of dead Germans, estimated at 100, in a communication trench west of Maedelstede Farm.

Orders appear to have been issued in some, if not in all, corps that helmets are no longer to be worn in the German Army. The red bands round the forage caps have been, in many cases, covered with strips of grey cloth. Prisoners of the 5th Bavarian Reserve Regiment have been taken wearing black greatcoats.

The Police Authorities all over Germany are issuing orders forbidding the waste of bread, and laying down regulations for its supply. They also decree

---

* On 13 December, Lt Cdr Norman Holbrook had daringly navigated the B11 into the Sea of Marmora. He avoided not only the moored mines, but also the searchlights and guns on either side of the narrow Dardanelles Straits. The *Messudiyeh* was sunk and the B11 escaped unscathed. For this feat, Holbrook was awarded the first naval Victoria Cross of the war. Geoffrey Bennett, *Naval Battles of the First World War*, p. 252.

that potatoes are to be cooked in their jackets, and no refuse is to be thrown away. No corn is on any account to be given to any animal. I wonder how the horses will get on.

FRIDAY DECEMBER 18

Had my squadron out at 8.30. Did a nice bit of squadron drill. The Reservists, if properly handled, are excellent. They drill with an intelligence and precision which is remarkable. A fortnight's quiet drill like this will entirely eradicate the result of a month in the trenches. Torrie came into the school about 11.30 and asked me to take over the job of Second in Command. So I bade a sorrowful farewell to my squadron which Malcolm Lyon has taken over.*

The motor car from Headquarters at St Omer arrived today about 11 with Stewart Menzies and his brother Keith, and Lyon. They also brought news of the death of poor Luxmoore's wife. This is really very sad for they were only married last April. What a lucky thing it was that he was able to get home a fortnight ago and was with her until the last.

More rumours about a move, but there is nothing definite. About 12 o'clock orders arrived from Brigade Headquarters saying that we were to be ready to move at 2 hours' notice.

This does not exactly mean standing to, which entails keeping the horses with their saddles on, but it points to a possible boost forward. The situation here is very mysterious. No one seems to know anything, least of all the General's entourage. We hear that Russia is not satisfied with the progress made on this side. She is annoyed with France, not with us, who only do what the French Staff decides, for not detaining more German 1st Line Corps this side. This is rather hard, since we have kept 20 out of a possible 22 1st Line Corps here since last August. Anyhow, I expect there will be a forward movement very shortly.

I never believe the rumours we hear of great attacks on certain dates. Those are certain to be spread for the purpose of deluding the enemy, and there has been far too much chat lately about moves. When the move does come, it will come like a thief in the night.

---

* Capt the Hon. Malcolm Bowes-Lyon resigned his commission in 1907 after twelve years' service. He rejoined the 2nd Life Guards in August 1914. He was a brother of the 14th Earl of Strathmore and an uncle of HRH Queen Elizabeth The Queen Mother. Later he commanded the 5th Battalion, Black Watch, the regiment in which her brother, Capt the Hon. Fergus Bowes-Lyon, was killed in action at Loos on 27 September 1915.

Every effort of 'man and horse' (to use the Kaiser's expression) is now devoted to keeping the war off German territory. What words for conquering nations to use. Although the situation on this side is to us very important, there is no shadow of doubt that the principal theatre of war is in Poland. It is Russia who calls the tune from that side, and it is Russia that will administer the *coup de grâce*.* The question is – does Germany consider that the primary theatre is in Poland, and has the western theatre been relegated into the second place? The reported arrival out East of six German Infantry Army Corps, and five cavalry divisions hitherto operating in France is significant.

We all know that the menace of Russia to Silesia is serious and imminent. When nations conflict in war they bring armies against one another for two objects.

a. To disarm and destroy the other army as quickly as possible.
b. To bring political and economic pressure on the other race, which indirectly leads to the same result as in a.

As an example of b. we have the German attack on Paris in 1870, not because Paris was an army, but because, when Paris was taken, French resistance was bound to cease.

Modern Germany has no centre corresponding to Paris, but Germany is a nation which has to a great extent industrialised itself. She possesses two main industrial districts, precisely in those regions which the first shock of an invasion will strike. The districts are Westphalia and Silesia.

To put pressure on Silesia is the alpha and omega of the Russian plan. The Russians are now nearing Silesia: the arrival of the Kaiser, and the furious efforts of von Hindenburg all show that the Germans thoroughly realise the menace. For four months the German army has bustled and racketed in the West, and has accomplished nothing except the destruction and plunder of a Neutral State** which Germany was pledged by international compact to protect.

The pet German surprise, the sudden deployment of unexpected reserves at a decisive point, failed. Germany cannot expect that the present stalemate could continue here, should she remove her first-line troops to Poland. The

---

* Not one of Crofton's more accurate predictions. But he could hardly have envisaged that Lenin would pull Russia out of the conflict in December 1917.
** Belgium. The Treaty of London of 1839 had committed Germany to upholding Belgian neutrality. The German Chancellor, Theobald von Bethmann-Hollweg, did not believe that Great Britain would go to war for 'a scrap of paper'.

German troops have undergone a dreadful disillusion in France and Belgium. They have had awful experiences; seen their ranks shattered, and their best officers killed. They know now what it means to face the modern fire of our rifles and field guns.

Then, whipped away, they have spent days in cold cattle trucks, to be finally detained in the frozen mud of Poland, without food or billets, to recommence fighting with a fresh enemy who continually reinforces and strengthens his armies. This is the prospect before these immature youths and old men that are being taken for the German ranks.

As far as we know Germany has not yet made this decision. The present teutonic burlesque Napoleon* knows that if he gives up his flamboyantly advertised conquest of Belgium, he would lose a powerful asset with which to bargain should overtures for peace come along soon. Also, the hoodwinked Germans at home would inconveniently ask for what purpose the losses in the West had been spent. In the third place he considers that a retreat in the west would turn the scales of the decisions of neutral powers. So Germany has not yet officially declared the Polish theatre to be the primary one, and instead has adopted the half measures of withdrawing from the West five Army Corps and five Cavalry Divisions. This transfer has equalised numbers in the West where hitherto she had a superiority, without equalising them in the East, where she is still in a minority.

SATURDAY DECEMBER 19

Rode round the D Squadron billets with Torrie and Menzies at 9 o'clock. The morning began by being too fine to last, and about 12 o'clock the usual driving rain set in. We still hear various rumours concerning our future. The chief one now is that the whole of the Cavalry is to move right back to the Base into winter quarters, so that the congestion in these billeting areas will be lessened, the horses will be more easily fed, and the hundreds of lorries which are now required for hay and oats will be used for other purposes. St Omer will decide definitely what is to be done with us this winter.

If this war should carry on over next summer, cavalry will certainly be required for its proper role again instead of in this damned mudlarking which fritters it away now. The papers seem full of the shelling of Scarborough, etc. This ought to wake up those fools who comprise the great majority of the Great British public. What a fuss over 20 minutes' shelling. Not a quarter

* Kaiser Wilhelm II.

the fuss was made over our 87,000 casualties of the last four months.* Every paper we have yet received is disfigured with the portraits of the very unattractive people who have been caught hoarding.

When will the Public understand that a shell is no respecter of persons, and that it whips off the head of the three-year-old child playing in the street, with the same gusto that it kills half a squadron of men. There will be many more such cases. The only remedy is, as far as I can see, *not* to live on the East Coast.

It is amusing to note the whine of fright that arises from gutter rags like the *Daily News*, and its bleating as to why the Fleet could not prevent this, when one remembers that if the *Daily News* had had its way there would have been no fleet at all.** All this should have a good effect on recruiting, but I imagine that the War Office now have almost as many men as they want. It is easy enough to get men; officers are the difficulty.

About tea-time an order came in from the 3rd Cavalry Division to say that 25 per cent of the officers in each Regiment may go home on 72 hours' leave.

This takes me, so I learn the very glad news that I can slip off home for three days. I can now rectify the many omissions which my hasty departure on November 5th occasioned. As one looks back now over the four and a half months during which the war has raged, one cannot help being thankful for the results achieved. The offensive against France has failed. For the dubious triumph of reading the annexation of Belgium from the steps of the fifteenth-century Cloth Hall of Ypres, the Kaiser has poured away in the flaming crucible of Dixmude the greater part of 200,000 men.

Steadily day by day the communiqués show that the Allies in the West have begun to reconquer the ground by this partial offensive which will lead to the final road of success.†

German maritime trade is dead, the ports closed, the crews are idle and unemployed. The defeat of the third Austrian invasion of Serbia is that

---

* The naval bombardment on 16 December of Scarborough, Whitby and Hartlepool by four German cruisers certainly removed any complacency in the British public. Rumours of an imminent German invasion were rife, prompting families to move inland and away from the east coast of Essex and Suffolk. Malcolm Brown, *The Imperial War Museum Book of 1914: the Men Who Went to War.*

** On 1 August there was an article in the *Daily News* by A.G. Gardiner entitled 'Why we must not fight'. Gardiner claimed there was nowhere that UK interests clashed with Germany. Niall Ferguson, *The Pity of War*, p. 216.

† True, the Schlieffen Plan had failed. But France had lost more than half her coal output and two-thirds of her steel capacity, and most of Belgium was occupied. Crofton here gives an oversanguine view of the situation just before Christmas 1914 which was, at best, a stalemate.

ulcer* which saps the vitality of the Austro-Germans, as assuredly as that Spanish ulcer, the Peninsular War, sapped the vitality of Napoleon.

Pensions, the relief of distress, the increasing cost of all commodities are an additional strain on the German war economy. We have yet to learn the results of the fighting, that for a month past has raged on the Polish theatre, but whatever the temporary German success may be, it will have no lasting favourable consequences.

The Russian advance has been delayed for a few weeks by the attack from Thorn which opened on November 12.** We have yet to hear full details of the Russian retreat from Lodz, and the withdrawal to within 20 miles of Warsaw. To my mind this shows the essence of the Russian strategy.† What is more effective than to lure the German hordes far from their strategic railways, out on to the trackless districts of Western Poland?

With every step in retreat the Russians draw nearer and nearer to their vast reinforcements and supplies, and the support of the line of the Vistula. *Reculer pour mieux sauter* is the motto. The Russian strategy of retreat is no new one. 1914 may be as decisive as 1812.††

England started to make her armies after the war had begun, and delayed her mobilisation for four days. But for the surprise defence of Liège, this would have wrecked the Allies' plan. History in the future will be interesting on that point. It is reported that at the Council when the Kaiser signed the declaration of war against Russia he threw his pen upon the table after signing, and said, 'Gentlemen you have compelled me to sign, but you will live to rue it.'

SUNDAY DECEMBER 20

A brilliant light sunny day. What a pleasant change!! Went for a long walk with Archie Sinclair, and we discussed the Russian operations. We sat in the

---

* But the ulcer lost its potency in 1915: by the end of the year Austria had conquered Serbia, and the Serbs were compelled to retreat to the Adriatic via Albania.
** An old fortress city, Thorn is located on the Vistula at the point it entered German territory in West Prussia.
† Crofton's optimism about Russian strategy might have been tempered if he had known that within ten days the Grand Duke Nicholas would send an SOS to London for help against the Turks.
†† In one sense, 1914 did prove to be a decisive year. It heralded the end of Tsarist Russia three years later. But that is far from what Crofton is predicting. By contrast, 1812 had been a triumph for the Russians and had seen the ignominious retreat from Moscow by Napoleon's Grande Armée.

sun and watched a German aeroplane being well shelled. The white puffs
looked very pretty on the blue sky. An English aeroplane shortly afterwards
appeared, and the German one disappeared at once.

My pass from the General returned, giving me 72 hours in England. At
3 o'clock church was held in the backyard of our school but I was too busy
writing to attend.

The owner of the house we mess in complained that our cook 'scorned'
him. Quite right too I thought. I don't like that fellow. I think that he is a
German spy, for he is always nosing about; however, he did not get much
change out of us. The man is a bit of mystery. When we were here last week
we asked if we could use the room opposite the one we feed in. It was the
usual parlour furnished with the total lack of taste, which is common to the
middle classes of most races, and as the shutters were never opened the room
smelt like twenty vaults. He said that he did not wish us to use it, as his wife
used it before she died and he had not disturbed it since. Out of respect to
her memory we did not use the room, but crowded uncomfortably into the
other one.

Our friend the schoolmaster, however, informed us two days ago that our
host had never been married. It was because he was a bachelor that he was so
'finicky'. The legend of the dear departed being thus rudely dispelled we
surged into the vault-like parlour, and the shades of the late lamented were
shattered by the song and laughter of the ribald soldiery.

At 6.30 I packed all my belongings into a haversack, and at 8 the motor
took eight of us swiftly into Hazebrouck to catch the 8.53 train to Calais. We
reached Calais about 11.30 pm. We had to walk about a mile from Calais
Ville to the boat which we boarded about 12.15.

A dilapidated man perambulating the decks said that nobody was allowed
on board, but we brushed him aside, and, seizing a cabin, bedded down.
Couldn't get into the Terminus Hotel as it was crowded.

MONDAY DECEMBER 21

The boat we were on is called the *Queen* and is a fast turbine. We had an
excellent breakfast of omelettes and coffee at 8 on shore. Boat sailed at 9 am.

The morning began by being very fine and bright, but turned into rain
later on. The sea was very choppy and inclined to be rough. Arrived at
Folkestone at 11.30.

Sent off wire announcing my arrival to my mother. The day now got finer.
Arrived at Victoria about 1.20. On arriving at 36 Buckingham Gate found
my mother out and my wire from Folkestone unopened. Mater turned up

about 2 and was astounded to see me. Went to the War Office at 3.30 to see George Arthur.

Tea with Marion* at Auto Club. Dined at home.

TUESDAY DECEMBER 22

Rose at 4.45 am. Quite like active service. No effort whatever, good training works wonders.

Caught 5.15 train at Waterloo for Blandford. Very cold and misty morning early. Snow at Basingstoke. Afterwards very bright and frosty like the day in the trenches on November 18.

Arrived Blandford 10.45. Mrs Walter met me at station and Walter outside village of Pimperne. They were just off to Wales for Xmas, so couldn't stay long. Filled up with Port and caught 12.20 train back to London. Reached Waterloo 5 o'clock. Train ran via Bournemouth, Southampton, right through New Forest. Wished I was out hunting there. Saw Marchwood from train.

Went to hear Hilaire Belloc lecture on the war at 8.30 at Queen's Hall.** He said the war in its present phase was essentially 'a siege of Austria and Germany'.

WEDNESDAY DECEMBER 23

Shopped all morning. Went to War Office and my lawyers in the afternoon.

Mater rather seedy, so spent the rest of the afternoon and evening with her.

THURSDAY DECEMBER 24

Caught 1 o'clock train at Victoria. Several people returning to the front. Very long faces and tears on the ladies' part.

Met Simpson the Interpreter who had got us places in the Pullman. Had a large lunch of chops and beer. Reach Folkestone about 2.45. Went at once

---

* Lady Marion Simpson-Baikie was his first cousin. In 1907 she married Brig Gen Sir Hugh Simpson-Baikie and his letters to her – both from Flanders and from Gallipoli – now form part of the Liddell Hart Military Archive.

** This lecture was fully reported in *The Times* on 23 December. French-born poet and historian Hilaire Belloc (1870–1953) was a master of modern English prose. He is best remembered for his humorous light verse, such as *Cautionary Tales*. After military service as a French citizen, he entered Balliol, Oxford, in 1894 and became a naturalised British subject in 1902.

on the steamer for Boulogne, the *Onward*. Sea like glass, but stiff breeze. Reach Boulogne about 5 o'clock – saw no warships.

We found at Boulogne that motor buses would take us to Hazebrouck, so we all crowded in and started off at 5.30. A very tedious journey, the only incident was when it got off the tarred road and stuck. It took us some time to get started again.

Brilliantly clear and very frosty night. Reach St Omer at 8.45. We then raced to a highly illuminated café for food and got some coffee, bread and butter.

Started off again at 9.30, reaching Hazebrouck at 10.30, where we succeeded in getting a car to take us back which was returning empty to St Omer. The air was very clear, and we heard a tremendous cannonade going on, and from time to time bursts of musketry fire.

Reached our beloved school about midnight and very pleased to see it. Woke up Hidden and Walker to chat. Found several letters and 5 parcels awaiting me. Slept like a log.

FRIDAY DECEMBER 25

Christmas Day, the third that I have spent on active service. First one in 1899, on outpost duty at Estcourt, Natal. Second one in 1900, on the staff at Dundee, Natal. Now this one at Staple.

A beautiful frosty day. I love a white Christmas – just like a Christmas card. Excellent breakfast of some delicious sausages, that I had brought back off leave. Church in the yard of our school at 10 o'clock. Very cold standing about and the mist came up and made it all very foggy.

Went for a long walk with Torrie until lunch time. At 6.30 we were all invited by Penn to go to the concert that he had got up for his squadron. His squadron had had a dinner previously of pork, geese and beer, and our arrivals were hailed with considerable hilarity.

Beer was being consumed out of anything that would hold it, cups, jugs, saucers and tin pots. Several of the leading villagers, chief amongst whom was the schoolmaster, also attended. They seemed very bewildered by it all, for it must have been to them rather as a singsong of some wild Arab tribe is to us. However, they smiled and seemed very pleased.

The songs were of various kinds largely sentimental with a topical verse at the end, which had evidently been invented during the afternoon. Everyone thoroughly enjoyed the show, with the possible exception of the Interpreter and Beaumont who from time to time were announced by the chairman as burning to sing various songs, the titles of which were

1. 'We are Painting Baby Yellow so We Can Find Him in the dark'.
2. 'Mary, Call the Lodger Down, He's Bathing in the Cistern'.

There was the greatest enthusiasm when these songs were announced and it was some time before order could be restored. But the disappointment of everyone was extreme when both Simpson and Bo declined to render these old ballads. Beer flowed (in every sense) pretty freely, and the notices on the wall of the school (for the concert was held in the girls' school) concerning alcohol seemed to stand out with biting sarcasm.

L'Alcool ne réchauffe pas kept catching my eye, and I was thankful that it is so, for the room was like twenty monkey houses in temperature. Another maxim *L'école est le grand atelier du progrès humain* had evidently been the cause of this building being selected for the smoker.

About 8.30 we managed to tear our way through to the door, and we left in the midst of a tumult similar to that which had occurred on our arrival. We went back to our house for the great event of the day – Christmas Dinner.

The menu which was as appropriate as it was varied was worthy of the company. The dinner was perfectly excellent in every particular, especially the Turkey which was a work of art. The chef, Lance Corporal Birch,* was suitably thanked, not only for his cooking of the dinner but also for the table decorations which were very clever.

After dinner we all received our Christmas cards which had been sent out by The King and Queen. These were much appreciated and we were told that we should get our present from Princess Mary tomorrow.

The day was a great success and our many kind friends in England who had provided the main articles for our banquet would have been very content had they seen the appreciation which they had caused. Our menu cards, which were made out of Active Service postcards, were all passed round for signatures of the eight diners present. They were Torrie (Commanding), Self (Second in Command), Stewart Menzies (Adjutant), Griffin (Machine Gunner), O'Kelly (Doctor), Walker (Vet), Hidden (Qr Master), Simpson (Interpreter).

SATURDAY DECEMBER 26

Still very frosty, but a very bright day, the country looked very pretty. Went for a walk with Torrie at 11 o'clock to visit the machine gun. Found the detachment hard at work playing football.

---

* Cpl Joseph Birch, from Lichfield, who joined the Army in 1902, was a Master Cook. The Army Catering Corps did not then exist, and every regiment had its own cooks, blacksmiths, saddlers, etc.

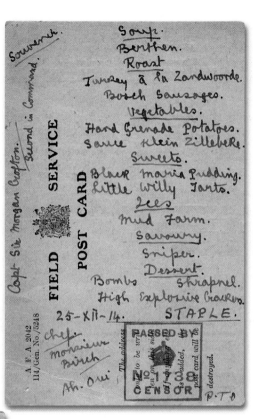

Souvenir.

Capt. Sir Morgan Crofton.
Second in Command.

FIELD SERVICE

POST CARD

A. F. A. 2042
114/Gen. No./5348

Soup.
Bertren.
Roast
Turkey à la Zandvoorde.
Bosch Sausages.
Vegetables.
Hand Grenade Potatoes.
Sauce Klein Zillebeke.
Sweets
Black Maria Pudding.
Little Willy Tarts.
Ices
Mud Farm.
Savoury.
Sniper.
Dessert.
Bombs   Shrapnel.
High Explosive Crackers.

25-XII-14.   STAPLE.

Chef.
Monsieur
Birch
Ah. Oui

PASSED BY
No 1738
CENSOR

P.T.O

Active Service postcard wittily converted into
a menu for Christmas Dinner 1914 and even
stamped by the Censor!

NOTHING is to be written on this side except the
and signature of the sender. Sentences
not required may be erased. If anything
else is added the post card will be destroyed.

I am quite well.

I have been admitted into hospital
{ sick } and am going on well.
{ wounded } and hope to be discharged soon.

I am being sent down to the base.

I have received your { letter dated
{ telegram „
{ parcel „

Letters follows at first opportunity.

I have received no letter from you
{ lately.
{ for a long time.

Signature
only.   To be filled in
after the
Repast.   Y.G. Gorrie.

Date

[Postage must be prepaid on any letter or post card
addressed to the sender of this card.]

(6464). Wt. W3497-293 1,000m. 11/14 F. T. & Co., Ltd.

With our best wishes for
Christmas 1914

May God protect you and
bring you home safe

Mary R   George R.I.

Christmas card from HM King George V and Queen Mary.

At 12 o'clock we received Princess Mary's present. There were two sorts, one for smokers, and the other for non-smokers. Each contained an embossed brass box which held in one case two packets of tobacco and cigarettes and in the other, a large packet of acid drops. To which was added a pipe and a case containing writing materials. I chose the non-smokers' present and got the brass box and acid drops and the writing case.

I was one of the lucky ones for inside the writing case I found an extremely pretty little photo of Princess Mary.[*]

There were only a few packets which had the photo. The brass box will make a very suitable companion to the chocolate box which I received from Queen Victoria on Christmas Day 1899 during the South African War.

About luncheon time the frost broke and a thaw and drizzle set in. Rather a pity. The nice hard roads, and the white hedges soon disappeared and we again returned to our familiar and infernal mud. Am dining tonight with C Squadron who are holding their Christmas Dinner which was postponed from yesterday owing to the concert.

The nibbling away continues on our side.[**] On Tuesday last the Indian Corps was attacked by some heavy columns of German infantry, and they apparently at once left their trenches in front of Givenchy and fled. The loss inflicted on the Germans was very slight, and the vacated trenches had to be recaptured by the Suffolk Regiment and the Manchesters which they only did after suffering considerable loss.

The odd thing is that Regiments, like the Gurkhas, with great reputations have done badly whilst others which were considered moderate have done well. There is of course something to be said on behalf of the Indians. The cold weather and the damp especially affects them. Also they have lost many of their white officers who are picked off by the snipers who have telescopic sights on their rifles. Few talk their language and they get very excited and ultimately lose their heads.

Then the food question is a difficulty. It is impossible to have the same facilities for preparing it, as can be got in peacetime, and the result is that they will eat nothing, and are therefore half-starved at times, for they only get a sack of oatmeal and tins of bully beef slung at them which they won't touch. Also the Indian Army possesses no native field artillery, heavy guns or aeroplanes with which to do their reconnaissance or bomb dropping.

---

[*] In 1914 Princess Mary – known from 1932 as The Princess Royal – was seventeen. She was the only sister of King George VI. Like her mother, Queen Mary, she took a keen interest in the welfare of the troops. She married Lord Lascelles in Westminster Abbey on 28 February 1922. She died suddenly on 28 March 1965 while walking in the park at Harewood House.

[**] 'Je grignote' (I nibble away), said Joffre. But no substantial gains were made by this strategy of attrition – only unlimited casualties – and in 1917 Joffre was replaced by Nivelle.

The French authorities yesterday published their hospital returns for Sept 15–Nov 30 (6 weeks). They were:

489,733 wounded of whom 54.5 per cent have returned to the front

26.5	will do so shortly
17.52	still under treatment
2.48	died

This low mortality for hospital cases must be almost a record.

Clive, at General Headquarters, estimated that the French losses in killed, wounded and prisoners from the beginning of the war up to now would roughly amount to 650,000.* This does not mean slightly wounded, but wounded men who will be of no more use in this war.

SUNDAY DECEMBER 27

A wet drizzly day. We had church at 12 o'clock; it took place in the concert room on Christmas night. The fumes of tobacco and beer plus the atmosphere of several troopers sleeping there for two nights made a not very clerical atmosphere. There was not much of the Odour of Sanctity about it. Communion was held afterwards and about 5 officers and 6 men attended.

The last few days have been marked by a general retirement of the Russians. This retirement has achieved the immediate objective of the Germans and Austrians, relieving the pressure upon Cracow, and the threat to the industrial region of Silesia.

In this connection it is evident that two critical factors may be taken as tests of German or Russian success in this theatre of war; one is the possession of the main Galician railway; and the other is the possession of Warsaw.

The reasons that Warsaw** is of such strategic value are:

---

* 'The slaughter of the French soldiers in the opening phase of the war was unmatched in the rest of the conflict: 329,000 killed in the space of two months and half a million by the end of the year.' Niall Ferguson, *The Pity of War*, p. 340. The total number of French dead in the war was 1,397,000. Lopez points out that this is an average of 900 men killed every day for 1,560 successive days. Jean Lopez, *Le Calvaire des Poilus*, pp. 14–18.

** 'Hold Warsaw and nobody can hold the line of the Vistula against you. Germany has made her great bid for Warsaw and has hitherto failed. Russia has twice had Cracow (the gateway to Silesia) within her grasp and twice has failed.' Hilaire Belloc in his London lecture on 22 December, underlining the ambivalent nature of the campaign on the Polish Front.

a. It is a vast depot.
b. A crossing place over a very difficult obstacle.
c. A railway centre in a land where railways are rare.
d. No other crossing place over the Vistula exists for 200 miles.

This is why the Germans have made these terrific efforts for a month past to obtain possession of the city. The Russian retirement corresponds to a belt 10 miles wide, or one day's march. Their line is still fed by the Vistula, and by the Warsaw–Lowicz railway. It still defends Warsaw at a distance of 3 days' march, and the fortress of Novo Georgievsk is upon the left flank of any further German advance.

Thus, notwithstanding enormous Austro-German losses in the battle in Central and Southern Poland during the last 3 weeks, no decisive result of any kind has yet been attained.

In addition, the weather in Poland continues to be a great disadvantage for the Germans. The roads are seas of mud, and their heavy guns can only move slowly. On the other hand the sudden cold, while helping their main advance, will imperil their position on the Western Vistula, by enabling the Russians to cross the ice and assault their flanks.

MONDAY DECEMBER 28

Went on a route march at 10 o'clock for about 2 hours. Weather inclined to be wet, anyhow dull but mild. At 2 o'clock we went out on bicycles for a staff ride to discuss a few simple problems with Torrie. Our start from this village was made the occasion of a good deal of levity on the part of the inhabitants and the troops, but we soon got down to riding our cycles with great skill.

General Kavanagh today went on seven days' leave to England. Not much news from our front. All four corps are in the line there now with the Indian Corps in reserve. The new 27th Division has also arrived. Torrie goes on a week's leave to England, leaving me in command here.

We received today Sir John French's Special Order of the Day for Christmas and the New Year.

The change of ruler in Egypt was effected very cleverly by the British Government.* The choice of the title of Sultan will direct the attention of the fellahin** from the one at Constantinople. The new Egyptian flag,

---

* At the outbreak of war, Britain proclaimed a protectorate over Egypt, annulling Ottoman sovereignty. Egypt was not recognised as an independent kingdom until 1922.
** Egyptian peasants (origin from Arabic *fallah* = tiller of the soil).

which is to be three white crescents with their backs to the staff, each with a five-pointed white star between the horns on a red field, will to the native population seem a more important flag than the old one with one crescent.

Am sorry to say that Simpson our Interpreter had to leave us today. He has been most excellent, and was most good hearted and obliging, and very useful to the officers and the Regiments although not quite in the way intended by the War Office. If we had been campaigning in China, no doubt interpreters would have been essential. But in France many have merely been a nuisance, for the majority of them are too old for subordinate rank, and also, never having done any soldiering, are usually hopelessly at sea. Some of them too were bad linguists, so there was little to justify their existence, and the War Office has wisely abolished this corps.

We are beginning to hear authentic accounts of what happened to the Indian Corps last week. There was apparently a gap of about 200 yards in our front line, and towards dark a number of 'Indians' appeared, and began to dig a trench there. This was highly approved by the trenches on either side, and on its completion it was considered that the gap was now secure. Soon however, a terrific rifle fire opened up from the new trench on the trenches on either side of it. It turned out that the 'Indians' who had dug this trench were disguised Germans.

The side trenches being enfiladed, the occupants left them hurriedly, and in the gap thus formed a German Army Corps advanced. A severe engagement then began, the 1st Infantry Brigade being now brought up in support which took the new trench, but failed to re-capture the others. However, after severe losses, especially amongst the Highland Light Infantry, the trenches were finally re-taken and the original line restored.

We hear today that the Scarborough Raid was not such a one-sided affair after all. The Admiralty had 1½ days' notice of it, and Warrender,* with 2 Dreadnought Squadrons, only missed the raiders owing to the fog by an hour. Also there was a submarine in Hartlepool Harbour during the shelling, which could have bagged at least one of the raiders, but it was waiting to cooperate with Warrender's squadron.

---

* Formerly a midshipman in the Zulu War of 1879, Adm Sir George Warrender rose to flag rank in 1908. In command of the 2nd Battle Squadron of the Grand Fleet at the time of the Scarborough attack, Warrender narrowly failed to intercept the German battleships under Adm von Ingenohl. He retired in December 1916 owing to ill health and died one month later. See Sir Julian Corbett, *Official History of the War. Naval Operations*, vol. II, 1921.

Robertson today told me that his brother, who is in the Flying Corps, and is now stationed at Eastchurch, said that the German raid of an aeroplane over Sheerness was an absolute failure. It was at once chased by two of ours, who got within 400 yards of it, when unfortunately a Corporal who was observing in one of them, jammed the gun and couldn't re-open fire, so the fugitive escaped.

We were given yesterday the profile sketch of the usual German trench, with the following remarks concerning it.

1. These trenches are to be widened so that one can easily move past men firing.
2. All communication trenches must be wide enough for a man to pass along with his knapsack on without touching the sides.
3. For observing and sniping, look-outs and loopholes of wood will be constructed.
4. Platoons that are resting will employ the time in repairing and cleaning clothing, boots, rifles. The ammunition will be counted and divided up equally. Every man must carry a tin of meat, one of vegetables, and a bag of biscuits.

These remarks tally very much with our own trenches. I suppose really they are the same in all armies.

On the sector of the line which is held by the British Army, the Germans have 2½ Corps only to our 4. The British Army out here consists now of Corps 1–4, the Indian Corps and the 27th Division, which is composed of troops from India, Aden, China, Jamaica, in fact from all quarters. When the 28th Division arrives these two will form the 5th Corps. So we shall have a total of 6 Army Corps. This is the first sign of our new reinforcements, and is a very welcome one.

The divisions of the first instalment of Kitchener's Army are numbered from 9 to 26. These 18 divisions are divided into the 1st, 2nd and 3rd Armies of 6 divisions each. We should see all these, and the 36th, out here in the middle of February or the beginning of March.

An Airman today reports that the Lille Aerodrome was empty this morning. There were no tents, and the landing T had been removed. Hangars and a landing T had been consistently reported for several weeks past.

Yesterday the Germans destroyed the Tour de Templars at Nieuport with a high explosive shell which killed the observing officer. They also threw 40 shells into Furnes between 7.30 pm and 9.30 pm on Christmas Day.

TUESDAY DECEMBER 29

About 3 am I was awakened by a tremendous thunderstorm. Even in the tropics I have never seen lightning more vivid. It seemed to be right over us. These outbursts were accompanied by a terrific gale of wind and sheets of hail, and from time to time, even while the lightning was going on the moon came out brilliantly and lit up the night like an arc lamp, making all the surrounding wet tiled roofs look like silver. I often thought that the windows were going to be blown in and smashed. About 4 o'clock the storm abated and I went to sleep again.

Torrie, Archie Sinclair and George Prescott all departed this morning at 10 o'clock in the motor from Boulogne, to catch the 3 o'clock boat for England on 7 days' leave. I took over command until Torrie's return.

At 2 o'clock this afternoon the Headquarters of the Regiment played the Machine Gun detachment in an Association Football match. I hadn't played for 10 years at least. There was a large attendance of the members of both units looking on. After ten minutes vigorous play I scored the first goal for the Headquarters and in doing so fell on my back in the mud. Great applause, both for the goal and the after effects. Stewart Menzies and Walker the vet both played very well, and after a most exhausting performance, the Headquarters finally won by 6 goals to 2. Feel very stiff now.

Speed returned off leave this morning and brought yesterday's *Times* with him. It contained the welcome news of the Aeroplane attack on Cuxhaven.* We seem to have acquired the command of the air to some purpose.

From all reports we seem to be making steady progress in our theatre of War. The advance has been most notable at Arras, Vermelles, and to the South of Ypres.

Both our positions, and those of the Germans were hastily taken up during the great movement which extended the opposing lines from the Oise to the Sea. The gradual advance of our line to the North and South of Ypres is important because it is diminishing the prominence of that salient. This salient was rendered necessary for the sentimental reason of not giving up Ypres to the enemy. But it was a source of weakness, for it was exposed to enveloping and converging fire, and it was liable to be outflanked on

---

* A port at the mouth of the River Elbe. The Zeppelins were attacked by nine seaplanes on Christmas Day. Dense fog obscured the exact location of the sheds. However, the raid caused part of the German fleet to be detached from Cuxhaven to other moorings on the Kiel Canal. Flight Commander Hewlett led the expedition and received a telegram of congratulations from King George V. *The Royal Air Force in the Great War*, pp. 47–8.

enfilade. Its radius of five miles however rather lessened the disadvantages incidental to it.

Our activity makes it impossible for the enemy further to weaken their army in France, in order to concentrate larger forces gainst Russia. Thus the advantage which Germany gains from being on interior lines is greatly neutralised.

WEDNESDAY DECEMBER 30

A beautiful fine frosty day. Held a Court Martial parade at 12.30 to read out some sentences on a few malefactors.

We were issued this morning with a diagram of the various types of German aeroplanes, to enable us to recognise them at once. They are however best recognised at once by people getting bombs on their heads. In the afternoon we went to watch a football match between C Squadron and the Headquarters and Machine Gun detachment. I acted as touch judge. It was bitterly cold. The match was a draw.

Our Intelligence Department informs us that the officers in C Squadron have a turkey. We decide on giving a banquet to see the New Year in, and inviting the C Squadron officers. The invitation is sent off and accepted with thanks, and a query as to whether we would accept a turkey. We reply in the affirmative. It is to be a great banquet lasting from 9.30 to midnight tomorrow night. We decide to use our last three plum puddings for it. Joicey who has just returned from St Omer makes us a present of four mackerel and a skate.* The doctor O'Kelly is dispatched into Hazebrouck to buy anything that he can. He returns with some beef with an undercut. The banquet is now assured.

We have been having the most brilliant moonlight nights lately, they are frosty and fine and so light that one can easily read a newspaper out of doors. They are like the nights at Eecke last month. I think snow must be in the offing.

The outlook is encouraging in the minor areas of conflict. Serbia has freed herself from the invader. The Turks before Erzurum have only crossed the frontier of Caucasia at one point. The banks of the Suez Canal are crowded with British Troops, and there is not a Turk in the Sinai Peninsula. In East

---

* Col Hugh Joicey (later 3rd Baron Joicey) had been adjutant of the 14th Hussars, but was attached in 1914–15 to the 2nd Life Guards. For the last three years of the war, he commanded the 1st Battalion, Royal Suffolk Regiment. His elder son David died of wounds received at Salerno in 1943, while serving in the Coldstream Guards.

Africa the Germans have failed to take Mombasa, or to cut the Uganda Railway. Tsingtao has fallen.[*]

THURSDAY DECEMBER 31

The last day of the old year.

We are told this morning that we are to play our tie today for the Football Cup. Our Headquarters and Machine Gun Detachment is to play A Squadron Leicestershire Yeomanry.

The team went off in a hay waggon drawn by 4 horses to Hondeghem, where the match is to take place in a field near the General's headquarters. Menzies, Walker and I motor over. I am to act as touch judge. The Chaplain referees. The match was good but we were outplayed. The field was very wet and muddy, and our men slipped about like horses, and the little Leicesters ran all round them. Leicestershire of course is a great place for football, and there were many excellent players in their team, including an officer, Macdonald, who is an Oxford footer blue. They beat us 6 goals to nil.

Great enthusiasm on the touch line, and each goal was hailed by a chorus of hunting noises, which were very appropriate as this squadron is made up from troops from Gadsby, Belvoir, Rutland and Melton. After tea preparations are made for the feast.

We have considerable trouble with some of our guests, who keep coming round and asking what we are going to give them to drink. We however, remembering the turkey, are coldly civil.

Brigade Headquarters today sent round to know, 'if, in the event of our returning to the trenches, it is considered necessary that the men should be equipped with entrenching tools'. We do consider it necessary, but we sincerely trust that we shall *not* be wanted for such work.

We have now six Infantry Corps or 220,000 men spread over our front which is only one of 14 miles. This works out at 80 men per yard, which should be sufficient to hold it, without calling on the cavalry. We hear very strong rumours that the cavalry is to go to Egypt. I shall not believe it yet, however anything is possible. I can't see that we are much use here during the winter.

[*] The Port of Tsingtao served the coastal region of Kiaochow and had been seized by the Germans from the Chinese in 1897. It was strongly defended by 3,000 Marines. Following an attack by the Japanese, Capt Meyer Waldeck, the naval officer acting as Governor, surrendered the garrison on 7 November 1914. John Keegan, *The First World War*, pp. 224–5.

The view that Germans are phlegmatic is incorrect. Under a phlegmatic surface they are a highly strung, nervous people, who react very easily to good or bad news. The present war has revealed them in their true colours. The shock and strain of fire action has completely broken down many of them.

Nothing shows the difference between the German and British characters better than their songs. The British soldier sings a song because he likes it, whereas the German soldier sings his war song, because it is the sort of song which a soldier ought to sing. The contrast is great between *Tipperary* and *die Wacht am Rhein*.

We decline to admire things unless we like them, whereas the Germans have always admired what they are told to admire. *Die Wacht am Rhein* for the German soldier is merely a vocal and mental goose-step. For his part, the German is extremely shocked by English ribaldry, in which there is, to him, something malignant.

We had a high tea today at 5.30 as we were dining late. Malcolm Lyon came up from his squadron, so we succeeded in getting together for our New Year Dinner all the real 2nd Life Guards Officers in the Regiment. Griffin bought some quite decent claret and Burgundy.

Was very sorry to lose my chestnut horse today, the one that I got at Rouen in November. He had become so lame, after being cut by brambles or wire on the night we were out at Berthen on the 15th that I had to return him to the Veterinary Hospital as he would have been of no use to me had we moved. I was lucky enough to get a very nice bay in exchange.

We dined tonight at 9.30. The table was decorated. There were ten present. Self, Bowes-Lyon, Speed, Beaumont, Stewart Menzies, Keith Menzies, Wilson, Griffin, Walker the vet and O'Kelly the doctor. Spirits were very high, and the beef and turkey were excellent, so were the plum puddings.

The time soon went, and before we could believe it we found that it was 5 minutes to 12. We had put the clock right by the church, so we were all ready when 12 struck. We downed a good tot of rum each to absent friends, then linked hands and sang 'Auld Lang Syne'. It all went off capitally, and we broke up about 12.15 and went off to bed. Such was the end of 1914.

FRIDAY JANUARY 1

The first day of the New Year. I wonder what it will bring. Let us hope that 1915 will be as destructive to Prussian militarism, as 1815 was to French. A bright cold morning which clouded over at lunch, and turned into a wet cold afternoon.

Went for a ride into Hazebrouck at 3 o'clock with Griffin to try my new bay. I like him very much, he is much the same stamp as my late chestnut, only younger. We got an order today stating that our division (the 3rd Cavalry Division) is on duty for 48 hours from 8 o'clock this morning.

We hear that the Germans made an air raid on Dunkirk,* two days ago, a feeble reply to our Cuxhaven one.

We also hear that the Canadians have come out here. They seem to have made England too hot for them and have created a reign of terror on Salisbury Plain. I wonder if they will be any good in the firing line. As a general rule this breed of brawler is not worth a damn, and I see no reason to suppose that these people will be any different to the ordinary common or garden swashbuckler.

I hope that the Americans are not going to make trouble over this contraband affair.** It is really too silly to suppose that with our whole existence at stake, we can bother about the so-called rights of these half-breed American traders. America stands to lose just as much as we do, if the Germans should win, let them be under no misapprehension on that count. A German victory and the elimination of the British could bring America face to face with the hard fact of a Europe dominated by German militarism.

SATURDAY JANUARY 2

We received orders today to send all officers into Hazebrouck on Monday next to learn how to throw hand grenades and bombs. This is most necessary, for no one here has the remotest idea of how to use these things. It will be a case of save me from my friends, when we get into the trenches again.

We arranged for a bathing parade today. We had previously sent our interpreter into Hazebrouck to arrange with a local brewery for the use of their tubs and plenty of hot water. The squadrons then marched in with intervals of an hour between them. The brewery was a capital place. We had the use of ten large vats each five feet across and two and a half feet deep, and two iron tanks. They were placed in a large shed with a brick floor, and we curtained off the sides with tarpaulins. Lots of hot water was supplied from the engine house, through a hose pipe.

Previously there had been some inclination, chiefly amongst the Lancer Reservists, to go sick and get out of the washing. In fact we had twenty to thirty people up to the hospital as soon as the news of the washing spread.

---

* On Kitchener's order, the Admiralty had established at Dunkirk on 1 September an airbase from which raids by 'naval aeroplanes' could be launched within a 100-mile radius. Twelve planes were intended for each of the three squadrons, but two or three were the most that a squadron could muster.

** The US Ambassador had protested against the seizure in mid-Atlantic of American exports deemed by the Royal Navy to be contraband. See 10 January.

This was very suspicious as we had, up to this, only been having two or three sick *a week*. However, O'Kelly the doctor told them that he prescribed a hot soaking for each ailment, and so they were all unwillingly led off.

It turned out a great success and all the men thoroughly enjoyed themselves, and splashed to their hearts' content. Plenty of soap was issued and we put creosote in the water. It was a remarkable sight to see three men in each tub, soaping and splashing like mad.

I think that they will look forward to their weekly wash in future. The regimental bath has become an important event, and days are allotted in orders, alongside reports of famous victories, etc., that such and such a regiment will have its bath on such and such a day.

The Turkish movement in Palestine against Egypt seems still to be hanging fire. Most of the carefully arranged demonstrations and processions of Holy Banners, carpets, etc. have utterly failed. On December 19 the Holy Banner arrived from Medina, escorted by a camel corps. The aged Mufti of the Great Mosque of Medina accompanied it. A procession escorted the banner to the Court of the Mosque of Oman, where a thunderstorm broke upon the cortège, drenching the banner. The Mufti, who took to his bed, died three days later. This was interpreted as an evil omen by the majority of the Arab population, who were never enthusiastic about the war.

The concert party, which came over from England during Xmas week under Seymour Hicks, has now returned, after giving several shows at Boulogne, Rouen and other places near the Base. They could not come, however, anywhere near Headquarters or the Front. Their performances were greatly appreciated in the hospitals.

SUNDAY JANUARY 3

A cold wet day again. Leaden skies and generally depressing outlook. Church and Holy Communion at 12 o'clock in the school.

After lunch a few papers were given us from which we learnt the loss of HMS *Formidable*.[*] A curious coincidence that she was the sister ship of the *Bulwark*. [**]

---

[*] HMS *Formidable* was torpedoed off the South Devon coast on 1 January. After signalling to another ship not to stand by, in case she too should be torpedoed, Capt Arthur Loxley went down with his crew, of whom only two hundred survived. He was last seen smoking a cigarette on the bridge, with his old terrier Bruce. Martin Gilbert, *Winston S. Churchill*, 1971, p. 185.
[**]The destruction of HMS *Bulwark* was not caused by the Germans. On 26 November a massive internal explosion occurred while ammunition was being loaded at Sheerness. Nearly eight hundred sailors were killed. Martin Gilbert, *Churchill*, p. 110.

At the time of the South African War, both these ships were considered the last word in naval architecture.

The news of the occupation of Walfish Bay* on Xmas day is satisfactory, and so is the news of the occupation on Dec 9 of Bougainville, the largest of the Solomon Isles.**

The Institution on Jan 1 of the new military decoration, The Military Cross, is a good idea.† A decoration of that kind was badly needed; it will rank with The Conspicuous Service Cross of the Navy.

The main feature of the second Austro-German invasion of Poland is the appalling death toll. The fighting has been unprecedented. For a fortnight past there has been no rest, no intermission from wholesale slaughter that must have strained the nerves of even the most hardened troops. It is said that the Germans were doped with alcohol or drugs, and, encouraged by the statement that this was their last fight (which it was for thousands), that Warsaw would be taken for comfortable winter quarters. For seven days and nights consecutively the German waves poured like a mighty tide upon the rock-like Russian defence, in a ceaseless sequence of attacks. The guns never ceased their roar day or night.

The effect of this failure to take Warsaw cannot be over-estimated. Between the Pilica and the upper reaches of the Vistula, the Russians took 200 officers and 15,000 men prisoner and 40 Maxims.††

Many signs point to Italy's inclusion in the war. The arrival of the Italian fleet, followed by the occupation of Valona and the landing there of two regiments of Bersaglieris is significant.‡ In other times that alone would have been regarded by Austria as a *casus belli*. The Austrians are very angry.

---

* Walfish Bay lies due west of Windhoek, capital of modern Namibia. The campaign in German South-West Africa ended with the surrender of the German Governor to Union forces under Gen Botha six months later.

** Named after the French navigator Louis-Antoine de Bougainville, this island, under German administration since 1898, was occupied by Australian troops until the end of the war.

† The MC was intended primarily for captains, subalterns and warrant officers in the British, Indian and Colonial armies. *The Times*, 1 January 1915, p. 8.

†† Machine gun named after Hiram Maxim (1840–1916), the prolific American inventor. Born of Huguenot stock in Maine, he settled in London where he produced the first fully automatic machine gun in 1884. Within a few years armies throughout the world were equipped with Maxim guns. 'His name is more deeply engraved in the real history of the World War than that of any other man.' Anthony Smith, *Machine Gun*.

‡ The second seaport of Albania, which had proclaimed its independence from Ottoman rule in 1912. Valona (or Vlore, its Albanian name) was occupied by Italian troops from 1915 to 1920.

MONDAY JANUARY 4

At 10 o'clock we all rode over to Hazebrouck to attend a demonstration of bomb throwing at the experimental field of the Engineers there. All the officers of the 3rd Cavalry Division were there.

One form of bomb was hand-thrown. A piece of wood was taken about 2 foot long and 4 inches wide. One end was fashioned into a rough handle, on the other end of which was fastened a slab of gun cotton. This was wired on, and in the wire were fastened about 15 long wire nails. On the guncotton slab was a primer with a detonator to which was attached the usual 5 seconds fuze. As soon as this was lighted it was hurled away, and exploded in a few seconds.

It would not be possible to throw this more than 50 yards. It did not seem very effective, though of course if it landed in a trench it would do damage. Most trenches are however by now protected in the front, and over the top by rabbit netting. Two other forms were used. One that was fired from a rifle and another made to throw with a long stick.

The grenade fired from the rifle was placed at the end of a long stick, which is placed down the muzzle. The bomb is fired by the action of the rifle being shot off, flies through the air about 250–500 yards, and bursts on falling on a trench.

This grenade is quite small and on bursting scatters about 15–20 small pieces of iron, which are made up of the casing of the bomb, which splits up on explosion. Like all these new inventions, they are not infallible.*

The London papers have been full of accounts for the last week or so of regiments of German infantry fraternising with our troops on Xmas Day. Apparently the Queen's Westminsters did so, but from many quarters there are the same reports of Germans and English soldiers mixing, shaking hands, exchanging cigars and cigarettes, even taking photos of each other. This is all very well but *ce n'est pas la guerre.***

Boshy papers of the halfpenny type slobber over this rubbish, but everyone out here condemns it. This is WAR, Bloody War, and not a mothers' meeting. I am glad to say that General French fired in a snorter which should put a complete stop to these unsoldierly antics.

---

* The need for these ingenious but rather Heath-Robinson weapons points to the shortage of industrially produced munitions. To judge from Crofton's bitter remarks later about the shortage of shells (see 5 June: 'if only we had shells', etc.), it appears that the French Army was far better supplied than the BEF.
** Crofton is quoting Gen Bosquet at Balaclava. As he watched the Light Brigade being decimated by the Russian guns, but advancing with beautiful precision behind Lord Cardigan, Bosquet said, 'C'est magnifique, mais ce n'est pas la guerre.' Cecil Woodham-Smith, *The Reason Why*, p. 247.

A.G.G.H.Q. B/698   C.C.H.Q. C/43

G.O.C.

   Cavalry Corps.

      The Commander-in-Chief views with grave
displeasure the reports he has received on recent
incidents of unauthorised intercourse with the enemy
and directs that the Officers concerned be so informed.

      It appears that troops, under an improper
use of a flag of truce and, on occasions, without that
formality, have entered into communication with the
enemy, it is to be clearly understood that on no
account will any officer or man take such action
except under the conditions laid down for flags of
truce in Section 120 Field Service Regulations, Part II.

      Any officer who may on his own responsibility
countenance the opening of communication with the
enemy, either on his own initiative or on that of the
enemy, will report the matter at once to higher
authority and will be held personally responsible for
his action.

G.H.Q.   Sd. C.F.N.Macready Lt General
                            Adjutant-General.
    1st January 1915.   British Army in the Field.

2nd L.C. *In your information.*
All officers must be
informed.

Gen Sir John French's Snorter, following the Christmas Truce.

Yesterday a small local attack took place between Neuve Chapelle and Bois Grenier, in which a German trench was captured and 20 Germans were killed. Our artillery today blew up either an ammunition waggon or a magazine to the South of La Bassée and also silenced a hostile battery NE of Auchy La Bassée.

The supply of meat in Germany is stated to be above normal. This means, however, that the maximum prices for fodder are so high that the farmer prefers putting his stock on the market to feeding it.

On Dec 31st General Joffre dispatched the following telegram to General French.

December 31st 1914

I send you, M. le Maréchal, my New Year's Greetings.

Five months of the brotherhood of arms have welded between the French and British Armies bonds which are everlasting.

We shall pursue with but one single purpose, the achievement of our common effort towards a victory which will be complete, and which from now onwards will be a certainty.

This will be our work in the year that is to come, and on the eve of which I beg you to accept the cordial good wishes of the French Army to yourself and the British Army.

To which the Commander-in-Chief replied.

In my own name and that of the British Army in France, I thank you with all my heart, for your cordial and kind New Year wishes. In offering you and the French Army our fervent and heartfelt greetings, I wish to express the honour and pride we feel, in having for five months fought side by side, with an Army which has so splendidly maintained the magnificent traditions of the past, and added so many fresh laurels to its glorious standards.

TUESDAY JANUARY 5

Received a note at 10 o'clock this morning to say that Ferguson was returning and asking me to send the motor for him to Hazebrouck. He arrived about 11 and resumed the reins of command which he had laid down so abruptly on October 21 last when he was hit in the leg.

I now revert from Commanding Officer to Signalling Officer, which will be an interesting billet. During my two months with the regiment I have played many parts:

Nov 12–Dec 10	Maxim Gun Officer
Dec 10–Dec 20	Commanding D Squadron
Dec 20–Dec 27	Second in Command
Dec 27–Jan 5	Commanding the Regiment
Jan 5	Signalling Officer

I think that Shakespeare must have had me in his mind's eye, when he remarked that 'one man in his time plays many parts'.*

The situation in the Western theatre is becoming very interesting. The front extends from the sea to the Swiss frontier, a distance of 350 miles. This extent is about as much as the German Army can protect. Its forces are spread out along its length, and the strain on their diminishing numbers is likely to become great.

True strategy should have obliged the Germans long ago to retire on a shorter line, such as the Liège–Metz line, supposing that the Allies respect the neutrality of Holland. To fall back upon this second line is to give up Antwerp and Belgium, and all thoughts of threatening us. This is the reason for the now persistent pressure by the Allies upon the immense stretch of trenches from Westende to the Swiss frontier.

Owing to our offensive action the enemy has been forced to take up a defensive attitude everywhere. The operations from the Sea to the Lys will be considered under the headings of the three areas:

1. Area opposite Nieuport
2. District N of Ypres
3. District S of Ypres

1.	*In front of Nieuport*
December 15	We debouched from Nieuport as far as outskirts of Lombartzyde.
December 16	Pushed forward to sea, occupied lighthouse and took more than 100 prisoners.
December 19	More progress. 200 yards gained along our front.
December 20	Hostile Trench captured.
December 21	Fresh advance of 150 yards towards Westende.
December 22	Counter attack repulsed, the whole of newly captured ground retained.

* From the 'All the world's a stage' speech by Jaques to the Duke in *As You Like It*, Act II, Scene vii.

2.	*North of Ypres*
December 17	Advanced 500 yards, captured several trenches, 4 machine guns, 150 prisoners. Captured Cabaret de Kortekeer.*
December 18	Cleared surroundings, took a wood, some houses and a field work.
December 22	Further 100 yards gained, making total advance of 700 yards.

3.	*South of Ypres*
December 16	Progressed 400 yards near Veldehoek and Zwarteleen.
December 17	Captured 2 machine guns, waggons and several groups of houses.
December 21–23	Ground gained everywhere without a single reverse.

Aircraft

December 17	Our Airship threw 15 bombs on Sarrebourg station and 5 on Petit-Eich station, as well as 5 bombs and 1,000 darts** on a train in the station at Heiming.
December 18, 20, 21, 22	German aeroplanes chased and forced to land.
December 18	One of our aviators shot a German pilot and saw his machine fall.
December 25	Our aviators dropped 20 bombs on Metz station and 12 on a company at Gercourt.
December 26	6 bombs dropped on Metz hangars.

This list of nibbles is characteristic of what goes on eternally every week, and is of such a character that it irritates and unsettles the German Headquarters Staff. It is being repeated along the whole of the French Sector to the Vosges and the Swiss Frontier.

---

* Or, more accurately, Kortekeer was recaptured; the hamlet had already been captured by the British on 23 October. This illustrates how minimal the gains over this period were and how these small areas were taken, lost again, then retaken. The greatest territorial gain recorded in the three areas round Ypres is 700 yards.
** Darts – called fléchettes by the military – are still used today, but are more lethal. The Israeli Army uses shells packed with 3,000 tiny metal darts, resembling one-inch nails with fins at one end. On bursting in the air, the shell produces a deadly hail of fléchettes, which on one occasion killed four members of the same Palestinian family, *Daily Telegraph*, 30 August 2002.

VOLUME III

JANUARY 6 – FEBRUARY 18, 1915

WEDNESDAY JANUARY 6

A fine day for once, and very mild. At 10.30 went for a ride with O'Kelly to see Cassel, a town about 8 kilometres off. Cassel is an example of the curious hills which are dotted about the country. They rise suddenly with steep slopes to a fairly high summit on which a town is built, the hill on all sides rises up sharply from the plain, and there are no gradual slopes. These hills look like puddings on plates. There are several about here, Kemmel, Mont des Cats, and of course, the best example Laon, which is crowned with a citadel, in which the German Headquarters is now located.

Cassel is now the headquarters of General Foch.* It is an extremely clean little place with well built, stonefaced villas, and narrow paved streets. At the very summit is built the cathedral, or rather parish church, which is very old, but I couldn't see any date on it.** It is built of old red brick and the glass seemed good. Round it grows a line of tall poplars, but the general appearance of the front of the church is ruined by a line of very common, inartistic men's lavatories. The French are really very odd.

Next door to the church was an old building 'Salle de St Joseph' dated 1631, which was full of French infantry.

Two large wireless stations are erected on the summit, which generally point to the whereabouts of a big bug in the military line. We didn't see where Foch lived, and we didn't like to ask. At this stage of the war the French have got very suspicious towards anyone asking questions. The town was full of sleek, well cleaned soldiers, mostly with new uniforms, which generally show that there is a staff in the town. From the summit we had the

---

* Cassel was situated 20km from the British GHQ at St Omer. From this high vantage point (175m), Foch could survey the Flanders plain. Today his magnificent equestrian statue looks out over the former battlefield. He lived at the Hôtel de Schoenbecque, where he was host to King George V and the Prince of Wales in August 1916 and July 1917.
** Collégiale Notre-Dame was the church where Foch came to pray and meditate.

Gen (later Marshal) Ferdinand Foch was appointed Supreme Commander of all Allied Forces in March 1918.

The Grande Place in Cassel – the tram is passing in front of the Hôtel du Sauvage. It still has the stylish restaurant that Crofton often frequented.

most glorious view to every point of the compass.* The roads stretched away, quite straight for 10–14 miles, like the spokes of a wheel.

It is really too funny censoring the men's letters. One gets a very great insight into their characters. Some write awfully well, and others grossly exaggerate. One today tells his best girl that he has 'killed in one place 500 Germans, and done other damage!' I can guess what the 'other damage' is.

Another, who has only left the base since we've been here, said that dead Germans were lying round him in heaps as he wrote, and that they were burning the corpses with petrol to get rid of them.

4,000 typhoid cases are reported from Spa, and cases are reported at Thielt, Ghent, and in all districts near the front. The British Army is extraordinarily free from disease.

In this Regiment there have only been 2 cases of typhoid since the war started, and neither of the men had been inoculated. There have been no cases of dysentery. How different from South Africa. Since we have been at Staple we have had practically no sick, merely one or two men every day, which isn't bad out of 590. The only exception to this was when the bathing

* 'From Cassel you can see the five Kingdoms – France, Belgium, Holland, England – and, above the clouds, the Kingdom of Heaven.' Thus runs a local proverb.

parade was ordered. On the morning on when it took place, the door of the doctor's quarters looked like the early door at Drury Lane in the Pantomime season. These delicate creatures were mostly Lancer Reservists.

Splendid news about the capture of the Turkish IX Corps, and pursuit of the X, at Ardagan by the Russians. What a damned fool Enver Bey* must feel. From the reports it appears that the Commander of the Corps, as well as all the Divisional Commanders, were captured. This makes it look rather like a put-up job, for these kind of people are hardly ever captured *unless they want to be*.

THURSDAY JANUARY 7

The usual pouring wet day. What damnable weather!** The drought really seems to have broken at last. The wind is blowing a hurricane. No chance of a ride or walk.

Some very interesting notes have been issued by the French Staff. Apparently the re-opening of their artillery fire created great consternation by its violence and effectiveness.

The men had been more or less quiet for the last three months; captured note books and diaries made mention in a casual way of a cannonade without serious effect; prisoners talked only of the dampness of their dugouts, and of the lack of variety in their rations. This arcadian existence seems to have been shattered by the re-opening of the French Artillery fire, since when the prisoners present an entirely different appearance; they appear bewildered, and two or three days after being captured they have not pulled themselves together again.

A soldier of the VIII Corps near Perthes: 'I am glad to think that I got out of that hell, and I do not think myself a bad German for saying that I have paid my debt to my country by having been exposed to such artillery fire; I wonder how it is that my reason has not given way; it was a perfectly damnable day.'

---

* A hero of the Young Turks who in 1908 had overthrown the autocratic Sultan Abdul Hamid and then taken control of the Government. In 1911 Enver turned to Germany for military advice. Churchill wrote to Lloyd George, 'What fools the Young Turks have been to put their money on Germany.' As Minister of War in 1914, Enver was highly influential and largely responsible for Turkey's decision to enter the war on Germany's side. He was killed in action in 1922. Martin Gilbert, *Winston S. Churchill*, vol. III, pp. 188–9.

** 'The winter of 1914–15 was the worst in living memory.' David Ascoli, *The Mons Star*, p. 206.

A Lieutenant in the Engineers, captured on Hill 200: 'We saw rifles and men flying through the air; the defenders are either blown to pieces or buried alive, the only ones to escape were those that took refuge in the mine galleries or in dugouts.' Men of the Reserve units tried to abandon the trenches which were being bombarded, but, in doing so, were all killed while running back to their reserve trenches. The prisoners say that it was better to stick to the bottom of the trench and trust to God, than to attempt to fly.

A plan which seems to have created discouragement and demoralisation, consists of bombarding the same trenches two days running. A man of the 65th Reserve Regiment says 'The man who comes to clean up the trenches that have been bombarded, and has seen the lamentable spectacle of his comrades buried or torn to pieces, works frantically all night and then feels his courage leaving him, when the guns open up again next morning.'

We continue to get further evidence of the decisiveness of the Russian victory on the Caucasus front. The official telegram of yesterday from the Russian General Staff gives us the results. The decisive victory occurred at Sarikamish when the IX Turkish Corps was annihilated.* The casualties of the Turks, and their losses in guns, stores and trains, were enormous.

On December 17 last some extremely interesting experiments were carried out by the XII French Army Corps Artillery. The Gun used was the famous 75mm gun firing high-explosive shell with percussion fuse. A Belt of obstacles was laid out consisting of: two lines of *Abattis*,** a line of Pheasant wire, a wire Entanglement 1 metre high 15 metres wide, *Trous de Loup*,† two lines of Rabbit Wire and, behind these obstacles, a line of fire-trenches.

Fire at a range of 1,400 metres continued for 35 minutes. Observation of fire was carried out on a trench 200 metres from the target. The result was that each of the four guns created a passage through the total length of the obstacles and wire entanglements of 3½ to 6 metres in width, a passage which was completely cleared.

---

* Even before the main Turkish attack took place on 27 December, the 29th Division had suffered 50 per cent casualties due to the excessive cold. In the Sarikamish area alone, the frozen corpses of 30,000 Turks were found. 'Throughout Asia, Sarikamish confirmed the image of Ottoman decline . . . It was a decisive battle.' Hew Strachan, *The First World War*, pp. 726–9.
** *Abattis* in the military sense were obstacles made from the boughs of fallen trees.
† Holes dug in front of the trenches intended to booby-trap would-be attackers.

FRIDAY JANUARY 8

For once a moderately fine day. Luxmoore turned up about 11.30 off his month's leave, so took him for a ride to Cassel. We went by a new route which was very pretty. On our way home the rains descended. It cleared up in the afternoon, but remained squally and dull. We hear from the American Consul, that Murray-Smith who was wounded and missing after the fight at Warneton on Oct 21 has since died of his wounds in a German hospital.

The card opposite is a good example of what kind people in England send us in *thousands*, often with woollens they have knitted themselves.

The following are details of the capture of a German trench to the North of La Bassée on the night of Jan 3/4, located in front of Neuve Chapelle:

Time 8 pm Jan 3rd *Artillery* Nil
Strength of attack 1 officer, 25 men
Distance between opposing trenches 200 yards
The enemy's trench consisted of a short trench which had been dug outwards from a sap head occupied by officers and 25/30 men with 2 sentries.
Attack The attack crept forward noiselessly to the trench – a short length of trench, without wire. 2 German sentries were awake and were bayoneted. All the occupants were asleep and were bayoneted; the officer's head was broken in with the butt end of a rifle – not a shot was fired – some men set to work at once, and cut the ground from the adjacent ditch thus flooding the trench. The attackers were only 15 minutes in the German trench and left the bayoneted Germans in the water.
British Casualties 1 wounded and 2 missing. The latter may have since returned.

I believe that this was carried out by the Worcester Regiment, and the DSO was sent up to the officer in the trenches by a motor cyclist.

The French are making further progress in Alsace. Burnaupt-le-Haut has been captured 18 kilometres west of Mulhouse. There is evidently a great deal of water in the German trenches opposite the centre of our line; their men were reported to be engaged in bailing the water out during yesterday. An Alsatian deserter of the 142nd Regiment, XIV Corps, gave the following information to the French troops near Notre Dame de Lorette* on January 5:

---

* About 7 miles south-west of Lens, the hill at Notre Dame de Lorette was one of Gen Pétain's command posts during the bitter fighting in the Artois region from May to September 1915. The immaculately tended cemetery has 20,000 named French graves and the ossuaries contain the remains of 20,000 more men with unknown graves. No breakthrough was achieved.

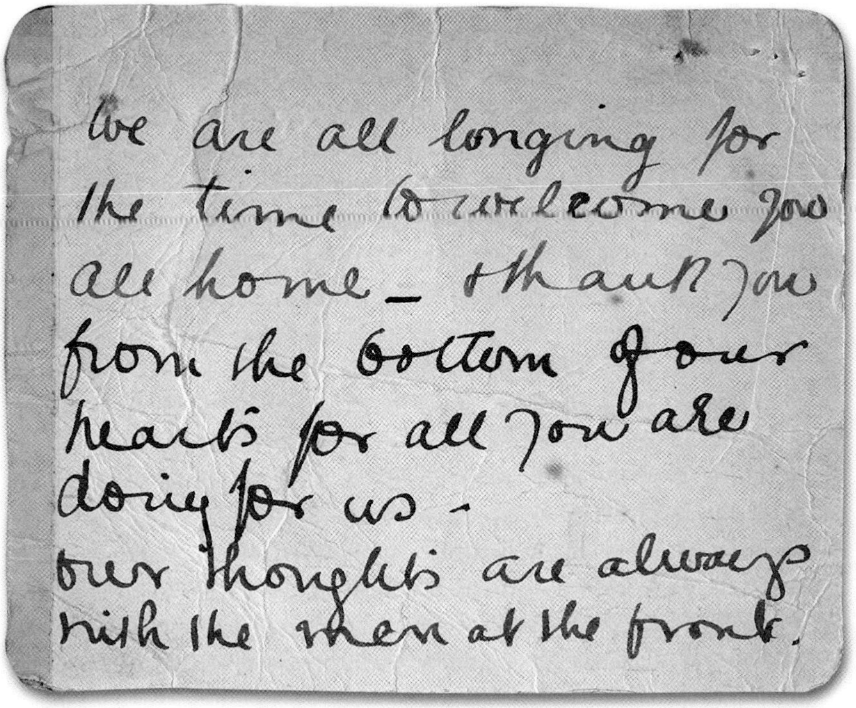

We are all longing for
the time to welcome you
all home – & thank you
from the bottom of our
hearts for all you are
doing for us –
Our thoughts are always
with the men at the front.

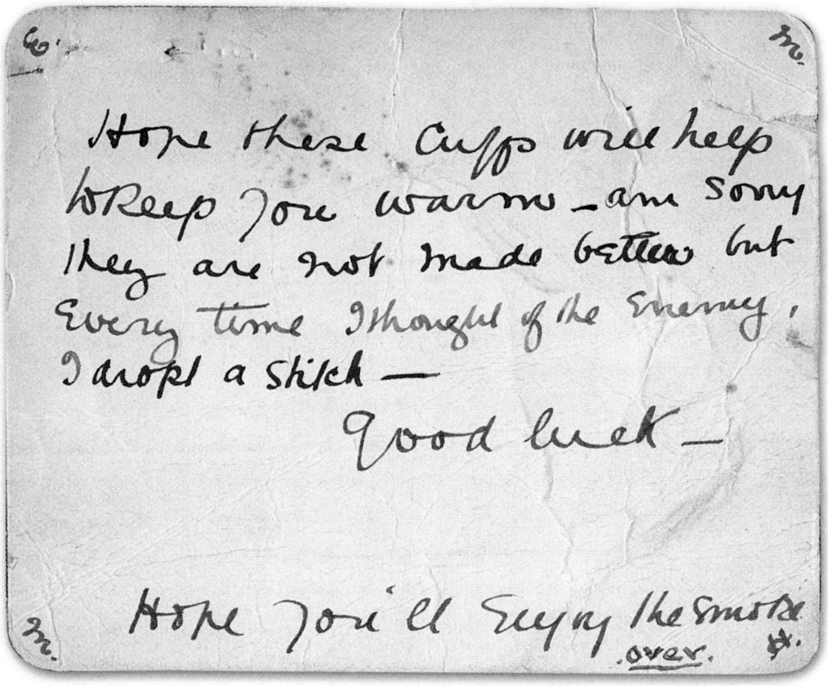

Hope these Cuffs will help
to keep you warm – am sorry
they are not made better but
Every time I thought of the Enemy,
I dropt a Stitch –
                    Good luck –

        Hope you'll Enjoy the smoke
                        over.

'We are all longing to welcome you home . . .'

A draft of 28 Germans arrived from the depot on Jan 4 without rifles but with their packs. They have to arm themselves with rifles which are to be found in the trenches. Shortage of arms and ammunition is reported in Germany, and recruits and Landsturm are reported to be drilling with old pattern rifles.

The following interesting State of Affairs in Germany was issued by the Headquarters of the Armies of the East on January 8:

I

Public Opinion on the War

Everything reveals a change in public opinion (enquiries by neutrals, press, captured German diaries and letters). In August, no German had any doubts of a crushing and rapid victory. In October, victory also seemed certain, but more difficult to obtain. Today the masses are very tired of the war. The talk is no longer of conquest but of the defence of the Empire. The Army Chiefs, when invited by the *Lokalanzeiger* at Xmas to express their feelings in one word, wrote *durchhalten* (Persevere) and *widerstehen* (Resist). Only one (Admiral von Tirpitz)* wrote *Vorwärts* (Onward!).

At the present moment the German leaders realise that the struggle cannot end in their favour, but they intend to maintain their hold on Belgium, the occupation of which will be their best security in the peace negotiations. They rely on obtaining 'peace with honour' owing to the Allies becoming tired of the war. The Imperial Government appeared at one time to have hopes of a separate negotiation with France (*vide* articles showing a friendly spirit towards France in the press and the mission entrusted to Monsieur Eyschen (Luxemburg Minister) to pave the way for Swiss or Dutch mediation).

The declaration of the President of the Council in Parliament,** has left no doubt as to the intentions of France to carry on the War to the end. This has caused a violent outburst in the German press, which betrays their disappointment and there were insulting articles in the *Frankfurter Zeitung* of Dec 24.

---

* Secretary of State of the Imperial Navy since 1897, Adm Alfred von Tirpitz (1849–1930) introduced the Fleet Acts in 1898 and 1900. His policy of building up the German Navy at a rate of four naval vessels a year led to the naval armaments race. An admirer of British education, he enrolled his two daughters at Cheltenham Ladies' College. Robert Massie, *Dreadnought: Britain, Germany and the Coming of the Great War*, p. 166.
** René Viviani was *président du conseil* (i.e. premier) for the first year of the war. A committed Socialist and a brilliant speaker, he was not an inspiring war leader. Criticised for a munitions shortage, he resigned and gave way to Aristide Briand in October 1915.

II

Germany and the Neutrals

Public opinion in Germany no longer has any doubts as to the hostility of the Neutrals. Constant efforts are made to win their sympathies (*vide* reply of Bethmann-Hollweg* to the French Yellow Book**). Their propaganda and attempts at justification lay stress on the following ideas:

i. That the war was forced on Germany.
ii. That Belgium having concluded a military agreement with France and Britain, had by this act, virtually ceased to enjoy the advantages of neutrality.

The responsibility of Germany in the development of the Austro-Serbian conflict and the violation of the neutrality of Belgium, appear to be inclining the sympathies of neutral countries towards the Allies. Germany endeavours to refute these two accusations, but the events of the past month show that she has failed in her attempt to stir up neutrals against the Triple Entente.

III

Economic Situation

The complete continental blockade of Germany is difficult to enforce in practice owing to the interests of countries engaged in the world's commerce. Germany can be hampered in her import of cereals but not to the point of starvation.

On the other hand, she can be caused considerable hurt, both from the military and economic point of view, by preventing the import of certain raw materials (copper, cotton, lead and the products of sulphur and nitrate).

SATURDAY JANUARY 9

A pouring wet day. I really think that it is a waste of time entering up wet days. Unless the fact is actually stated that the day is fine it may be safely presumed that the day is the usual stinking wet one.

---

* Theobald von Bethmann-Hollweg had been Chancellor since 1909. He favoured a negotiated peace and tried to secure the mediation of the USA in 1916. Failing to convince his military chiefs of the benefits of an early end to the conflict, he resigned in July 1917.
** *Le Livre Jaune Français* was published on 30 November 1914. It recorded the diplomatic negotiations between Germany, France and Russia during the week before war broke out. It is one of a number of booklets, issued by the Entente Powers, in the series 'Les Pourparlers Diplomatiques' held in the Library of the Musée de l'Armée in Paris.

Took over the duties of Censor. A very boring job although in the performance of this duty one gets a great insight into the character, habits, customs and opinions of the men. It confirms what I have always thought, that soldiers' letters are extraordinarily inaccurate as regards facts. Modesty, also, is not a virtue common amongst the rank and file. Many members of this Regiment claim to be the cause of the deaths of dozens, and in some cases hundreds, of Germans. It also confirms the impression that no rumour is too wild or too fantastic to be believed.

From time to time, we get many interesting communiqués from the French Intelligence Department. One today deals with a recent French attack near St Menehould. This account is an excellent example of the preciseness of detail of all French orders for warlike operations and also brings home how we are drifting back to the style of fighting which predominated in the Peninsular War, a century ago. As one reads these orders, one sees how remarkably similar they are to those issued by Wellington for the attacks on Badajoz,* Ciudad Rodrigo,** and San Sebastian.†

This attack was carried out by the IV French Army and was completely successful. Success was mainly due to well-organised artillery preparation and support and to a definite objective being allotted to each body of troops.

SUNDAY JANUARY 10

A fine day at last!

We had church at 12 o'clock in the School. The Colonel was in a great hurry, so the Service began 5 minutes before the scheduled time, with the result that two squadrons arrived after the Service had begun and were shut out.

After lunch Luxmoore and I went for a ride to Cassel. The Colonel joined us just as we reached the town. We dismounted at the church and went to look over it. It is an old Dominican Priory built in 1687, and has some very beautiful old windows. The organ too is beautifully carved. The tower of the

---

* The ancient capital of Extremadura, the largest province in Spain. It was deemed to be the key to Portugal, playing strategic roles in both the Peninsular War and the Spanish Civil War.
** Named after Count Rodrigo Gonzalez who founded it in 1150, this medieval city in Salamanca province was captured by the French in 1810. It was recaptured by Wellington's British troops and Spanish guerrillas in 1812.
† San Sebastian – old Basque name Donostia – was formerly the residence of the Spanish Royal Court. It was burned after Wellington had taken it from the French in 1813, albeit controversially. 'The horrors which attended its capture were never surpassed during the Peninsular War', writes Elizabeth Longford in *Wellington, The Years of the Sword*, p. 405.

church is very remarkable in that all its bells, eight in number, hang on the outside of the building.

We next went over the Salle de St Joseph, which is quite close to the church. This hall was an old church, and still retains on its roof the Cross, but it has long since been turned into a school. A floor has been built half way up the pillars of the Nave, and on this floor we found three classrooms. It is quite easy to see where the altar stood, and there were several niches, where presumably figures and statues have stood.

As usual the town seemed full of French Staff Officers.

Before long Germany will be seriously inconvenienced by lack of copper. This is evident when we consider the uses of copper in war material. First and foremost are the cartridge cases for rifle and machine guns, made of copper and zinc alloys, which must be pure to ensure against flaws in the thin drawn metal. This is especially necessary with machine gun cartridges, which have to be exact to the 500th part of an inch. Pure copper alone will give satisfactory results. Field telephones and all electrical fittings require copper. Here again there is no alternative substance.

Besides this there is a band of copper on every shell to take the rifling, so it is not to be wondered that Germany is prepared to pay £160 a ton brought over the frontier, whilst in England the cost is only £60. This large profit explains the hostility of Americans to our seizures of contraband copper. Normally Germany consumes about 250,000 tons of copper annually. Her internal production is about 25,000 tons.

German copper supplies have in the past largely been drawn from the United States, and there are some very significant figures in Sir Edward Grey's reply to the American Note.* In this he shows that Italy has imported from America over 36,000,000 pounds of copper as compared with 15,000,000 pounds for the same period of 1913.

MONDAY JANUARY 11

Another fine day, though not so bright and mild as yesterday. Rode out at 11 o'clock with Archie Sinclair to make up some simple problems for his

---

* The American Note from the ambassador, Walter Page, was published in *The Times* on 1 January under the heading 'A Friendly Protest'. It deplored 'the present condition of American foreign trade resulting from the frequent seizures of American cargoes destined for European neutral ports'. The resulting furore dominated the press early in the new year, but was handled very skilfully by Grey, so that crucial USA/UK trade relations were not jeopardised.

NCOs. A political argument developed and few schemes or problems were arranged.

We hear rumours of Romania entering on the side of the Allies. Her intervention will be followed by that of Italy.

A glance at the map will show the gradual closing of the frontiers of the Central Empires by these interventions. When these have taken effect, there will only be Denmark, the Baltic Sea Coast and Switzerland, through which to get contraband. I hear from most reliable sources that Greece contemplates intervening too, and is being well financed by us for that purpose.

à Court Repington[*] in *The Times* has told us that the Germans, in addition to what they already have put into the field, have about four million men to draw on. This number he divides up into three classes:

a. Men who have just reached their 20th year. This class will supply a million.
b. Men who are of military age (i.e. 20–55) and who have never been called up for training. This class will produce about two million.
c. Men who are over military age, that is over 55. He considers this class will produce another million.

Now out of a population of 62 million, 30 million are males, of whom 14 million are of military age, i.e. the 20–55 age-group.

But no country, even in the greatest straits, can put all its men capable of military service into the field. Food, clothing, arms and equipment, and transport are necessary. Therefore an army in the field must have an industrial population at its back.

The strain upon Germany in supplying her Active Army is considerable, but the strain of carrying on the necessary industries when 60 per cent of the workers have been withdrawn would be almost insupportable.

The systems of Germany and the Allies are totally opposite. Germany on the outbreak of war withdrew almost the whole of the pick of her manhood, for her plan was to gain rapid success. The Allied system (France perhaps excepted) was to use moderate material to stave off the

---

[*] Lt Col Charles à Court Repington (1858–1925) was the brilliant but controversial Military Correspondent of *The Times*. A capable staff officer, he had an intrigue while in Egypt with Lady Garstin. As co-respondent in the ensuing divorce case, he had to resign his commission. This did not prevent him achieving fame with his pen for *The Times*, but also notoriety for making public more than was discreet in wartime. See W. Michael Ryan, *Lieutenant Colonel Charles Repington, passim.*

The Siege of the Empires: the Royal Navy tightens the blockade noose around Germany and Austria-Hungary.

German threat, using the *crème de la crème* later. England and Russia still have unlimited reserves of the finest calibre up their sleeves. To obtain men, Germany will now be obliged to withdraw them from her industries, whereas British industries are practically at normal strength.* As regards Russia, her hordes of men are so ample, that all her military requirements can be more than met, without dislocating any of her industries,** or utilising medical misfits.

---

* This was largely thanks to the advent of women in factories, whose contribution to the industrial war effort, especially in the area of munitions, was crucial.
** Very debatable. The relatively backward industries in Russia were incapable of producing rifles and shells in the quantities which the 'hordes of men' in the Russian Army so urgently required.

TUESDAY JANUARY 12

It is unnecessary to say what the day is like. The Reader is allowed one guess; if he guesses wrongly he ought to be shot and stuffed. Not much news.

There are 900 cases of typhoid reported in hospital at Froyenne near Tournai.

The Russian victory in the Caucasus seems to have been conclusive. Now that we have more information on this subject, it is interesting to review the whole of these operations.

The German masters of the unfortunate Turk compelled their victims to begin hostilities against Russia on October 29. We were aware that there were in Trans Caucasia, within reach of the Russian frontier, three Turkish Army Corps, with a total effective strength of probably 100,000 men. The Russian General Staff were prepared to act vigorously at the first sign of aggression. As a result, a few days after the first Turkish attack on the Black Sea Littoral, Russian troops crossed their frontier.

WEDNESDAY JANUARY 13

The first thing that one notices in connection with the Turkish offensive, is that the general plan was an envelopment of the Russian Army of the Caucasus.

The Turkish Army was under German direction. Many people regard it as the third of the great failures of this enveloping strategy in the present war. The first was von Kluck's failure to get round the Allied Army in front of Paris last August. The second was von Hindenburg's failure to get round the Russian line in front of Warsaw last October. This Caucasian battle was fought on the old plan and failed in the same old manner.

Heavy fighting took place during Xmas week. For three days there was a violent struggle between Turks and Russians with Sarikamish at the centre. The entire corps which consisted of the 17th, 28th and 29th divisions, was captured, together with the German officers attached to them.

This disaster will not be easily retrieved. There are no railways at the disposal of the Turks to bring up reinforcements within 200 miles of the front. But the fighting has been decisive. As a result the Russians have saved their Caucasian province from a Turkish invasion and, more important still, have safeguarded their oil fields at Baku.

THURSDAY JANUARY 14

Dull but fine, a biting wind which is most unpleasant, but seems to be drying up the country wonderfully.

No change on the British Front!! The accounts of the French check at Soissons* show that the whole affair was greatly exaggerated. It is annoying to hear that the Germans have 1,000 prisoners and captured several guns, but it is an affair of no importance. The Germans make so much out of this, it shows that they are beginning to be thankful for small mercies.

The French troops involved were Territorials. The reason for their misfortune may be found in the climatic conditions, a rising of the Aisne which swept away the pontoons and cut off all troops on the North bank from reinforcements. The German attack, which took place under the eyes of the Kaiser, consisted of 2 Army Corps.

Rode into Cassel this afternoon to buy meat with Luxmoore. We bought a leg of mutton which half-killed us with its weight carrying it out.

FRIDAY JANUARY 15

Field Day today. We started at 9 o'clock to reconnoitre an area from Staple towards Aire. Day was fine but cold.

Got back into billets about 4.30. Found Teck waiting for us.** He had just come over from Furnes, which is the Headquarters of the King of the Belgians. He did not seem very struck with the Belgian Army. They had, he said, about 80,000 men in the field, and two Cavalry Divisions. They seem to have done nothing much since Liège. The amount they effected there was entirely due to the idiocy of the German Commanders.

Teck said that he had seen a case lately of 40 men leaving the firing line to bury one officer. When the war broke out they had practically no ammunition at all. The situation was saved by the Belgian Attaché in London finding 500,000 rounds of big gun ammunition at Vickers Maxim works, which had been destined for the Turkish Government. By altering the driving band at the back of the shell they were able to adapt it for the Belgian gun.

I hear that the Portuguese are sending us a division of 15,000 men to serve with us under the French. There is a rumour that these are Royalist troops and the Portuguese Government is rather anxious to get rid of them.

---

* Soissons, on the south bank of the Aisne, has endured the fortunes of war for two thousand years. A garrison town under the Romans, it later suffered in both the Hundred Years' War and the Wars of Religion. Severely damaged by bombardment in the First World War, Soissons was not captured by the Germans until May 1918.
** Prince Alexander of Teck, brother-in-law of King George V. See 15 December.

Count Berchtold's resignation is very significant.* It will have a great effect on the strategy of the future war in Austro-Hungary. It shows amongst other things that the Hungarians are getting the upper hand, as his successor is a man, for whom the wants of Hungary come first.

Berchtold's policy was to allow Berlin to dictate the strategy regardless of the well-being of Austria or Hungary. To Hungary the proximity of the Russian menace is very real and she is demanding more and more protection against it.

SATURDAY JANUARY 16

Fine, but dull and cold. Went to watch the final in the Football Cup given by the Brigadier at 2.30 this afternoon. The match was between our D Squadron and C Squadron of the Leicestershire Yeomanry. A very good match, during which three footballs burst, and which ended in our victory by 3 goals to nil.

We hear more definite news about the Soissons fight. The fighting began on January 8 with a French offensive with two battalions against some German trenches on Hill 132; the French hoped to establish some artillery on the hill to prevent the German guns shelling Soissons.

From the 9th to the 12th the Germans delivered a series of counter attacks on Hill 132, all of which failed, and the French were able to take some more German trenches, including a number of prisoners. With the help of substantial reserves the Germans forced the French back on to the original line of trenches held by the British in September. All this time the Aisne was rapidly rising and some of the pontoon bridges were carried away. On the 14th the French were withdrawn south of the river but they still hold St Paul.

Such in a nutshell is the French official account of this incident. It is to be regretted that the British Authorities did not see their way to be equally candid, regarding the Givenchy episode on Dec 20.**

---

* Count Leopold Berchtold (1863–1942) resigned on 13 January and was succeeded by Baron Stephen Burian. He had been Austro-Hungarian Foreign Minister since 1912. His reaction to the assassination of Archduke Franz Ferdinand led to the fateful fifteen-point ultimatum to Serbia on 23 July, which Sir Edward Grey described as 'the most formidable document that was ever addressed from one state to another'. Serbia mobilised two days later. Martin Gilbert, *Churchill*, p. 22.

** Four days previously, costly and ill-conceived attacks had been made in foul weather near Givenchy by the Indian Corps and Scots Guards. The few yards of muddy terrain gained were only held until 20 December. Crofton shows his disapproval by giving no details of this episode, like the British authorities he criticises.

SUNDAY JANUARY 17

At 10 o'clock we had church in the School, and at 11, Torrie and I went into St Omer in the motor, dropping Penn and Beaumont on the way for the pheasant shoot. We got to St Omer about 12.30, and had lunch with Livingstone-Learmonth and several other people in the Adjutant General's department. They hadn't much news.

The day was rather bright and fine but cold. After lunch we walked about and saw various people, and tried to find out where Hugh Baikie was living.* We found out that he was acting as liaison officer to the 2nd Army, but nobody knew whether he was living at St Omer or Hazebrouck.

About 3 we motored back, stopping on the way at the Artillery barracks to see Jack Speed, who is doing a Maxim gun course there. We found him in the midst of a lecture in the Riding School, which was so enthralling that we stayed until the close. There were a great number of officers doing the course. On the way home we picked up Penn and Beaumont, at a point near where they had been shooting. They had had an altercation with some keepers in the woods and had all their pheasants taken away from them, so the day as far as they were concerned was a failure.

The question of shooting is a much debated one. There is no doubt that it much annoys the French inhabitants, who are themselves forbidden by law to carry shotguns during the war. It irritates the owners of these estates when they see British Officers mopping up all their game, while they are obliged to look on. It is only a question of time before the whole thing is forbidden.

MONDAY JANUARY 18

Three German airmen have been killed at Johannisthal as the result of an accident.

It is reported that the Commander of XI Turkish Army Corps, which was recently compelled to retire on Erzurum after the Battle in the Caucasus, has been executed by order of Enver Bey. This appears to have caused a great deal of dissatisfaction among the Turkish officers.

WEDNESDAY JANUARY 20

Fine and cold. Left my billet at 8.15 for the station at Hazebrouck, in the motor, to catch the 8.50 train to Boulogne. Picked Parker up on the way, who

---

* Brig Gen Sir Hugh Simpson-Baikie. See 21 December 1914 and 13 February 1915.

was also going to England on Leave. Arrived at Calais about 11.30, and found that owing to a breakdown on the line there was no train to Boulogne until the next day, nor a boat to England until 9 o'clock the following morning.

I at once proceeded to the office of the Governor of the town, and demanded a motor to take me to Boulogne, so I could catch the 3 o'clock boat to England. The Governor was very civil, but unable to spare a car. He gave me a pass which would enable me to leave the town, and advised me to go to the harbour, and try to borrow a car from the Embarkation officer there.

We therefore withdrew with our pass to the Harbour, where we were lucky enough to find Captain Foster RN, the Naval Embarkation officer, who at once offered us his car. However, the chauffeur was nowhere to be found. He had gone out for lunch, and was not returning until 2 o'clock. This wouldn't leave us much time to get to Boulogne to catch the 3 o'clock boat.

Captain Foster's servant, a Marine, was dispatched into the town to find him, which he did by 1.30. Great rejoicing. We set off at once in the car, and after being stopped at barriers nine times en route, we reached Boulogne at 2.45. It was a delightful drive on the long straight road, which stretches over the hills from Calais to Boulogne. Everywhere we could see masses of Belgian recruits drilling. From the road on which we were travelling, we could see for miles on either side.

On reaching Boulogne we found the steamer, and went on board, Parker going ahead with our leave warrants to have them exchanged for tickets. We embarked on the steam packet *Onward*, and sailed about 3.15. We reached Folkestone about 5 after a very cold, but calm passage. The boat was crowded with soldiers going home on 72 hours' leave, and all very merry. Delysia the famous French Actress was on board,* and caused the men considerable amusement. I got to Victoria at 7.15, and drove at once to Buckingham Gate where I found Tiger Tim waiting.** Very good dinner.

THURSDAY JANUARY 21

Shopped most of the day. Had the usual haircut and manicure. Lunched with my mother at 1.30, then went off to see Tiger Tim at his gymnasium.

---

* Alice Delysia (1888–1979) was not only a famous actress, but also a singer and a designer of costumes for the stage. In 1916, she played the role of the mystical cavewoman in the silent film *She*, based on the best-selling Victorian adventure novel by Sir Henry Rider Haggard.
** His son. See 18 April.

We all walked home, stopping en route at Hamleys. Dined at Buckingham Gate and went out afterwards to see the Hippodrome. Very good show. Supper afterwards at the Savoy.

FRIDAY JANUARY 22

Snowing and sleeting. Bitterly cold. Caught the 10.15 train from Waterloo to Totton. Met by Fuller at station, and drove off to Woodside, which I reached at 12.30. Saw all the improvements, the bow window, trellis, newly papered nursery, etc. Saw man from Shepherd and Hedger about new curtains. The snow and wet made the garden very sloppy.

Caught 2.40 train at Totton to Bournemouth, en route to Blandford. Train very late owing to fog and snow in London, so missed the connection at Bournemouth, where I arrived at 4.50 and had to wait until 6.10. Reached Pimperne* finally about 7.30.

Very tired, and after good dinner went off to bed about 10.30.

SATURDAY JANUARY 23

Beautiful warm sunny day. After breakfast Walter, Mrs Walter and I went for a long walk on the Downs to see the camp of the Naval Division.

Ping pong was very amusing in the garden after lunch. Caught 2.40 train to London. Train very late, only reached London at 7.30. Found Brooks waiting for me at the flat. Dined at flat, went to the Alhambra** afterwards.

SUNDAY JANUARY 24

Dull but fine. Caught 1 o'clock boat train to Folkestone. Several people going back to the front. Reached Folkestone about 3 o'clock. Sailed almost at once for Boulogne on the *Invicta*. Stiff breeze and sea inclined to be choppy, but otherwise a good crossing.

The weather very clear and about 4 o'clock the sun came out. Reached Boulogne about 4.45. Here I found Gage of the Divisional Staff, who offered me a lift back in a motor.

---

* A small village in Dorset about a mile north-east of Blandford Forum, close to where the Royal Signals Regiment Museum and Blandford Camp are now located.
** The famous theatre and music hall in Leicester Square. In 1858 it was renamed the Alhambra (signifying in Arabic 'the red') after the citadel built at Granada by the Moorish kings. It was demolished in 1936.

Had tea at the Folkestone Hotel. Started off to Staple about 6 o'clock. A very fine frosty night. Reached Staple about 7.45 pm.

MONDAY JANUARY 25

Frosty, clear, and very bright. A rumour was spread today that we are to go back into the trenches for 10 days, on or about Wednesday Feb 3. Each Cavalry Division is to do 10 days and hold a front of one kilometre, supplying also the supports and Reserve. What an infernal nuisance it all is. This evil rumour was very shortly confirmed by an official despatch.

It appears that the French inhabitants are very irritated by our hounds and by officers shooting. They say that we don't take the war seriously enough; that all of their mankind relations are at the war, and that we have done nothing lately, except to ride over their crops, smash down their fences and shoot their game. And that if we can't do anything more useful, we had better go to into the trenches for a bit. So French gave way and there we are.

Fortunately the weather of the last few days has made a great difference to the ground, and we hope that the trenches won't be entirely full of water. The spot where we are to go is I believe Klein Zillebeke again. Ypres is the refilling point for our supply waggons.

As the whole country round here is full of typhoid, we are not to be billeted, but are to leave our horses here, and to the number of 250 are to go up in motor buses, dismounted. We presume that we shall return here after our ten days. It is a pity, for nothing more is calculated to ruin cavalry than trenches. We are sending up 80 rifles per squadron.

TUESDAY JANUARY 26

Another fine bright day. The ground is drying wonderfully. A good frost has started. We hear great news about the sinking of the German Cruiser *Blücher* by our fleet on Sunday last.* The German cruiser *Kolberg* is also reported sunk.

This is a very good reply to the bombardment of Scarborough. The Germans were either trying to bring off another similar coup, or else were trying to get out of the trade routes. The *Derfflinger*, sister ship to the

---

* The *Blücher* was sunk at the Battle of the Dogger Bank on 24 January, described by Churchill as 'a solid and indisputable result'. 954 Germans were drowned or killed, and only 15 British. The other German battle-cruisers escaped back to base. It would have been more decisive had Adm Beatty not lost close command of the battle when his flagship, *Lion*, was hit and forced to lag behind. Geoffrey Bennett, *Naval Battles*, pp. 142–5.

Goeben, was also very seriously damaged, as was the *Moltke*. The flagship *Seydlitz* seems to have escaped damage.*

A German Zeppelin flew over Libau** yesterday, and dropped 9 bombs. As it flew away, however, it was hit by gun fire and fell into the water, where it was destroyed by tugs from Libau.

A loan of £5,000,000 has just been issued to Romania by our Government. This looks like business. Their intervention now is only a question of a few weeks.

WEDNESDAY JANUARY 27

Fine and frosty. The Kaiser's birthday, on which a great hostile demonstration was expected.†

Regiment paraded in full marching order at 7 o'clock. All kits were packed, and the waggons loaded. The whole Division stood to until after midday, when the few sporadic and abortive attempts made by the enemy to provide their voracious War Lord with a suitable birthday present were beaten off and all troops returned to their billets.

The Kaiser's birthday must have cost the Germans in one way and another 20,000 men. The essence of our system is to compel the Germans to attack us, instead of wasting our men in assailing the Germans in carefully prepared positions.

THURSDAY JANUARY 28

Dull and very frosty but fine. A lot of chat goes on about our return to the trenches. I cannot help thinking that people depress themselves very much long before they go in by talking like this. It is like the discussion which

---

* Not so. The *Seydlitz* sustained a serious hit from the *Lion* in the aftermost turret. But for the swift action of an officer who flooded both magazines, she would probably have sunk. Learning from this near-disaster, the Germans modified the design of their warship gun-turrets to ensure that charges were delivered to the guns in a flash-proof covering. The significance of this change in design – of which the Royal Navy was unaware – became all too clear at Jutland. Geoffrey Bennett, *Naval Battles*, p. 146.

** Libau, now Liepaja, is a city and port on the Baltic coast of Latvia. It had been in Russian hands since the Third Partition of Poland in 1795. As a naval base, it was strategically important in both world wars.

† The fifty-sixth birthday of Wilhelm II, a grandson of Queen Victoria. He had become Kaiser in 1888 at the age of twenty-nine, following the premature death from throat cancer of his father, Frederick III.

invariably precedes a point-to-point or steeplechase. People reduce themselves to a state of nervous collapse by continuing to say how awful the jumps are. But when the race is being run no one notices the jumps, which before had appeared so ominous.

I trust that this will be our last appearance in the trenches, but now they have got us there again, the authorities are quite capable of keeping us there. I am sorry if they do, for trenches ruin the cavalry spirit, and should we be wanted later in the war to act as Cavalry, we shall have greatly deteriorated.

The enteric out here is increasing, largely because of the total ignorance of the inhabitants, especially in Belgium, of the most primary and elementary ethics of sanitation. Round Ypres there are 2,000 Belgian civilians down with it. In addition 300 outpatients are being attended to from 'Friends Ambulance'* which has established a temporary hospital in the Asylum on the NW corner of Ypres.

In the village of Vlamertinghe nearly every house shelters an enteric patient. In Poperinghe 30 houses are infected. There have been 18 deaths recently amongst the inhabitants, and there are 40 cases in the civil hospital of the town. A second hospital in Château St Elizabeth contains 70 beds, mostly enteric cases.

The sources of the water supply in Ypres and the other villages are contaminated.

FRIDAY JANUARY 29

Owing to enteric there is to be no billeting anywhere near Steenvoorde and Winnezeele. All men going up to the trenches are being sent there by motor bus. General Smith-Dorrien** recommends that drastic steps should be taken to clear all the sick and suspected cases from the Ypres area, and farther north.

Depots have been established in Ypres where water can be boiled for the troops to drink in the trenches.

---

* The FAU was largely founded by Quakers. Geoffrey Winthrop Young gives an account of their work in *The Grace of Forgetting*. The water supply in Ypres had been destroyed in November 1914 and one of the FAU doctors in Ypres reported that the inhabitants of the town had been drinking water from the moat, the canals, pits and old wells. *The Friends Ambulance Unit, 1914–1919 – A Record*, p. 31.
** Gen Sir Horace Smith-Dorrien, who had served on Lord Kitchener's Staff at Omdurman, commanded II British Corps. He had played a crucial role at Le Cateau in August 1914 (see 30 November). But he did not see eye to eye with Sir John French, who removed him from his command in May 1915.

SATURDAY JANUARY 30

Snowed in the night, but fine this morning. Went over the signalling equipment which we shall want in the trenches, as we are going to take good care that we are not left, as we were in November, without any communications between the front and rear trenches.

In the afternoon Torrie, Luxmoore and I went on a ride to Cassel. Coming back we stopped and looked at a farm which was one of the C Squadron billets, and which was burnt down last week.

The front of General Smith-Dorrien's Army was heavily shelled yesterday. 250 shells passed over the 10th Brigade line alone.

SUNDAY JANUARY 31

Snowed all night, very dull and cold this morning, snow fell continuously until midday when it cleared up, and began to thaw. Sun came out about 2.30 and turned into a beautiful day.

At 10.30 we had church in the usual place, followed by Communion. At about 3 o'clock Torrie and I rode into Hazebrouck to try and find out where Hugh Baikie lived. After wandering about a good deal we discovered where he lived, 61 rue des Clefs. But he was out, and as he wouldn't be back until 5.30, we didn't wait.

MONDAY FEBRUARY 1

Paraded at 9 o'clock with the Regiment, which went out with the rest of the brigade under General Kavanagh to practise making counter attacks in view of possible happenings while we are in the trenches.

We attacked in the form laid down by General Gough,[*] i.e. two regiments attacking, with the third in support, the whole with bayonets fixed. The advance over the ploughed fields leading up to the wood was very exhausting under the hot sun, as the soil stuck to our boots in the most awful way. Each foot had a lump on it as big as a football and weighing 20lb.

There seems to be considerable activity with the German submarines; three merchant vessels have been sunk off Fleetwood, Lancashire by

---

[*] Maj Gen Sir Hubert Gough, always known as 'Goughie' in his Regiment, the 16th Lancers, commanded the 2nd Cavalry Division in 1915. At forty-seven, he was the youngest of the Army Commanders when he was promoted to command the Fifth Army in 1916. After the German offensive of March 1918, he was replaced by Gen Sir Henry Rawlinson.

submarine No. 21.* It looks as if they are hanging about to catch some of our transports which are to bring over the four new infantry divisions due within the next ten days.

TUESDAY FEBRUARY 2

Raining, dull and cold, in fact a perfectly damnable day. All trace of the snow and frost has gone, and we have reverted to the usual slime and damp.

The General went up last night to visit the line of trenches which he will take up tomorrow with his brigade.** The line is about 1,200 metres in length. The German line runs close, being never more than 60 yards away, and usually about 20. There is an advantage in being so close, for the enemy dare not shell our front line, and this section of the front has not been shelled for a long time. The line lies to the East of Ypres, and is reached through Zillebeke. It is to the left of the trenches we occupied last on November 18.

Our right is supported by our 28th Division, and our left by the French. The trenches are dry, and well provided with head cover and dugouts. In these there are braziers formed out of oil drums with holes pushed in them, making stoves very like the buckets containing burning coke which workmen use in the streets in London.

The General said that the heat of the dugouts was, in some cases, so great that he couldn't go into them. Some of the communicating trenches leading to the trenches have water in them. The sanitary arrangements are reported to be excellent.

The German trenches being so close there is danger of sapping, and we shall have to have 'listeners' lying out to spot any digging.

Five regiments, ourselves, 1st Life Guards, Leicestershire Yeomanry, the Blues, and Essex Yeomanry, are to occupy these trenches for five days and nights. We will be relieved, I suppose, by the 10th Hussars, North Somerset Yeomanry, Royals and 3rd Dragoon Guards.

---

* *U-21*, commanded by the German U-boat ace, Otto Hersing, had nosed its way round Land's End up into the Irish Sea, to the busy shipping lanes off Liverpool. The first merchantman victim was the 6,000 tons collier, *Ben Cruachan*, followed by the *Linda Blanche* and the *Kilchuan*. However, each time warning shots were fired and the crews were permitted to launch the lifeboats. Edwyn Gray, *The U-boat War 1914–18*, pp. 78–9.
** The 7th Cavalry Brigade under Brig Gen Sir Charles Kavanagh comprised the 1st and 2nd Life Guards and the Royal Horse Guards. It was popularly known as the Fire Brigade, as it was constantly having to turn out to deal with some alarm.

Whale oil and grease has been issued for every man to rub his feet and legs with before he goes in. New socks and a spare pair of boots will be carried on each man. Officers will discard their swords, revolvers and Brown belts, and go in with rifles, bandoliers and bayonets. The General said that the support trenches were one mass of little chimneys smoking, and a considerable amount of cooking was going on. We have taken a large box of 'comforts' in the food line.

We are to start from here tomorrow at 2 pm in motor buses,* which land us in the great square at Ypres. From there we march four miles to the trenches. There will be a good deal of sniping I expect. It is believed that the troops opposing us are Alsatians.**

WEDNESDAY FEBRUARY 3

A beautiful day. At about 10.30 orders arrived that the signallers were not to go to the trenches, so I find I have to stay behind in billets with Torrie, and one officer per squadron, to look after the horses and the 250 men who are not going up to the trenches. Rather a bore as all one's preparations were made.

The motor buses, 15 per regiment, arrived about 11.30. The men paraded about 12.30. They all looked as if they were equipped for a polar expedition. There was a great deal of badinage between those going and those left behind plus the civil inhabitants of this village. About 20 were told off to each bus, the officers going on the top. The blankets had gone on to Ypres the night before, and were to be waiting in the *Grande Place* for them tonight.

The 1st Life Guards were waiting at the top of our main street, and were picked up by the 15 buses following us. I took several photographs. They got off about 1.30. The long line of buses looked most effective as they trailed away 10 yards apart, along the road to Hondeghem.

This village seems very quiet and empty now they have all gone. They are apparently to be away 10 days, but no one quite knows. It is certain that we are in the front trenches five days, and we may spend five in reserve, or else return here.

The owner of our lodging house could scarcely contain his delight at the departure of the Regiment for the trenches. But his pleasure was muted when

---

* See 14 November.
** Formerly Alsatians had been French citizens. But Alsace (along with Lorraine) had been in German hands since the Franco–Prussian War of 1870. Those who wished to remain French had to leave the province at that time: those who stayed became Germans and now had to fight against their former compatriots.

Capt F. Penn, 'The Nib', about to board the bus for the trenches.

he discovered that four of the Headquarters had been left behind. He wishes to go and visit his relations (he says) and so we decide to allow him to do so. Meanwhile we shall go and live in the house occupied by the Composite Squadron officers. The Patron has been given leave from after lunch on Saturday next to after lunch on Tuesday following.

One of my duties during the absence of the Regiment is to sort out and pack into bundles the letters for officers and men who are in the trenches.

THURSDAY FEBRUARY 4

Another glorious fine day. If only this weather will continue, what a difference it would make. At 12.15 sent up several bundles of letters and newspapers by motor cyclist to the trenches.

Went for a ride in the afternoon to Cassel with Archie Sinclair. I am very fond of that side of the country. I can't stand the Hazebrouck side.

We have received several large cases of cigarettes from Mexican admirers. Each packet is contained in a rather flamboyant and patriotic paper case.

B Squadron leave for the trenches, with Lt F.N. Griffin (left) and Lt F.D'A. Blofeld, who was killed on 13 May at Frezenberg.

The last of the General Omnibus Company buses leaves the main street of Staple.

One would have thought that all their cigarettes would be required for their own soldiers, who have been fighting on one side or the other, for or against various Presidents and Dictators, for several years.

FRIDAY FEBRUARY 5

Went up on the church tower to have a good look round, especially towards Hazebrouck as we heard that a German aeroplane was dropping bombs there. Too misty to see much, but took some photos of Staple. We examined also the old clock in the tower, which has no face but only strikes the hour. It was made 200 years ago by a clock maker in Cassel, a town famous for clocks, as all the ones round here were made there. This old clock seems much the same as it was on the day on which it was made. The weights are made of lumps of very old hewn stone.

In the afternoon Archie Sinclair and I went to Cassel. We put our horses up and did the sights of the town. It really is a most interesting old town. On the top of the highest hill* we found the Casino, a most repellent building full of French Soldiers.

We bought a lot of postcards and cakes and had tea at a magnificent hotel. While tea was being got ready we visited the old Priory church. There are two good windows in it, but the rest of the decoration is tawdry. As we went out an elderly French lady came up to me and gave me two small silver medals as *porte-bonheurs*,** one for me and one for my comrade. Archie and I were very touched.

SUNDAY FEBRUARY 7

A dull day, inclined to rain and cold.

Am going up to the trenches tomorrow to take mail, changes of clothes etc., so have arranged with the Brigade Chaplain to go with him in his motor. Went to Cassel in the afternoon with Walker, where we put up our horses, and went round the town buying picture postcards and looking at the view. Had tea at the Hotel, where we found two men belonging to the Flying Corps also having tea. The conversation was interesting so we listened to it from our corner.

---

* Reputed to be the hill up which the 'Grand Old Duke of York' famously marched his 10,000 men – and marched them down again – during the Flanders Campaign of 1793–5.
** Good-luck tokens.

One said that we had lost from accidents 5 aeroplanes last week. 2 Henri Farmans,* 2 Voisins and another kind, which I did not hear the name of. He also said that the French produced a flying boat, which can climb 6,000 feet in 4½ minutes. He said that he had seen it, and that it was a wonderful machine, and that it only went about 20 yards before it started climbing.

No more news from the trenches but shall soon find out when I see the Regiment tomorrow. There are at this moment about 94 German divisions in the Western theatre, and 43 in the East. What we may expect, however, is that Germany may make a last violent effort in the West before the Allied Armies are all assembled.

Between Arras and the Oise is not an unlikely front for such an operation, and March is the most likely month for this attempt. The state of the ground now is awful and it will require three weeks of drying winds before operations *en masse* can be undertaken. We may also have confidence in the knowledge that General Joffre fully realises what Germany is about and is quite prepared for her.

MONDAY FEBRUARY 8

A beautiful sunny morning. Had an enormous breakfast, and collected all my kit, six mailbags, and many parcels of food and clean clothes.

At 10.30 the motor ambulance arrived which was to take me into Hondeghem where I was to pick up the Chaplain and the motor which should take us to Ypres. We reached Hondeghem about 11 and there we had to wait a considerable time. We heard news there from the trenches. A shell had burst very near Kavanagh's headquarters and had deafened Kavanagh and slightly wounded Potter his ADC, and Labouchère, the Brigade Interpreter, in the face.

They had both been brought back to Hazebrouck to the hospital. Cowie the Surgeon Major of the 1st Life Guards, who so often used to hunt in the New Forest, was hit in the chest by a ricochet bullet, and seemed to be much worse than he really was.

As the motor from Ypres didn't turn up I went off and took several photos of General Kavanagh's quarters in the village. It is a pretty little house surrounded by a moat. About 1 o'clock we had lunch with the Chaplain and several doctors in the 7th Cavalry Ambulance. About 2.30 the motor from

---

* These early aircraft are described as 'Henri Farman pushers (engine behind pilot, skeletal and transparent, more like kites than aeroplanes)' by Ralph Barker, *The Royal Flying Corps in France*, p. 23.

Ypres arrived and at 3 we loaded up all our kit and set off. We took the road to Ypres via Steenvoorde and Poperinghe. It was a topping afternoon and our car actually raised clouds of dust.

The roads were covered with masses of transport, both for food and ammunition, and along its whole length bands of Belgian soldiers were endeavouring to repair the very evident signs of wear and tear. We went to Poperinghe about 4 and had a look round. The town is compact, with a large *Place* in the middle of which stands the inevitable bandstand. This is always filled with tins of petrol and other *disjecta membra** of the supply columns. On the west side of the square stands the Town Hall, a pretentious stone building with the Belgian flag hanging out of the first-floor window. The town is full of typhoid patients, but of course we saw nothing of them.

The streets were crammed with French infantry, many in new French grey uniforms,** which are smart when new, but we have yet to see how they will wear in the trenches. The streets were packed from end to end with these heroes, and the crowds were every now and again cleaved asunder by a British motor cyclist or a French Officer on his horse, who with a look of great dignity and at the same time uncertainty as to his balance in the saddle was making his way precariously down the street.

The motor slowly threaded its way through the busy streets and we got out at last on to the high road for Ypres. This road is one of the most important in this theatre of war. It is the main artery for supplies, both of food and ammunition, for all the troops in front of Ypres; should this road ever come under shell fire, it would render the existence of our whole line in front of Ypres most precarious.

We entered the approaches of Ypres about 4.30, passing several large and flamboyant villas, which are now filled with sick and wounded. As we passed through the gates of Ypres we saw the first evidence of the severe bombardment of last November. The first streets of houses had all collapsed like packs of cards.

We went slowly down between two long heaps of rubbish, which had formed, a few months ago, one of the main streets. We came out into the main square whose western end is bordered by the remains of the old 13th century Cloth Hall which is backed by the ruins of St Martin's Cathedral.

---

* Throw-outs, empty shell-cases, etc.
** The French still wore their colourful uniforms with *pantalons rouges* in the early months of the war. 'The khaki of our column struck a discordant note as it mixed with the red and blue uniforms of French soldiers who swarmed in the town.' Paul Maze, *A Frenchman in Khaki*, p. 33.

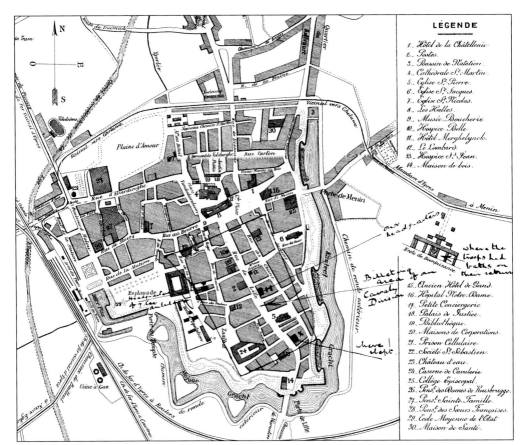

Street plan of Ypres in 1915.

Here the effects of bombardment were awful. Nothing remained either of the Cathedral or the Cloth Hall but bare, cracked, and scratched walls. Every house in the *Place* was either in total ruins, or else badly damaged. There was not a single unbroken pane of glass in the entire square. We went down the rue de Lille until we came to a side street with the high-sounding name of Lombard Street, and finally reached the Headquarters of the 7th Cavalry Field Ambulance. Here we deposited the Chaplain and I was invited to stay until my Regiment returned from the trenches.

These Headquarters, although sadly damaged, were palatial. They were evidently the town residence of some enormous local Bug. Having had tea, I piled up my kit and mailbags in the hall under the guardianship of a plaster lady, very scantily attired, who was occupied in holding aloft a smashed lamp, and sallied out to see the sights.

In the square I met several acquaintances, and saw groups of 10th Hussars and 3rd Dragoon Guards wandering about waiting to relieve us in the trenches in the evening. I went at once to the ruins of the Cloth Hall. I took from one of the doors some pieces of glass in its leaden frame. The whole of the ground floor was one huge heap of bricks and rubble. The courtyard was filled with debris and looked like a builder's yard. I went on through the wreckage and came to the Cathedral which was in a similar parlous condition.

After considerable difficulty I got hold of the Concierge who let me into the Cathedral. The interior was awful. I got some pieces of glass from the East Window* which were lying about the floor. As it was now getting dark I returned to our residence in the rue Lombard, where I was given an excellent dinner.

After dinner I wandered out and found our street, the rue de Lille, and the parallel one, the rue des Chiens, full of our troops preparing to go up to the trenches. The rattle of musketry was deafening for the trenches were only about 3 miles off, and the night was lit up like the day by the flare shells which were fired by both sides. These shells largely composed of magnesium give a strong white light, lighting everything up most clearly. They are so powerful, that, although fired 3 to 4 miles off, they lit up very well the square of Ypres.

Towards 9 o'clock I walked out towards the trenches along the road leading through the Porte de Lille. It was now pitch dark and the rattle of the musketry and the flare of the starshells made the situation very thrilling.

After walking a mile, falling into shell holes, running into odd troops and being challenged, I thought it best to return, so came back to the rue Lombard. Very shortly afterwards Kearsley the Brigade Major** came in, and offered to show me where the Regimental Headquarters were to be. They were in a large empty house in the rue de Lille, to which I transferred all my kit and mailbags and sat down to await the Regiment's return.

TUESDAY FEBRUARY 9

The Regiment was very long in coming. The relieving regiments, the 10th Hussars and the 3rd Dragoon Guards,† had only paraded at 10.30 pm, so as the trenches were 3 miles off, it would be 1 o'clock at least before they got up

---

* On 14 May 2003, along with the key of the West Door, these were formally returned to the Dean of the Cathedral by Maj Edward Crofton, son of the diarist. See 'Ypres Then and Now', Editor's Note.
** Maj R.H. Kearsley, 5th Dragoon Guards.
† Along with the 1st Royal Dragoons, the 3rd Dragoon Guards and the 10th Hussars formed the 6th Cavalry Brigade. This was commanded by Brig Gen Sir Ernest Makins. A veteran of the South African War, he served throughout the First World War, after which he was MP for Knutsford, Cheshire, from 1922 to 1945.

to them. The work of actual relieving would take an hour or more, so I settled down to wait. The house had been badly damaged by shellfire and the front door was riddled with shrapnel bullets. A good fire however was burning in our room, and the Colonel of the 3rd DGs* who had occupied the house for the past five days, had left his Mess Corporal there and some rich stew. I opened some bottles of port which I brought with me.

About 4.30 the squadrons appeared and were put into billets along the rue de Lille. We had several cans of cocoa ready and gave everyone who came to our house a mugful. The rich stew was so excellent and the five of us, the Colonel, Stewart Menzies, Luxmoore, Griffin, the machine gunner, and myself, thoroughly enjoyed it. It was like supper after a ball. They said that they had had a very quiet time and our casualties were only one killed, one wounded, and seven with frostbite, after our five days in the front trenches. There had been little or no shellfire.

At 5 o'clock we turned in. The Colonel had a room upstairs, and Menzies and Luxmoore shared a tiny room in the front on one mattress spread on the floor. I went off down the street to where C Squadron was billeted.

It was a Nunnery, but all the Nuns had fled except two who had remained throughout the bombardment. Penn, Wilson, Keith Menzies, Beaumont and I slept in one of the dormitories. It was a large room with a stone floor and containing about 10 beds, each only large enough for a child of 12. We were so tired, that we took off our boots, climbed in between the very rough sailcloth-like sheets, and soon slumbered.

At 9 o'clock we woke, and began to get up, which is a very simple matter when one sleeps in one's clothes. In fact it merely means standing upright. We took ages to get hot water and then found it very difficult to wash in basins which were only the size of teacups.

After breakfast, taking my camera, I went off to find the Chaplain, with whom I had arranged to walk out to Zillebeke, the little village near which we had spent the night of November 19. At the Chaplain's door was a motor which dropped us near the railway crossing to the SE of the town.

We started off down the road leading to Zillebeke, to the right and left of which we could see the French busily engaged in building large redoubts for heavy guns. The road was full of shell holes and the fields on each side were honeycombed with them. To our left on the crest of the wooded slopes about 1½ miles off lay the German trenches.

---

* Lt Col O.B.B. Smith-Bingham commanded the 3rd (Prince of Wales) Dragoon Guards from 1912 to 1916.

A Belgian farm-hand hacks the legs off dead horses with an axe – to make them fit into the grave.

Carcasses of horses lying in shell holes on the road from Ypres to Zillebeke.

The fields were uncultivated and looked most desolate. Our road led us past several small farms and cottages which were mere heaps of rubble. The road was peppered with old rifles, broken carts, limbers, heaps of cartridges, and bits of shell. As we approached the village which lay in the hollow we could see the difference in damage which had been done since we were last here in November.

The body of Zillebeke Church had almost disappeared, and so had the steeple, the ruined tower alone remained. Every single house had been smashed to atoms. In some cases the entire front had been torn away and the house stood open like a doll's house. The furniture was hanging out over the edge of the floors. In the ground-floor rooms the book cases were full of books, china, crockery, etc. covered in dust, and left just as they were when their owners fled three months ago. The debris from the houses was in heaps on each side of the road. The smell was awful.

In the porch of the church, the only habitable place, lived a French Guard of a corporal and four men, though for what reason they were there nobody knew. Inside the church lay the remnants of a 10th century font, and several broken plaster saints. The Church Yard had several enormous shell holes in it, which had uprooted the monuments, smashed open the vaults and laid bare the coffins and the dead. These vaults were half full of rainwater, and in many cases the zinc or tin coffins were floating about, with their occupants exposed or bobbing over the sides.

The stench was too bad to stay long, and as stray bullets were humming over, and six or seven shrapnel shells had burst over the village, I hastily took several photos and departed.

I picked up a few relics, and the Chaplain took several, especially from the church. I was very glad to see that the graves of Bernard Gordon-Lennox, Congleton and Stocks of the Grenadiers,* and Peterson of my Regiment were untouched, though their names, which had been written in pencil on wooden crosses, were in danger of being washed out by the rain and bad weather.

As we hastened back along the road towards the railway, more shrapnel came over us. We reached the railway cutting in safety. Close to the cutting were the dugouts made by the Engineers in which we spent the night of November 19 when we left the trenches. The French troops had removed every particle of wood from them with a result that they were entirely destroyed, and were now little more than holes in the railway bank.

---

* All four officers had been killed in the German attack on 6 November. See 20 November.

The ruins of Zillebeke church.

A vault in the graveyard burst open by a shell.

We walked along the railway line back towards Ypres. The whole line was dotted with little heaps of French cartridges in packets and from time to time large heaps of empty brass cases of the French 75mm shell, which had been collected prior to removal for refilling.

On our left the fields were pock-marked with the craters of high-explosive shells. Some hundreds of thousands of these must have been thrown into and around Ypres. A field the size of Trafalgar Square would have 20 such holes, each large enough to bury a motor bus in it. As we got towards Ypres we discovered several batteries of British Artillery dug in, and disguised in such a complete fashion that they were absolutely unnoticeable at 10 yards off. We regained Ypres by the Porte de Lille.

After lunch we started out on a tour of inspection. We again visited the remains of the Cloth Hall, and this time succeeded in climbing to the first floor where formerly the Banqueting and Reception Halls were situated. Traces of fine mural paintings were still on the wall, but irretrievably ruined. The floor which was composed of black and white marble squares like a chess board, was heaped with bricks and plaster, and the charred beams of the six century old roof trees. The tower, though damaged, still stood, and under it lay the melted masses of metal which had formerly composed the famous Carillon chimes. The gilded clock face still remained on the walls, but one of our party secured as a souvenir the figure V which had dropped off.

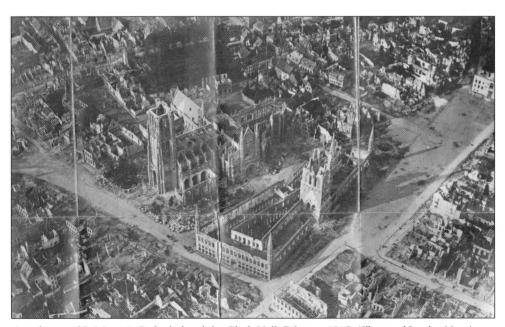

Aerial view of St Martin's Cathedral and the Cloth Hall, February 1915. (*Illustrated London News*)

We then went on to the Cathedral. Here they seem to be making some spasmodic efforts to effect local repairs. The canvases of the pictures still hang dismally, rotted with rain and damp from their frames which are equally dilapidated. In one case only has a chapel been boarded up to preserve it, the remaining ones being filled with charred wood, broken marble, twisted brass railings and candlesticks.

Three columns which supported the roof on the right of the nave have fallen together across the body of the church, covering the carved oak 14th Century choir stalls and raising a heap of masonry 16–20 feet high. The bells were lying, broken in fragments in a heap in the porch. Not a window remained unbroken and the East Window and many of the other stained-glass ones were scattered in broken bits over the floor of the Cathedral. These pieces were very popular as souvenirs, and the entire church was by now filled with soldiers clambering over heaps, or digging about for mementoes. I secured several.

It is surprising that efforts have not been made by the Belgian authorities to try and save some of the flotsam and jetsam, such as the chairs, the font, the pulpit, the brass fittings, the pictures and the organ, which is mostly composed of wooden pipes. If some effort is not made to safeguard the remains, the British soldier, as souvenir hunter, will complete the utter destruction of the Cathedral which was begun by the Germans.

As we came out we saw a soldier on a ladder, busily engaged in removing the last vestiges of some glass in a window, and being urged to further efforts by a Belgian priest who held the bottom of the ladder. In an estaminet or tavern close to the Cathedral we discovered a most beautifully carved chest three or four hundred years old, which had been carried there for its safety. Lying across the zinc counter of the shop was the embroidered altar cloth of 16th Century work which was full of shell holes. It was the most beautiful piece of embroidery I have ever seen, heavy gold bullion on white woven silk, in the centre of which, and surrounded by massive lumps of gold embroidery was a panel of the Holy Family in tapestry with the faces painted in, like miniatures.

Menzies and I offered a man who was mending the windows £2 for it but he explained that he would certainly sell it, but it wasn't his. I wonder what its end will be. Probably stolen, while the Belgian Authorities are waking up.

WEDNESDAY FEBRUARY 10

Slept with difficulty in the Nuns' dormitory, and washed with yet greater.

It poured with rain during the night, and the everlasting rattle of musketry kept on without ceasing. During the night several shells landed in various parts of the town, but we are now above such trifles.

The water from the moat supplies all the water that the British troops drink in Ypres, for all other sources are too foully contaminated for words. The water is pumped up into the public baths and then chlorinated, which causes all doubtful substances to sink to the bottom. The water is then cleaned with alum,* and issued to the men. The work is very well done by one of our new sanitation companies, under the direction of the most extraordinary character called Maloney, who is in peacetime a Medical Health Officer. Though rather a rum bird, I must say he does his work most capably. His men are extremely good.

One of his corporals is a Bachelor of Science at London University. This war has brought out many odd men into the Army. The Supply Officer for our Cavalry Brigade in peacetime is in charge of the Butterfly Department at the South Kensington Museum. An official out of the Mummy Department in the British Museum is in our Cavalry Field Ambulance, and one of the chauffeurs in the Ammunition Column attached to our Division is chauffeur to Jack Johnson the pugilist.**

About 10.30 I collected Penn, Beaumont and a few others, and made a tour of the town again. Several German aeroplanes were flying about, and being heavily shot at with no apparent result. I wondered that they did not begin dropping bombs, but they only seemed to be making reconnaissance. We bought several picture postcards and a *Guide to Ypres*. There is an extensive manufacture of lace in Ypres, and considerable quantities are on sale in the shops. But the bulk of the lace makers have fled to Poperinghe.

In the Middle Ages the town was famed for its cloth as well as its lace, and the English word 'diaper' arose from Ypres† and was applied to a species of linen or fabric made in this town. The history of Ypres shows that this is not the first occasion that it has been bombarded, burned, taken by assault or sacked. It has always suffered grievously from its position close to the French frontier.

Today Ypres is (or was) a town of 18,929 inhabitants, and is the judicial and administrative centre of the surrounding district. It also contains, or did contain when the war broke out, the Cavalry School of Belgium, corresponding to Netheravon for us, and Saumur for the French. The Belgian

---

* One of a series of double sulphates, especially that of potassium and aluminium, used industrially not only for water purification (as here), but also in the production of medicines, textiles, paper, paints, matches and deodorants. They are also used in fire-extinguishers.
** He unwittingly lent his name to the all too well-known German shell. Jack Johnson shells were also known as 'coalboxes'. See 16 November.
† Or, more precisely, 'diaper' is derived from the Flemish Ieper.

Cavalry Officers have for some time gone in for *Haute Ecole* in horse training, and one of their most successful officer riders is very well known at our Horse Show at Olympia every summer.

Every time that I see the Cloth Hall or Cathedral, the wreckage makes an ever starker impact. The worst bombardment took place on November 22, two days after we had left it. The loss of civilian life must have been considerable, but I couldn't find out any details about it.

We made a careful inspection again of the ruins, and it was curious to note, that, amidst the debris of fallen columns and heaps of charred wood and broken stone, there remained untouched a horribly modern commonplace statue of some local swell, who had been a benefactor of the town. It was the sort of thing that one sees in Birmingham.

Some steps are, I believe, about to be taken, towards cleaning the rubbish and safeguarding the remains. All the troops who had just come out of the trenches were marched up to the Reformatory or 'Bienfaisance' just outside the town, where every man had a hot bath. This building, when we were here before, was the No. 3 Clearing Hospital and had many miraculous escapes.

After dinner about 9 o'clock we received an unpleasant reminder of the German ability to use large shells. They had brought up very secretly, on a train, two 8 inch guns. They took up a position to the SE of the town, on the railway behind Klein Zillebeke. They opened fire exclusively on that section of the town occupied by our billets.

The frequent cruises of their aeroplanes during the afternoon were intended to find our position. Or else they had very good spies, for they seemed to know exactly where we all were. The first thing that we heard were two of these very large missiles crash over our headquarters and fall with a roar in the rue des Chiens which was occupied by the 1st Life Guards. The shells fell in pairs, and arrived every five minutes. The third and fourth fell in the rue Lombard very near the 7th Cavalry Ambulance headquarters. On bursting, they entirely destroyed a large four-wheeled waggon, and killed four horses and two men, belonging to the Northumberland Territorial Engineers. Another struck a house occupied by the 1st Life Guards, causing it to collapse like a house of cards, killing six men and wounding eleven.

The inhabitants were by this time running screaming with terror about the streets. Several got into cellars, but many more ran for some arches which were made in the fortifications of the NE part of the town. Here a shell pitched, and exploding killed or severely wounded three women and eight children. The Germans fired altogether about twelve shells, of which three or four did not burst. After about half an hour's firing the French guns,

Ypres Post Office before the war . . . *(Nels)*   . . . and destroyed by German shells. *(Nels)*

which up to now had been locating the guns, suddenly opened and completely silenced the enemy.

We called a squadron out at once to help with the removal of the wounded. The arch in which the shell exploded was an awful sight. The men and women were screaming with terror, and we couldn't get them to do anything. We finally cleared them out, and searched for the casualties. Three women were carried out dead, and several children. One little boy of about five had all his entrails hanging out, another a fearful gash on his thigh, which exposed the bone and the femoral artery.

Luxmoore attended to him and I think made a good job of him. He cried a good deal, but more noise was made by a lot of women who crowded round to soothe him. Luxmoore soon quietened him by the simple procedure of giving him a new franc. He clasped it tightly in his fist and seemed quite satisfied. Our men had to carry the wounded to the Civil Hospital, and the dead to a Nunnery, for the Belgians wouldn't go near, nor could they be induced to touch the bodies.

Ypres Hospital, 1914. *(Nels)*

The ruins of the same building, 1915.

No further excitement occurred during the night, but the sight in the arches is one not easily forgotten. The motionless bodies, the crowd of middle-aged terror-stricken women and men, and the gloomy depths of the arches with khaki-clad figures standing round, the whole lit up from time to time by the fitful gleams of my electric torch. We did not feel sorry that our sojourn in Ypres was nearly over.

THURSDAY FEBRUARY 11

A beautifully fine day with a sharp wind.

About 10.30 I went round to the rue Lombard to see the 7th Cavalry Field Ambulance. There I found Molyneux the Supply and Transport officer for our Brigade, who was shortly returning to Staple. He offered to take me and I accepted his offer.

I walked back to the Nunnery across the fortifications which in this part of the town have been laid out as boulevards. At 11.30 I collected my kit, said goodbye to the Nuns, and left for Staple in the motor. The Regiment is by way of coming back in motor buses tomorrow night. I expect they will be very late.

We soon got out of Ypres and got on the road to Poperinghe, where we were to lunch. We passed numerous convoys of food and ammunition, and swarms of French soldiers. Reached Poperinghe about 1.

Had lunch at Poperinghe and went out with Molyneux to see the supplies issued to the Brigade, a job which took over an hour. The supplies of hay, oats, beef, candles, cheese, bacon, rum, etc., etc. are dumped on the road side by motor lorries, and are then divided up and removed by our light wagons. The Belgian inhabitants crowd together at a respectful distance and when all is finished descend on the spot like a swarm of locusts, and remove the remains. Everything is removed, nothing is too unimportant, all the wooden cases, bits of meat and cheese, even the sawdust. The job completed, we returned to Poperinghe, and at 3.30 set out for Staple.

We returned via Steenvoorde and Cassel. Near Steenvoorde we passed the Belgian frontier post, a twisted iron, very dirty and battered post, sticking up in the ground at an angle of 45 degrees. It was more like a dilapidated lamp post.

Reached Staple, at 5.30. Found Archie Sinclair and Torrie to relate all my adventures to. Very glad to get back.

FRIDAY FEBRUARY 12

Very windy and cold, but otherwise fine.

Village usually very quiet here, but now full of excitement at the prospect of the troops' return. The people here have now got thoroughly used to us, and in most cases will miss us very much when we go.* They are now all busily engaged in preparing, in the various billets, some sort of gastronomic welcome. What they call 'Lapin' soup is the favourite. It is a sort of Irish Stew made out of rabbit and vegetables.

We hear the Regiment is to leave Ypres at 6 o'clock tonight in motor buses, and that they will be back here by 10, but I very much doubt it; anyhow everything will be ready for them at that hour.

The entire population of all these villages is now engaged in cultivating the fields. The inhabitants seem to love the soil, they cultivate every field up to within one inch of the ditch. The total absence of hedges is one of the most marked characteristics of this part of the country.

At 10.30 tonight there were no signs of the Regiment's return, so we went to bed.

SATURDAY FEBRUARY 13

Was woken up at 5 this morning by the return of Luxmoore with the Regiment from the trenches. Having thoroughly roused us, he told us that the journey out here in the motor buses had been awful. They had paraded in the square of Ypres at 6 pm yesterday, and had stood about there until 8.30 when they began to get on the buses. It was very lucky that the Germans didn't shell the town, as they had done the night before, for they would have had a very big bag.

The buses started and progress was very slow, and from time to time ceased altogether as the buses got in the ditch, or off the pavé, and they did not arrive here until after 4. But notwithstanding the early hour, most of the villagers were up and out to meet them.

I had a letter from Hugh Baikie in the morning, asking me to go over to Hazebrouck to dine and sleep. About 4.30 I rode over there, my servant bringing my kit on my spare horse.

I found Hugh's house, 50 rue des Clefs, a most palatial residence and very comfortable. It was the property of a Belgian lawyer. After tea I read all the papers until Hugh's return, which was rather late, it being nearly 8 o'clock before he turned up. He had had a long day in the trenches, where he had slept the preceding night. He is Liaison Officer on the Second Army Staff

* 'There was one village even where it was popularly believed that our names were entered on the electoral roll, although no election furnished an opportunity of putting the theory to the test.' Sir George Arthur, *Household Cavalry*, vol. III, p. 36.

and moves continually between Smith-Dorrien's headquarters and V Infantry Corps, of which two divisions, the 27th and 28th, being lately arrived, were a little unsteady and causing some anxiety in the trenches. He lives in this house with Lewin, Lord Roberts' son-in-law,* and a Belgian duke, the duc d'Urcel, who is also attached to the Second Army Staff.

I shared Hugh's bedroom, and slept very well in an enormous and very comfortable four poster.

SUNDAY FEBRUARY 14

Valentine's Day. Hugh had to be off by 9.30 to his job again, so we breakfasted at 8.30, and having read all the communiqués, I saw Hugh off and started to ride back to Staple. The morning was cold, and as I started, the rain began and continued for the rest of the day. A most depressing day. I reached Staple about 11.

I fear we may lose our school, for an order has come out from the French Government, that all schools, which are not actually in the war area, are to re-open for teaching again.

An episode has occurred which shows how very seriously some people at home in England are taking the war. Some little time ago there was a discussion at dinner at the General's headquarters as to whether, if an advertisement was put in the paper purporting to come from an officer who hadn't got many friends, saying that he would like someone to write to him, it would have any effect.

An advertisement was concocted and sent to the *The Times* stating that a young officer called Lieutenant X, through circumstances not entirely under his control, found himself on active service with very few sympathetic friends who would write to him. He asked if some kind person would do so, and also send a photograph.

For a few days nothing happened. Then suddenly about 30 letters arrived at Army Post Office 60, which is our Brigade Post Office. Then they poured in, in torrents: 200 the next day, then 500, and finally on Tuesday last Lieutenant X received two entire sacks for himself which contained over 2,000.

General Kavanagh, who had at first regarded this as a joke, now began to get angry. This was increased by the arrival at his billet of the Post Office official who had been sent there by the Head Official at Boulogne to ask

---

* Col Henry Lewin, CMG, Royal Artillery. He married Lord Roberts' second daughter, Lady Edwina Stewart, in 1913.

what the deuce it was all about. He stated that the postal arrangements were being badly deranged by the unexpected flow of letters addressed to one man. He also asked if they were all going to be answered for, if so, he must supplement the staff at the Post Office.

These letters now nearly filled up Headquarters, round the chief room of which sacks were filled, and each corner had a heap in it. They opened several which were found to contain tobacco, jam, cigarettes, socks, scarves, shirts and even slices of cake. Many of the letters were pathetic, some gushing, some utter drivel, some clever, and written by every conceivable class and status of society, 99 per cent being women. I suppose these are the sorts of people who write to actors.

We don't know how to stop this. Lieutenant X is rapidly becoming a national asset. We are going to put another advertisement in the The Times saying that he has been killed in the trenches. I wonder if half suburbia will go into mourning.

MONDAY FEBRUARY 15

Mr Tennant* today in the House of Commons announced that the cases of frostbite up to January 24 last inclusive in the Expeditionary Force amounted to 9,175.

THURSDAY FEBRUARY 18

A fine day at last. Went for a ride to Cassel. The sun was beautifully hot and there was a real touch of spring in the air.

The new descriptive plate of the French uniforms is issued today, from which it will be seen that the familiar and conspicuous *pantalons rouges* are now relics of the past. The new French light blue shade is extremely smart, when new. In the spring it is expected to harmonise more with the surrounding country than our khaki does. *Nous verrons!!!*

---

* Harold John Tennant, son of Sir Charles Tennant, was a Liberal MP from 1894 to 1918. 'Jack' was Private Secretary to Asquith when the (future) Prime Minister married his sister, the brilliant Margot Tennant, in 1894.

VOLUME IV

February 19 – April 14, 1915

FRIDAY FEBRUARY 19

Wet and beastly as usual. In the afternoon rode into Hazebrouck to see if we could get any news about the boats sailing to England, as we hear they are stopped because of the ridiculous German decree about the submarine blockade.*

Hear definitely that we must turn out of our school, as the parents (but not the children) are beginning to object to this prolonged holiday. Has now lasted 11 weeks tomorrow. How time flies. It certainly doesn't seem as long as that since we rode in here that very wet Monday afternoon early in December. We must hunt around and find some suitable quarters, which will not be easy.

SATURDAY FEBRUARY 20

Fine and cold. Very busy getting my traps together to go home tomorrow. My leave for 7 days has just arrived. Rode to Hazebrouck during the afternoon with Walker to see if I can find out any arrangements about trains, etc. for tomorrow. Find that my train will leave about 5 pm but no one can tell what time it will arrive.

Had some very interesting information from a friend of mine in Armstrong Whitworth & Co's works.** He says:

1. The comparative failure of German submarines is that they are so vulnerable when they come to the surface. 12 have been destroyed since the beginning of the war.

---

* On 4 February, the German Government announced that the waters round the UK would be treated as a war zone from 18 February, and even merchant vessels would be at risk from this new 'sink on sight' policy.
** This Newcastle upon Tyne engineering company branched out in 1913 into supplying aircraft for the War Office and airships for the Admiralty.

2. HMS *Iron Duke* is said to have sunk 4 German destroyers that had slipped through the line into the North Sea.*

3. HMS *Queen Elizabeth* is now ready for sea, as are also the sister-ships *Barham* and *Warspite*; these ships each have eight 15 inch guns.

4. 60 aeroplanes are being made in England a month.

SUNDAY FEBRUARY 21

A list was issued today showing the very heavy death toll of officers in the four** Regiments of the Foot Guards for the first six months of the war.

As my train was due to leave Hazebrouck for Boulogne at 5 pm, I left Staple about 4.15 in the motor. Archie Sinclair, Keith Menzies and Walker came in to see me off. A long hospital train, which had about 400 wounded and frost-bitten soldiers on board, was in the station and made my train rather late. I got off about 5.30. The train stopped at every station, and the journey was most tedious. We arrived at Boulogne at 11 o'clock. 5½ hours to go 30 miles. We were told on arrival there that we were not to go on board until 1.30 am. This delay was enlivened by a fairly good dinner at the station restaurant about midnight. I went and got my warrant changed for a ticket from an old Captain who looked very like a goat with his long white beard.

MONDAY FEBRUARY 22

A beautiful fine night. Went on board the lugger about 1 o'clock. Went at once to the Ladies' Saloon where I spread myself on the divan, as a novel would say, and slept. They tell me the boat sailed at 4.30, but I only recovered consciousness as the boat was entering Folkestone Harbour at 6.30.

It was a fine crisp morning and the red flush of the dawn looked very pretty over the sea. We were escorted over by French destroyers. The train waiting for us was very soon crowded, and no place was to be had in it for love or money. So I decided not to rush and fight, but to wait half an hour for the next train, in which I soon got a very good seat in a Pullman and had an excellent breakfast.

A very interesting gunner major sat opposite me, who was in command of one of our Siege Batteries and was stationed at La Bassée. He showed me all

---

* HMS *Iron Duke* was the flagship of Vice Adm Sir John Jellicoe, Second Sea Lord and Commander of the Grand Fleet.

** The 5th Foot Guards Regiment, the Welsh Guards, was formed six days later on 27 February 1915.

his sketches and notes, and explained fully the system now used by our heavy guns to search the enemy's positions. It seems most effective. He said that our new 9 inch gun beats anything that the Germans can bring up and told me a lot about our new 15 inch surprise which is shortly coming up.

We reached Victoria at 9.30. I walked with my kit bag to 36 Buckingham Gate, and as I was totally unexpected created some surprise. Reading *The Times* on the way to London, my eye was caught by an announcement (foreshadowed) of the awful fate of Lieut. X.

Requiescat in Pace

Lieutenant X begs to thank the 3,677 Correspondents who have so kindly written to him and regrets that owing to a nervous breakdown he will be unable to answer all of them.

Got home about 9.45 and found the house still under the aegis of the housemaid.

Another breakfast at	10.15
Haircut and Bath	11.00
Manicure	12.00

Lunched at home and took Tiger Tim out to Cinema. Household Brigade Lodge at 6.* Dined at Savoy with Marion, 8.30.

TUESDAY FEBRUARY 23

Wet and beastly, but no matter if it snowed red ink. Shopped most of the day. Dined Marlborough Club with Archie Carlton, went to Hippodrome and on to Savoy for supper, thence to 400 Club.

WEDNESDAY FEBRUARY 24

Heavy fall of snow during the night, very dull and beastly cold.

Rung up by Keith Menzies to say that we should probably be recalled on Friday. Also told me of the disasters to the 16th Lancers, who were

---

* Freemasonry. At the time he was Worshipful Deputy Master.

occupying some trenches which had been held by the Blues when we were in the trenches February 3–8. We should be holding them now if it were not for us having to send 150 men to groom the 9th Lancers' horses while they were in the trenches: Lucky escape!!

At 3.30 received a wire from the Adjutant telling me to return on Sunday night February 28. Dined Berkeley Grill and went to *Country Girl*. Supper at 400 Club.

FRIDAY FEBRUARY 26

Very fine but cold. Caught 10.15 from Waterloo for Woodside. Met Henry Powell in train going home to Lyndhurst on a weekend leave. Had a great chat. Got to Woodside 12.30. Everything in good shape. Caught 4.40 to Bournemouth and arrived at 6, when I got a motor and motored out to Pimperne to stay with Cazenoves.

SATURDAY FEBRUARY 27

Beautiful fine day. Went for a walk in the morning and watched the Naval Division marching to Blandford, en route to the Dardanelles. Very fine body of men. News of the bombardment of the Dardanelles forts, excellent.

At 3 o'clock motored to Salisbury and caught 4.15 train to London which I reached at 6.30. Dined at home and went afterwards to Hippodrome.

SUNDAY FEBRUARY 28

Dull but fine. Spent morning writing letters and settling up various matters.

Went to Victoria at 5.30 to catch 6 o'clock train. Station simply packed, not a place to be had in the first train. Succeeded, after much fighting, in getting a place in the 2nd class saloon with 21 others, in the second train. Arrived Folkestone 8 o'clock.

Went at once on steamer the *Onward*. Same crowd there. Over 1,140 officers and men were on board. A great struggle in the dining saloon. Succeeded at last in getting some dinner which did not profit me much.

Boat sailed at 9.15. Total darkness on ship, which was escorted by two French destroyers.

A most brilliant moonlight night, so could see as clearly as in the day. Very strong wind NW and the most awful swell. Too cold to stay on deck, so retired to the Ladies' Saloon which was in total darkness. Everyone there being violently sick. I did my share. Felt like death, could not have moved an eyelid if we had been torpedoed ten times. However, after getting rid of my 3s 6d dinner I felt better, and fell asleep hugging my tin basin.

We arrived at Boulogne at 10.30 after a very fast trip. The lights being turned on revealed the awful condition of the Ladies' Saloon. The horrors of war were indeed brought home.

MONDAY MARCH 1

Arrived at Hazebrouck Station at 6.30 am. Very dull and cold. Found motor waiting for us. The train apparently had left Boulogne about 1.30. Our compartment was filled by our returning people, Keith Menzies, Archie Sinclair, Self, Blofeld and Townsend, and a man belonging to the Indian Cavalry who got out at St Omer.

Archie and Keith were in a state of collapse from the crossing. At Hazebrouck we all packed into the motor, until its springs groaned. Our baggage was put on top and Mr Howard the RCM* and Corporal Button,** who were also returning off leave, crowded into the front seat with the chauffeur. Fetched up in Staple about 7 and found my servant on the look-out for me, as we had left the school during my absence in England.

My new quarters were at the Brewery halfway up the main street and opposite to the house occupied by the officers of C Squadron. It is certainly the best house in the village, and very comfortable. The proprietor is most kind and he loves soldiers. Nothing is too much trouble for him to do for us.

He and his wife had cleared the furniture out of their dining and sitting rooms, and let us have them to spread our valises in. Luxmoore had a bedroom upstairs. I found Walker stretched in a condition of oblivion on the floor of the dining room. Sleep for him is an orgy and not a relaxation! My room was beyond, where my fleabag looked most inviting. After a cup of very nice hot coffee I turned in and slept soundly until 9.30.

At about 11 I had a long interview with the Patron. He seemed most friendly and took me over his house. The whole place was extremely neat and clean. He told me that he makes beer 120 times a year. Each brew is worth 900 francs (£36) and he is allowed to keep one-third of the profit,

---

* Regimental Corporal Major.
** Cpl Ernest Button, a grocer by trade, lived at Louth, Lincolnshire. Aged twenty when he enlisted in the 2nd Life Guards in 1904, he transferred to the 2nd Machine Gun Regiment in May 1918 and served on the Western Front throughout the war.

about £12 a time, so his income is roughly about £1,500 a year. As he is very careful and thrifty he probably saves a good deal and is therefore now very rich. His cellars are filled with very good Brandy, Madeira, Claret and Burgundy, and he occasionally presents us with a bottle. Every morning at 8 o'clock he sends us in cups of delicious coffee. We are indeed in clover.

TUESDAY MARCH 2

An account of the crisis in the Austrian food supply has been issued to us.

Austria-Hungary is confronted with difficulties in the matter of her food supply no less than Germany. But the measures which she has taken to protect herself against a shortage, have been carried out with less energy.

1. Because the Austro-Hungarian Government has neither the organising ability of the German Government, nor their power of coming to a quick decision.
2. Because the inhabitants of the Dual Monarchy are less disciplined than the Germans.
3. Because on this point there is a clash of interests between Austria, who imports wheat, and Hungary who grows it.

WEDNESDAY MARCH 3

Fairly fine, though cold. Took advantage of the cessation of rain to ride to Cassel with Keith Menzies. We found there signs of the arrival of the North Midland Territorial Division. Every village round Cassel is now filled with the troops of this division.

The Headquarters of General Stuart-Wortley* who commands, is now situated in the nice white château with the ornamental water, just outside Cassel. We found Granby and young Stuart-Wortley his ADCs there. Coming home we passed the three Field Batteries under Hill Child's command. Both men and horses looked very workmanlike and in excellent condition, very different from the Territorial of pre-war days.

---

* Maj Gen Edward Stuart-Wortley was a veteran of the Afghanistan Campaign of 1877–80. He then served in Egypt, the Sudan and the South African War. Capt Archibald Stuart-Wortley, 2nd Life Guards ('Young S-W'), was his nephew and later ADC to Viscount Buxton, Governor-General of South Africa.

Read Asquith's speech in the House on the War and measures to combat the German blockade.* Thought it good. His references to finance were also very interesting. He pointed out that the costs of previous wars seem very trivial to the one in which we are now engaged. The 22 years of the Napoleonic Wars (1793–1815) cost us approximately £831,000,000.

Crimea (1854–5)   £70,000,000
South Africa (1899–1902)   £211,000,000
This War   £730,000,000 *a year*
or only £100,000,000 less than the whole cost of 22 years of the Napoleonic Wars.

The News from the Dardanelles seems very satisfactory. Its passage by the British Fleet will have the greatest effect on the war. In any case a successful passage will drive a wedge between Turkey and her allies, will cut off all her supplies for her troops in Egypt or the Caucasus, and will turn the Heathen Turk out of Europe.

It will give us Adrianople to tempt Bulgaria with, and will open up a line from Russia to send out her corn and oil. The former will greatly cheapen the price of the loaf in England. It will also give Russia a far more easy means of obtaining the equipment she so badly needs for her other two ports, Archangel and Vladivostock. Neither is very satisfactory, the former because it is now ice-bound, and only joined to the centre of Russia by a single narrow gauge line, and the latter is so far distant. There are now 80,000 tons of wheat waiting to pour through, should the Dardanelles be opened, none of which can trickle through Archangel or Vladivostock.

Having put our hand to the Dardanelles plough we cannot turn back. A failure here would cause us the greatest setback and loss of prestige amongst those nations – Greece, Romania, Bulgaria and Italy – which are now hovering on the brink of coming in. A success here would probably force their hand. So it *must* be done, now it has started, and so far things look favourable, though it is a tough nut to crack.

---

* The measures were in response to the more aggressive German maritime policy, which had started on 18 February. Seven British merchantmen were sunk in the following week by U-boats. Asquith stated that the British and French Governments would now 'hold themselves free to detain and take into port ships carrying goods of presumed enemy destination, ownership or origin'. This speech by the Prime Minister was reported in *The Times* of 2 March 1915.

THURSDAY MARCH 4

A beastly day. Wet and cold. Rode as far as St Marie Cappel to look at the new artillery. Just missed being bowled over in the village street by a runaway horse, ridden by a terrified Corporal. It was a miracle that his horse didn't slip up on the pavé which was very greasy, but it managed to get out all right into the fields, where the man fell off on the soft ground.

The Dardanelles operations seem to be progressing very favourably, although the Narrows, which is the hardest part of the work, has yet to be reduced. The range of the HMS *Queen Elizabeth* (25,000 yards)* is such that it is now possible for her to attack the rear of these ports. The famous Bulair Lines are now being reduced by gunfire from the Gulf of Saros, and when they are completely overcome they will presumably be occupied, and put in a state of defence by our landing parties.**

These Lines were built during the Crimean War under British supervision by the Turkish Authorities, to guard against a Russian advance on the Dardanelles forts. Thus they face northwards, which will allow their reduction by long-distance indirect fire by the Fleet from the South.

FRIDAY MARCH 5

Wet and beastly cold as usual. Managed to get a ride in. While we were at Ste Marie-Capelle another runaway horse, this time riderless, tore down the village street. Walker stopped it. This really is a most dangerous village.

SATURDAY MARCH 6

Wet again and very cold. Spent the afternoon acting as touch judge in a football match, and slipping about in frightful mud: the wind is simply bitter.

Not a great deal of news. The French have issued a communiqué concerning the embarrassment of Germany over the food question. It is a sort of rider to the one they issued about Austria–Hungary a few days ago.

---

* Most of the ships earmarked by the Admiralty for the Dardanelles operation were pre-Dreadnought vessels and launched before 1906. The *Queen Elizabeth* was a shining exception, being the newest and most powerful battleship in the fleet. Martin Gilbert, *Churchill*, vol. III, pp. 249–50.

** Crofton presumes that the Bulair Lines, at the neck of the Gallipoli Peninsula, will be chosen as the best spot for military landings – and explains why on 8 March. Ellis Ashmead-Bartlett was also a strong proponent of this strategy. See *The Uncensored Dardanelles*, pp. 127–8.

Potatoes

The potato crop of 1914, amounting to 47 million tons, shows a decrease of 7 million tons on the 1913 crop. The Government is attempting to diminish the amount used by distilleries and starch factories. They have even gone to the lengths of forbidding the use of starch for stiffening shirts. But the obligation to add 10 per cent–20 per cent of starch to bread involves increasing the consumption of potato flour. The existing stock of potatoes will prove insufficient for the normal demand.

The German people, already obliged to eat less bread than before,* would be still more affected by a dearth of potatoes. Some disturbance took place at Schöneberg, a suburb of Berlin, at the time of the potato sale.

To sum up

The Imperial Government is adopting the measures of State Socialism. But it is not possible to regulate in its most minute details, the economic life of a whole people. Henceforth it is certain that it will not suffice for the Germans to economise; they will be obliged to go short of food. The *Kölnische Zeitung* of February 15 does not conceal from its readers their 'new duty'; it is printed in capitals:

EAT LESS.

SUNDAY MARCH 7

Bright sun, but *very* cold wind. The last few days have been colder than any time previously. Church at the usual hour in the usual place.

At 6.30 gave a lecture in the girls' school to C Squadron on the part taken by Russia in this war. There seems to be an idea here as well as at home that *we* are doing everything, and the rest of the Allies nothing. I suppose the Allies think the same about us. Lecture was well attended and lasted an hour.

There are many signs now that we are not going to stay in Staple for ever. In my opinion the time is not ripe even now for a renewed offensive on our part. The ammunition question is still serious, and if we could wait until June, we should have another 250,000 men out, and a still greater superiority in guns. The French too would have larger reserves of equipment and ammunition.

---

* Bread and flour rationing had been introduced on 1 February. Under an earlier decree (25 January), all stocks of grain and flour were confiscated. These measures point to the effectiveness of the naval blockade, even at this early stage in the war.

I do not think that the Germans will allow us to wait for our own time, at least it would be very silly of them if they did. I rather imagine that they will attack us, and endeavour to break through to Calais or Paris at the earliest moment and when the going is better.

I am confident that they will fail. For I cannot believe that they will succeed in doing what they failed to do in November last when the French Armies have improved 100 per cent in numbers, equipment and morale. Then we were all out, and hanging on by our eyelids, while they, the Germans, had the advantage of numbers and guns.

MONDAY MARCH 8

Fine and bright, but a piercing and Arctic wind. Went for a ride in the afternoon to look at the new North Midland Division in their billets. The ground is drying very fast, and the roads are already in beautiful condition. There is a good touch of frost in the air, and what puddles there are, are frozen hard.

The Dardanelles affair goes on all right. The French ships have been shelling the Bulair Lines again. These Lines are extremely important, as they seal the neck of the peninsula, and, in our hands, would effectively stop any reinforcements coming from Turkey to the forts on the Dardanelles.

The Bulair Isthmus is, generally speaking, occupied by one lump of hill with three summits 433, 489 and 436 feet high respectively. There are entrenched lines reaching across the narrowest part. But this line can be turned by anyone in command of the sea.

The whole operation of occupying this little belt of land, or of sweeping it from the sea to prevent its being crossed by the enemy, closely resembles that which the Japanese undertook when they made untenable by their men-of-war the isthmus of Nan Shan which unites the Peninsula of Port Arthur to the mainland.*

TUESDAY MARCH 9

A fine and bright day. Very cold East wind. The roads have dried up, and this morning were very dusty owing to a good frost during the night. Went for a

* Port Arthur, or Lu-shun as it is now known, has a deep-water harbour free from ice throughout the year. The Treaty of Portsmouth, which ended the Russo–Japanese War in 1905, transferred Port Arthur from Russia to Japan, but today it is an important Chinese naval base.

ride into Hazebrouck after lunch with Torrie, Griffin and Walker. Found Hazebrouck very full of rumours. Some say that we are going to attack, and some say that the Germans are concentrating at Courtrai and may be expected to attack shortly.

It looks as if there is a move on. Ferguson and the Adjutant saw General Byng at 3rd Cavalry Division Headquarters this afternoon. They returned just before dinner and both seemed full of mystery. We couldn't get anything out of either. During dinner the Colonel announced that all accounts for forage and requisitions were to be settled at once. We were to stand to at 6 am tomorrow, saddled up ready to move off at an hour's notice. All baggage to be packed in the waggons and ready to move by 8 am. There was immediate summoning of servants. Most of us went to bed at 9.

Things seem to be going well; a new 15 inch gun has been mounted near Kemmel, which is called *Grandmother*. This is in contradistinction to the 9.2 inch gun which is called *Mother*. This new 15 inch throws a shell containing nearly a ton of high explosive a distance of 12 miles. It should surprise the Boche. An enormous crowd collected yesterday to see it fire its first shell. It fired three and behaved very well.

WEDNESDAY MARCH 10

Called at 5 o'clock. Was up, packed by 6, then had breakfast. A dull grey morning not too warm, but not so bitter as yesterday. We still sit and wait, the whole village is roused with the excitement of our apparent departure. The Maire is besieged by people making claims for damage. Even in his or her grief at our departure, the business side of the French race is never forgotten.

At 8 o'clock we could hear a terrific bombardment taking place towards La Bassée. We could distinguish the deep thunder of *Grandmother* amidst the general hubbub. Dundonald turned up during the morning and said he was staying with French, and had motored out to see us.* He looked rather seedy, I thought, and incidentally he let out that French had invited him over to see a big battle which was just going to start. He did not enlarge on this information.

---

* Lt Gen the Earl of Dundonald, formerly Lord Cochrane (1852–1935), was a resilient character who had retired in 1907. In 1884, he led a contingent of the 2nd Life Guards in the campaign to relieve Khartoum, and it fell to him to ride with the despatch telling of the death of Gordon. In the South African War, he commanded the 2nd Cavalry Brigade which entered Ladysmith in February 1900. At the age of seventy-seven, he sailed a 14-ton boat across the Atlantic to South America. See *The Times*, 13 April 1935.

Special Order.

To the 1st Army.

We are about to engage the enemy under very favourable conditions. Until now in the present campaign, the British Army has, by its pluck and determination, gained victories against an enemy greatly superior both in men and guns. Reinforcements have made us stronger than the enemy in our front. Our guns are now both more numerous than the enemy's are, and also larger than any hitherto used by any army in the field. Our Flying Corps has driven the Germans from the air.

On the Eastern Front, and to South of us, our Allies have made marked progress and caused enormous losses to the Germans, who are, moreover, harassed by internal troubles and shortage of supplies, so that there is little prospect at present of big reinforcements being sent against us here.

In front of us we have only one German Corps, spread out on a front as large as that occupied by the whole of our Army (the First)

We are now about to attack with about 48 battalions a locality in that front which is held by some three German battalions. It seems probable, also, that for the first day of the operations the Germans will not have more than four battalions available as reinforcements for the counter attack. Quickness of movement is therefore of first importance to enable us to forestall the enemy and thereby gain success without severe loss.

At no time in this war has there been a more favourable moment for us, and I feel confident of success. The extent of that success must depend on the rapidity and determination with which we advance.

Although fighting in France, let us remember that we are fighting to preserve the British Empire and to protect our homes against the organized savagery of the German Army. To ensure success, each one of us must play his part, and fight like men for the Honour of Old England.

(Sd.) D. HAIG, General,

9th March, 1915.   Commanding 1st Army.

1st Printing Co., R.E. G.H.Q. 673.

Gen Sir Douglas Haig's Special Order on the eve of Neuve Chapelle.

At lunch the Colonel said that he didn't think that there was any further need for secrecy. A big attack was taking place at La Bassée to seize a ridge which lay at right angles behind Neuve Chapelle. The attack was to be carried out by the First Army, of which IV and Indian Corps were to attack, and I Corps was to demonstrate and act as support. 200 Guns were massed to prepare the advance.

Our advantage is that we outnumber the Germans by 2½ to 1. No further news, except that we are to be ready to start tomorrow morning at 6 am.

THURSDAY MARCH 11

Got up at 4.30. Pitch dark. Had breakfast, and was all packed and my valise on the waggon by 5.30. Mounted at 6 and rode off to join Torrie who had gone on to the rendez-vous. Still very dark, and a heavy mist settled on one's cloak like falling rain. All the village was up, and the lights from open doors and windows splashed across the road, and enlivened the otherwise depressing gloom of dawn. I wondered if I should ever see Staple again, and was sorry not to be able to say 'goodbye' to it by daylight.

We reached the rendez-vous through a stream of shouting, arguing men. The hubbub of an early start is always extraordinary. The waggons rumble louder than any other time, people always seem to have such a lot to say and nobody ever dreams of listening. The civil population added their share to the commotion. We got clear of the village and slowly wended our way towards Hondeghem.

By the time we had reached the main Hazebrouck–St Silvestre road it was daylight. We proceeded to La Kreule, where the whole brigade was to assemble. At 7 o'clock the Brigade moved off and we walked our horses most of the way with very rare and short trots to the little village of Borré.

From Borré we marched towards the village of La Motte. Here is the Château in which live General Allenby and the Headquarters Staff of the Cavalry Corps. We soon passed through the Bois de Nieppe. In the middle of the wood, we were ordered to dismount and wait. It was about 10.30 when we dismounted.

We heard a great cannonade going on towards La Bassée but couldn't get any news as to what was happening. We stayed in the wood until 4 o'clock, when we were ordered to saddle up and go into billets. When we got to the edge of the wood, about 2 miles from Merville, Torrie told me to trot on and find a house for our headquarters in a small village called Les Puresbecques.

I trotted on and found the billeting party and a house which I at once inspected. It was a house of four large rooms, and an old man and woman were living in it. In my best French I explained that we should require this of them. They were most dreary rooms and not entirely devoid of damp. I sent the interpreter into Merville to buy meat and eggs, and we got some milk from a farm opposite. We soon had a blazing fire going, and things didn't look so bad.

Wallace,* who had been wounded at Warneton on October 20, joined us today, and for the present was attached to the headquarters. This made our party eight, as Ferguson was acting as Brigadier, while Kavanagh was on leave in England.

We got some bundles of straw and spread it out along one side of the room. Then we put our blankets, which we took off the saddles, on it. At

---

* Lt Euan Wallace had come out with the Composite Regiment in August. Now back with his Regiment, he served as Adjutant of the 2nd Life Guards for two years from December 1915. After the war he joined the General Staff in Washington.

7.30 we had a meal of eggs, tea, jam and tinned foods of various kinds, which filled us up well. At 8.30 we all turned in, for we had no idea, when we should be wanted, and we had had a long and tedious day.

FRIDAY MARCH 12

Woken up during the night by the orderly coming into our room and flashing his electric torch on our five recumbent bodies. The orders he brought were not very pressing, and might easily have been sent later, instead of waking us all up at 1.30 am. We slumbered on until 5 o'clock.

We had breakfast and were packed again and saddled up ready to move on at 6 am. As we stood about in the road we could hear the artillery beginning to get to work, for it was very still, and the sounds came to us in increasing bursts. Our orders were to remain ready to move at an hour's notice.

The Brigade Major turned up about 10 and gave us a little information about yesterday. It appears that on Wednesday morning, the 11th Jäger Battalion held Neuve Chapelle. From documents taken from prisoners, it appears that our attack came as a complete surprise. At Lille there were only Reserve formations, and prisoners state that there is no line of trenches between the trenches we took on the 10th, and the Lille defences, running through Eghlos.

On Wednesday evening the village of Neuve Chapelle was in our hands. We captured about 800 prisoners, and all the 3rd Battalion of their 16th Regiment was either killed or wounded. On Wednesday night the enemy were reinforced by the 6th Bavarian Reserve Division. The rapidity with which they were hurried down, and the way in which miscellaneous units were thrown into the fight, are evidence of the complete surprise of our attack last Wednesday.*

A wounded German officer stated that he thought the counter attack must have gone wrong, as he and his men found themselves alone with no support. A man of the same regiment said that the Bavarians had surrendered because the 153rd Saxon Regiment had left them in the lurch. This suggests that the Saxons and the Bavarians did not work well together. There is no doubt that the Bavarians suffered heavy losses; many of their

---

* A.J.P. Taylor underlines the great opportunity which was missed. 'The British broke the German line – for the only time in the war. Nothing of any significance followed . . . they waited for reinforcements: but by the time these arrived, German reinforcements had arrived also. The gap was closed.' *The First World War*, p. 62.

prisoners had had no food for 36 hours. The battle continued and we could hear how tremendous the cannonade was.

Not being called out yet, we ventured to have a light lunch at 1 o'clock. About 4 o'clock we were still standing to and several of us walked into Merville. The streets were full of motor ambulances containing wounded in various stages of severity. Many were being sent on to Boulogne en route to England, but many more were being helped and carried into various convents at Merville. They were on the whole cheerful and conveyed a sense of relief. We walked down the two main streets and bought some tinned peaches and eggs. The *Place* or Square was occupied by 6 armoured cars with guns on board.

We returned to our billets for tea, and spent the rest of the day walking up and down the road and waiting. Towards the end of the day a consignment of about 500 German prisoners came into Merville and were incarcerated, pro tem, on two large barges on the canal.

We had a cheery dinner at 7 o'clock, and about 8 took shelter in our blankets on the straw, as we were again to be ready to move at 6 o'clock in the morning.

SATURDAY MARCH 13

At 5 we hauled ourselves off the straw, opened the windows and took turns at washing in the one solitary bucket. By 6 we were ready to move. The same waiting then took place. We loitered as usual in the road, listening to the thick muffled noise of the guns which came through the clammy morning mist.

At 10.30 the Brigade Major appeared but he did not seem to know much. We heard definitely that Neuve Chapelle was in our hands, and that we were now attacking in a NE direction on Aubers.

About 3.30 Walker and I went into Merville to look at the German prisoners. We found them on two barges, on a branch or backwater of the canal. There were about 480 of them. Out of this number there were perhaps a dozen of the same appearance and physique as the NCOs of this regiment. The remainder were undersized, of poor physique, and anaemic-looking, and looked like the sort of fifth-class waiter one sees in restaurants at the White City. They seemed quite satisfied with their lot. Their clothes were quite new and consisted of trousers with a thin red stripe down them, and large waders or jack boots. Their greatcoats were the new blue grey of the German infantry, and they wore flat caps with scarlet bands round them. I did not see one helmet. Their clothes, although new, were caked from head to foot in mud. The men were obviously the 1914 conscripts with which the German ranks are now filled.

There were a few officers on board who kept religiously to themselves, and refused to be contaminated by any contact with such cattle as they consider their men to be. They were chinless, putty-faced youths. After staring at them for about 20 minutes we departed into the town and had our hair cut.

At 4.30 we returned to our billets, and found that we were under orders to return to Staple, since the operations had not progressed far enough for us to bring off a Cavalry coup. The roads leading from the front were now full of motor ambulances, for our casualties had become very heavy. Most of the ones I saw in the motors had head wounds and several wounded Germans were also brought in. All the prisoners had a great weight on their minds from the danger of crossing the Channel infested with German submarines. The estimate of the German casualties for the fighting on Wednesday, Thursday and Friday is about 2,000 prisoners, 4,000 killed, and 12,000 wounded. Our toll too must be heavy. There are all sorts of rumours.

At 5.30 we paraded, and said *adieu* to our old couple. Having made some money out of us, they blessed us in loud tones, and we rode away towards the Brigade rendez-vous, Vieux Berquin. We made very slow progress for the roads were choked with baggage columns. For miles we could only go at a slow walk. From Vieux Berquin we crossed the railway line at Strazeele, then we marched on Hazebrouck which was reached about 9.15 pm. From here we could trot a little and we finally reached our billets at Staple at 10.30 pm.

The village was out to a man to meet us, and the greatest excitement prevailed. In some places Chinese lanterns were hanging out, for they all knew of our return, from the orderlies we had sent back earlier in the day, and from the motor which we sent back with our food. Everyone seemed very glad to be back.

We had a most excellent cold supper, and returned to our billets. I found the worthy brewer and his wife delighted to see me, and an enormous fire blazing in my room.

SUNDAY MARCH 14

A beautiful warm spring day. Breakfasted at 9.

Our troubles were not over yet. An order arrived shortly after breakfast, that we were to get ready to move at an hour's notice. We couldn't get much news but we heard that the Germans were attacking at St Eloi, probably in return for our attack at Neuve Chapelle, and had captured the village.

From what we can hear about the offensive of Wednesday last on Neuve Chapelle, it appears to have been partially successful. The idea was to capture the ridge on which Aubers stands, then send the cavalry round by a circular move, to fall on the German position at La Bassée from the rear. For several reasons, the infantry failed to do more than capture one-third of the ridge. Although the Cavalry were brought up, and the Scots Greys actually got into position for the gallop round, it was impossible to execute the plan, without enormous losses, so the last part of the plan was abandoned. But at the same time the station at Don was bombed by our airmen and great damage done.

We stood to all day, and about 3 pm were allowed to off-saddle, but otherwise to remain ready to move in an hour.

MONDAY MARCH 15

Awakened at 5.10 am. Howard banging on the window. Packed and ready to move by 6 am, but got no orders. The German attack on St Eloi seems to have fizzled out, for we have recaptured any ground we lost yesterday. The fact of the matter is that the Germans haven't the men on this front now. The attack on Wednesday last was an eye-opener. It showed that they were very short of reserves.

The country has dried out in the most wonderful manner and very soon it should be fit for any operations required. It is the most beautiful day again today. About 12 o'clock orders came in that we were to be ready to move in half an hour. The Squadrons were therefore concentrated in this village, which was filled from end to end with men and horses. At 1.30 we got the order to off-saddle, but to remain concentrated. At 4 pm came the order to saddle up and return to our billets, but to remain ready to move in an hour.

I wish they would either use us or leave us alone. For a week they have been messing us about, saddling up, standing to, etc. and nothing has happened.

During dinner, orders came that in future we were to remain ready to move in 3½ hours from the time that the Brigadier received the order. That would give us 3 hours' notice, which practically means that the status quo of ten days ago is resumed.

Euan Wallace has come to live with me in my house. I am sorry to say Archie Sinclair departed today for England to go on Seely's staff as ADC.*

---

* Brig Gen John Seely (1868–1947) had switched from politics to the Army. He served in France from 11 August 1914, gaining the reputation of the 'luckiest man in the British Army', until he was gassed in 1918. Later he was Under-Secretary to the Air Ministry, but resigned in November 1919, when Lloyd George refused to give the Air Ministry a separate Secretary of State. See The Times, 8 November 1947.

Seely commands a scallywag brigade of Canadian Cavalry and King Edward's Horse.* Archie's departure leaves Penn as the sole survivor of the Composite Squadron which left England on August 14 to form part of the Household Cavalry Regiment, which served through the Retreat from Mons in the 4th Cavalry Brigade under Bingham.**

Bethell and Wallace have now returned here, but Penn remains the only one who has been out since the beginning of the war. With the exception of a few days leave, he has, so far, not missed a day.†

TUESDAY MARCH 16

A dull cold morning. As usual stood to and saddled up at 6 o'clock.

The casualties amongst the officers in the fighting at Neuve Chapelle from March 10–13 are getting heavier and heavier. They now amount to 191.

Killed	46	
Died of wounds	10	
Accidentally killed	2	
Died	1	Total deaths 59
Wounded	117	
Wounded and missing	5	
Missing	10	Total wounded and missing 132

There are many more I fear yet to come.

THURSDAY MARCH 18

Beastly day. Snow storm during the night, very dull and biting wind now!

More Casualties continue to come in over Neuve Chapelle and St Eloi on Sunday last. An analysis shows that 6 Lieutenant Colonels, 17 Majors, 65 Captains, 49 Lieutenants and 45 Second Lieutenants, were in the lists. I hope that this is final but I fear that it is not.

---

* Not the first time that Crofton has expressed his scepticism about the Canadians. But he changes his tune after the gas attack at 2nd Ypres.

** Maj Gen Sir Cecil Bingham had been formerly ADC to Sir John French in South Africa and had commanded 1st Life Guards. He served in the First World War from 1914 to 1917 and commanded 4th Cavalry Brigade.

† Capt Frank Penn maintained this remarkable record for most of the war. Previously Adjutant of the 2nd Life Guards from 1910 to 1913, he was indeed a survivor, being on active service continuously from August 1914 to April 1918.

Some of the Regiments have suffered massive casualties. The Cameronians with 15 officers killed and 9 wounded, and the Worcester Regiment with 13 killed and 12 wounded easily top the list. Poor John de Blaquière* was killed with the Cameronians. I have known him since he was a baby. When he joined the Army in 1910, his father wrote to me with reference to him going into the Irish Guards.

The offensive from March 10–14 was very nearly sensational. The first attack was due to come off about 8 am and the objective was timed to have been reached about 1 pm. The second attack was timed for 3 pm, but although the first objective was gained at 10.30, nobody thought of altering the time of the second attack. By 3 o'clock the Germans had collected enough reinforcements to stop any further progress. At one time there was nothing in front of the Indian Corps as far as Lille. Better staff management would have enabled us to acquire that town. The authorities seem satisfied. But to us the casualty lists seem very heavy for the results attained.

FRIDAY MARCH 19

Still dull, but much warmer. Usual routine still goes on here. There is a sort of easy going on all fronts, largely due to the exhaustion after the fighting of the last ten days. We are, I believe, very short of ammunition. It is reported that the French have six weeks' supply in hand, but our reserves at present are nil, owing chiefly to the enormous amount sent to the Dardanelles.

Wrote to Hugh Baikie today and said I would ride over and see him and stay the night tomorrow. He may have some news.

The casualty list today shows another 207 casualties amongst officers, of whom

Killed	76
Died of wounds	9
Wounded	118
Missing	4

---

* Descended from a Huguenot family, John de Blaquière was a nephew of Georgiana de Blaquière, the diarist's grandmother. Her husband, Col Hugh Crofton, was severely wounded at the Battle of Inkerman. In 1861, while commanding the Depot Battalion, both he and his adjutant, Capt Hanham, were shot dead by a disgruntled (British) soldier of the 32nd Regiment at Fulwood Barracks, Preston. Both officers were heirs to baronetcies.

This brings the total casualty list up to 726, of which 73 killed and wounded belong to the Indian Corps.* I hear on very reliable information that the St Eloi casualties were about 50 officers and 900 men killed, wounded and missing.

The Germans got hold of Douglas Haig's proclamation which was issued to us before Neuve Chapelle; they must have taken a copy off a prisoner. We have seen many ingenious attempts to turn it to their advantage. In one they point out that 3 of their battalions withstood and beat back 48 of ours, and they quote this in order to show how very strong we have to be before we can make a small impression on their line.

They recognise that we have cooked their goose, and it is this fact which has stirred the whole Teutonic race into a blind ungovernable fury against us, as their Gazette shows:

Effusions of this kind are getting more and more common. They are pathetic and ridiculous. It is only to be supposed that the man who vomits this muck is paid by the yard for doing so. It is a penny a line with a vengeance. To my mind, one of the worst traits in the German character is their lack of humour, without which it is hard to redeem their unattractive characters. Poor Devils!

SATURDAY MARCH 20

We heard today of the latest result in the bombardment of the Dardanelles fortresses on March 18. The *Ocean* and *Irresistible* and *Bouvet* were sunk. The *Invincible*, the battle-cruiser which took the leading part in the Battle of the Falkland Islands, and the *Gaulois* were damaged more or less badly. Fortunately as regards the first two, very few lives were lost. But several Turkish forts were silenced, though whether permanently or not it is too early yet to know. It is to be noted that these ships were *not* sunk by gunfire, but by floating mines,** so that the question as to whether a battleship or a fort is the top dog is still undecided.

---

* At the outbreak of war, the Lahore and Meerut Infantry Divisions of the Indian Army were selected for Europe. From October 1914, the Indian Corps was involved in some of the fiercest fighting round Ypres. They provided a high proportion of the attacking force at Neuve Chapelle, where the finest memorial to the Indian Army on the Western Front, designed by Sir Herbert Baker, stands today.
** The *Ocean*, the *Irresistible* and the French battleship *Bouvet* all fell victim to the minefield laid a few nights before by a small Turkish steamer, the *Nusret*. Several of the twenty-nine mines sown were laid parallel to the shore of Eren Keui Bay, as German observers had noticed that Allied ships had been manoeuvring in this bay when preparing to make further bombardments. This trap worked all too well. Michael Hickey, *Gallipoli*, p. 73.

TRANSLATION FROM "LILLE WAR GAZETTE," 3rd MARCH, 1915.
(This is a weekly newspaper, issued by the Germans in LILLE, in German).

FIRE.

(BY LIEUTENANT-COLONEL KADEN.)

As children many of us have played with it : some of us have seen an outbreak of fire. First a small tongue-like flame appears, it grows into a devastating fury of heat. We out here in the field have seen more than enough of it.

But there is also the fire of joy, of sacred enthusiasm ! It arose from sacrificial altars, from mountain heights of Germany, and lit t the heavens at the time of solstice and whenever the home countries were in danger. This year fires of joy shall flare from the Bismarck Columns throughout the length and breadth of Germany, for on 1st April, just one hundred years ago, our country's greatest son was born. Let us celebrate this event in a manner deep, far-reaching and mighty ! BLOOD AND IRON.

Let every German, man or woman, young or old, find in his heart a Bismarck Column, a pillar of fire now in these days of storm and stress. Let this fire, enkindled in every German breast, be a fire of joy, of holiest enthusiasm. But let it be terrible, unfettered, let it carry horror and destruction ! Call it HATE ! Let no one come to you with " Love thine enemy ! " We all have but one enemy, *England !* How long have we wooed her almost to the point of our own self-abasement. She would none of us, so leave to her the apostles of peace, the " No-War " disciples. The time has passed when we would do homage to everything English—our cousins that were !

" God punish England ! " " May He punish her ! " This is the greeting that now passes when Germans meet. The fire of this righteous hate is all aglow !

You men of Germany, from East and West, forced to shed your blood in the defence of your home-land through England's infamous envy and hatred of Germany's progress, feed the flame that burns in your souls. We have but one war-cry "GOD PUNISH ENGLAND !" Hiss this to one another in the trenches, in the charge, hiss as it were the sound of licking flames.

Behold in every dead comrade a sacrifice forced from you by this accursed people. Take ten-fold vengeance for each hero's death !

You German people at home, feed this fire of hate !

You mothers, engrave this in the heart of the babe at your breast !

You thousands of teachers, to whom millions of German children look up with eyes and hearts, teach HATE ! unquenchable HATE !

You homes of German learning, pile up the fuel on this fire ! Tell the nation that this hate is not un-German, that it is not poison for our people. Write in letters of fire the name of our bitterest enemy. You guardians of the truth, feed this sacred HATE !

You German fathers, lead your children up to the high hills of our home-land, at their feet our dear country bathed in sunshine. Your women and children shall starve; bestial, devilish conception. England wills it ! Surely, all that is in you rises against such infamy ?

Listen to the ceaseless song of the German forest, behold the fruitful fields like rolling seas, then will your love for this wondrous land find the right words, HATE, unquenchable HATE. Germany, Germany above all !

Let it be inculcated in your children and it will grow like a land-slide, irresistible, from generation to generation.

You fathers, proclaim it aloud over the billowing fields, that the toiling peasant below may hear you, that the birds of the forest may " away with the message : into all the land. that echoes from German cliffs send it reverberating like the clanging of bells from tower to tower throughout the country-side : " HATE, HATE, the accursed English, HATE " !

You masters, carry the flame to your workshops ; axe and hammer will fall the heavier when arms are nerved by this HATE.

You peasants, guard this flame, fan it anew in the hearts of your toilers, that the hand may rest heavy on the plough that throws up the soil of our home-land.

What CARTHAGE was to ROME, ENGLAND is to GERMANY. For ROME as for us it is a question of " to be or not to be." May our people find a faithful mentor like Cato. His " ceterum censeo, Carthaginem esse delendam " for us Germans means.—

"GOD PUNISH ENGLAND."

N.B.—A copy of this newspaper was found on a German prisoner captured during the recent fighting at NEUVE CHAPELLE. It is of interest as showing the hatred for Great Britain which is being sedulously cultivated in Germany. This hatred is being encouraged and fostered officially by every possible means.

1d Plain.
2d Coloured.

'God Punish England!' *The Lille War Gazette*, found on a German prisoner, dated 3 March 1915.

Six battleships in the Straits were being relieved by the *Vengeance*, *Irresistible*, *Albion*, *Ocean*, *Swiftsure* and *Majestic*. Then on the way out the *Bouvet* was blown up by a drifting mine and sank in 36 fathoms north of Eren Keui village, in less than 3 minutes, with a loss of about 740 men. At 4.09 the *Irresistible* quit the line, listing heavily; and at 5.50 she sank. At 6.05 the *Ocean* also struck a drifting mine and sank. The crews were safely removed under a hot fire.

We have been badly handicapped by the weather, and during the month which has elapsed since the operations commenced the bombardment has only been possible on about 10 days. This setback has been enormous for it has enabled the Unspeakable Turk assisted by the Impossible German to erect more effective resistance. This will very shortly be put to the test.

About 4 o'clock I rode over with Walker to Hazebrouck to stay the night with Hugh Baikie. I found him very fit and well, and far more cheerful than when I saw him last on February 14.

SUNDAY MARCH 21

The official first day of Spring.

The room I slept in was one borrowed from the Staff Officer whose turn it was to sleep in the office. The house Hugh Baikie lives in belongs I believe to a lawyer and is one of the most important in Hazebrouck. My room looks on to a garden with a few good trees and nicely laid out shrubs and paths. It really is a grand day, the birds were singing, and I felt as if I had come into an extra thousand a year. I almost longed for a big battle, for it is so easy to be brave upon a day like this.

Hugh's house is shared by the Second Army Staff. Windsor Clive, and three others, the French liaison officer, and the Belgian duc d'Urcel, who is a kind of liaison officer for the Belgian Army.

I heard a good deal about the German attack at St Eloi last Sunday. The Germans were contemplating an attack here by 13 battalions, when we pre-empted them by attacking at Neuve Chapelle. But as we started our attack first they had to use the 6th Bavarian Reserve Division as a reinforcement at Neuve Chapelle. Their large attack couldn't come off, and they were obliged to attack at St Eloi with only five battalions. They began their attack with a terrific military fire, and afterwards rushed our first line of trenches, but were driven out by the Irish Fusiliers and Cornwall Light Infantry. They appear to have treated our wounded well, dressing their wounds and feeding them. They allowed our stretcher parties to come out and collect the wounded, but they would not allow any dead to be moved, supposing that they would find information on them.

Last Monday the Germans made an isolated attack with 100 men. Most of them were shot down. Over 37 were killed at once. No one knows why they made such an attack. The only plausible reason is that they were malefactors, and they were sent out deliberately to be shot.

A German aeroplane came over Ypres yesterday. Dropping a bomb to attract notice it also dropped a bag with a letter in it. This stated that two of our airmen had had to descend behind German lines owing to engine trouble, and although prisoners, were quite unhurt and were being well looked after.

At 9.30 am Hugh went off to see his boss to get orders, and I walked about Hazebrouck until 10. Then Walker turned up with my horses and we rode home together. In the afternoon, Griffin, Walker and I had to attend a wine party at our landlord's. We had a quantity of very sweet Champagne and then several wonderful liqueurs.

WEDNESDAY MARCH 24

A filthy day. Pouring hard and very cold.

During the day we get great news of the fall of Przemysl.* What a difference this will make to the Russian campaign in the Carpathians. It must release a considerable force of Russians for the offensive against Hungary. It will also allow the Russians to make full use of the railway system. The new advance on Cracow can also begin now, or at least as soon as the snow melts. This is the Allies biggest success in the war so far.

THURSDAY MARCH 25

Another foul day. Pouring and bitterly cold. Spent the morning getting up a lecture on the War to B Squadron.

The list of prisoners captured by the Russians at Przemysl far exceeds one's most sanguine expectations. They are reported at 9 Generals, 2,500 Officers and 117,000 men. The number of guns and the amount of material captured has not yet been estimated.

---

* The fortress town of Przemysl is 65 miles west of Lemberg in Galicia, on the south-west Front. It had been under pressure from the Russians since 10 November, when one corps of Gen Brusilov's army had resumed the siege, which lasted all winter. Hew Strachan, *The First World War*, p. 372.

Przemysl contained the beaten remnants of the Austrian Third Army, which was defeated at Lemberg last September. One important result of the fall of this stronghold will be the effect upon Austrian morale.*

Przemysl held out for five months and its capture must have been due to exhaustion of supplies. Disease also may have played some part in the reduction, for all the prisoners are to go into quarantine for 21 days at Lemberg, before being taken to Russia. This points to the presence of sickness in the fortress.

At 6 o'clock, lectured B Squadron for an hour and a half on the War, and what our Allies are doing. The lecture took place in a very draughty barn and although under difficult lighting and hearing conditions went off all right.

FRIDAY MARCH 26

Parade at 7 o'clock for purposes of quiet and steady drill. We proceeded about 7.15 to a field about a mile away where a few evolutions were pretty badly performed. The mist prevented one seeing much of what was going on and the rain on the semi-ploughed field in which we drilled made the going very difficult.

We hear that the naval attack on the Dardanelles has been temporarily stopped owing to the strong gale and heavy seas. This is most unfortunate as it allows the Turks to replace their destroyed guns, and repair their shattered forts. The whole business may have to be done again.

One of the many advantages of forts is that their permanent destruction is practically impossible, unless landing parties intervene. This is a difficult matter for a fleet which has only a strictly limited number of men available. The military forces dispatched by France and England should by now be available for this duty.** It would save a great deal of bother if Russia captured Constantinople, for she has been after it for centuries, and she would certainly claim it, in event of success, as her prize of the war.

MONDAY MARCH 29

Another fine bright day, but very cold. Damn this infernal wind. About 9 o'clock a German Taube dropped six bombs on Cassel, hoping, I suppose, to

---

* The news was a great boost to the morale of the Allies, at a time when casualties continued to rise on the Western Front and the naval bombardment of the Dardanelles had not succeeded.
** In fact, the first wave of military landings did not take place on the Gallipoli Peninsula until 25 April. By then the Turks, who had expected the naval attack to be renewed on 19 March, had had ample time to bolster their defences.

catch General Foch, but like the seed which fell on stony ground, the result was abortive.

At 9.30 the Regiment paraded and marched to an outlying field formed up *en masse* for an inspection by General Kavanagh. After shivering in the icy blast for about 2 hours we returned to billets, somewhat warmed by the heated comments which were showered on us by the irate brigadier. His chief complaint was about the horses. But it is impossible to get the appearance customary in England, where warm stables, easy work and plenty of food are the conditions which prevail. Here the horses have been standing in draughty barns for over four months, surviving despite insufficient food.

However, the rebuke will filter down through the Regiment, everyone damning the next person junior to him, so in the end the village cat will certainly get it in the neck as being entirely responsible for this deplorable state of affairs.

I was very glad to see in the *London Gazette* that Airman Lieutenant Pretyman, who dropped bombs on the station at Don on March 11, has been given the DSO. By his action in dropping a 100lb bomb on this junction, which is in rear of the German lines at Neuve Chapelle, he materially hindered the enemy bringing up reinforcements by rail.[*]

TUESDAY MARCH 30

Bright sunny morning but very cold wind. At 10 o'clock the Regiment paraded and marched out to the same field that we were inspected in yesterday, to be inspected again – by General Byng this time. He commands the 3rd Cavalry Division, of which our Brigade is one of the three.

The General took a considerable time over each squadron, so we shivered longer than ever. I sought shelter with Luxmoore and Walker under the lee of a straw stack, where to keep my flagging circulation going I engaged in a rough and tumble with these two worthy people. Luxmoore and I rolled in a heap of chaff until he disappeared from view in it. At last we were looked at and got home about 12 o'clock.

Contrary to Kavanagh yesterday, Byng today was pleased with our horses.[**] This only shows what can be done with horses in one night!!!

---

[*] Pretyman scored a direct hit on the centre carriages of a train. He was also one of those who saw the potential of aerial photography for identifying enemy emplacements. Many pilots had brought their own cameras to the war. They strapped them to the outside of the aircraft and changed the plates by hand during the flights. Anne Baker, *From Biplane to Spitfire*, p. 45.

[**] But not, apparently, with the men. See 31 March.

At 6 o'clock I lectured in the school to C Squadron on the 1870 War. It was very well attended by an appreciative audience.

WEDNESDAY MARCH 31

General Byng's report on yesterday's inspection arrived during the morning. He seems very displeased with what he saw, and I believe Ferguson got it hot. Anyhow, we are to be inspected all over again next week.

Went on a ride in the afternoon to look at our old Billets of November last in Eecke. Top hole ride of about 10 miles. The village looked very smiling and pretty, quite different to those days. Those days seem years ago now. Our school which we slept in was now full of children, but our mess looked much the same. I Battery Royal Horse Artillery was billeted there, and there was an ammunition pack there. These troops, I fancy, belong to the 1st Cavalry Division. Got home about 6.30.

The Russians have begun to bombard the forts at the entrance to the Bosphorus. This should bring the war home to these damned Turks. From Cape Rumeli* to Constantinople is only about fifteen miles. But the Bosphorus passage is tortuous and surrounded by hills from which a plunging fire may be delivered.

THURSDAY APRIL 1

The hateful north-east wind has disappeared. Went for a ride in the morning to look for a suitable place to put a heliograph station.**

At 2 o'clock the Regiment paraded and marched to Ebblinghem, about 3 miles off, to take part in a Service taken by the Bishop of London.† He wished to see the Household Cavalry, as he regarded them rather as his parishioners in London. The Blues marched in from their billets to join us. They now belong to the 8th Cavalry Brigade. We had a short and impressive

---

* Cape Rumeli commands the entrance to the neck of the Bosphorus, on the north-west (European Turkey) side.
** A heliogram is a signal sent by reflecting flashes of sunlight from a movable mirror.
† The Rt Revd Arthur Winnington-Ingram (1858–1946) was a remarkable prelate. Already very popular in the East End when appointed Bishop of London in 1901, he held the see for thirty-eight years. Fulham Palace became a byword for warm hospitality and care extended to all sorts and conditions of men. In his *DNB* tribute, Cuthbert Thicknesse writes: 'His visits to the troops in Flanders, France and Salonika were a marked contribution to the morale of a citizen army.' There is a portrait of him by Sir Hubert von Herkomer at Keble College, Oxford.

service, rather spoilt by continual hoots by passing motors, and incessant whistling from engines on the railway which ran past quite close by. Afterwards we were all given a leaflet which the Bishop had compiled, entitled *Thoughts and Prayers for Good Friday and Easter Day for Soldiers at the Front*. The Bishop seems to be putting in a good deal of work, for he holds 12–14 services a day. He is going to spend a night in the trenches at Ploegsteert, and also is going to visit Ypres.

Letters seized on a dead German officer predict the possibility of Germany finding herself after the war with empty hands and pockets turned inside out.* An officer of the General Staff who was made prisoner on January 18 said: 'Perhaps this struggle of despair has already begun'.

The German authorities have made a sustained effort to create in the Army an artificial state of mind based entirely on lies. The German authorities cover their ranks with a veil of deceit. The French have found

---

* In view of the extortionate reparations bill presented to Germany after the war, this prediction proved uncannily accurate.

Thoughts and Prayer for Easter Day.

CHRIST rose from the grave to-day, then death is not the end.

My dead comrade who lies on the stretcher will live again.

Christ said, "He that believeth in Me, though he were dead, yet shall he live, and he that believeth in Me, shall never die."

Death is the "gate of life."

However violent the stroke which liberates the soul, "the soul is born into the other world as quietly and peacefully as it is born into this."

But as I look at the Angel giving the triumphant message in the picture, Easter means more than this; it means that Right must triumph in the end.

"Heaviness may endure for a night, but Joy cometh in the morning."

HELP me, O Risen Lord, to bear what I have to bear now, certain that a morning is coming full of joy and victory for all that is good in the world.

Prayer leaflet issued by the popular Bishop of London to all those who attended the service at Ebblinghem, 1 April 1915.

---

prisoners in possession of postcards in German entitled *Souvenir of the Capture of Warsaw*. On the other hand the Russians found postcards entitled *Souvenir of the Capture of Calais. Quos Deus perdere vult, prius dementat.*[*]

FRIDAY APRIL 2

Good Friday. Fine and inclined at intervals to be sunny. Warm. Went for a ride in the morning to find more signalling positions. Played football in the afternoon.

Claud Hamilton who is attached as bear-leader to The Prince of Wales came to tea.[**] He told us some interesting bits of news. The new 15 inch gun is a great success. Last week half the village of Aubers was destroyed by a shot

---

[*] 'Those whom God wishes to destroy, he first makes mad.'
[**] Lord Claud Hamilton, a young Grenadier captain, became ADC to Prince Edward in May 1915. The Prince of Wales poured out his frustration to Hamilton at not being allowed to fight in the trenches. Hamilton became his close confidant and introduced him in 1916, after a bibulous dinner in Amiens, to a celebrated *fille de joie*, Paulette. Given Prince Edward's later reputation, especially with married women, Hamilton may have come to regret this episode, since 'from that moment, sex became one of Prince Edward's most urgent preoccupations'. Philip Ziegler, *Edward VIII – The Official Biography*, p. 89.

fired from it. He also told us that young Marshall of the Grenadiers who was killed at Neuve Chapelle was walking across a field when he was hit through the heart by a bullet. The moment he was hit he started off to run and ran 100 yards at top speed before he dropped dead. He also told us that an Artillery observing officer witnessed the attack of the 60th Rifles at Givenchy on March 12. He said that he saw the Regiment advance at the double across a field, on the far side of which was an uncut wire fence. When they were about 100 yards from it, he saw the whole line 'lie down' together, as if they had been ordered by some officer to do so. He afterwards found that the Germans had got some Maxim guns on them. All the men who lay down were killed or wounded.

Hamilton also said that the great losses of the Cameronians at Neuve Chapelle were caused by Maxim gun fire when the Regiment was stopped by a wire fence. The casualties for the month of March as published yesterday show a loss of about 20,000 men, or the equivalent of an infantry division. The officers total is very high, but this number includes all trench losses, and the demonstration against La Bassée, as well as St Eloi and Neuve Chapelle.

SATURDAY APRIL 3

Drizzly rain, very dull, and inclined to be cold. Went for a ride in the afternoon with Torrie to Renescure, and home by Sercus and Ebblinghem. On the way home we looked at the very strong line of trenches which have been dug near Sercus. They are part of the line which extends in a NW–SE direction right over this part of France. They are beautifully made, very well sited, and form part of an exceedingly strong position, which we are to fall back on to, should we ever retreat from here, which is most unlikely. Very little news, the calm before stirring events.

SUNDAY APRIL 4

Easter Day. Dull and inclined to rain. Rather chilly. It has been raining during the greater part of last night. Church was held in the school at 11 o'clock, followed by Communion.

About 12.30 Hugh Baikie's groom turned up with a horse which he wanted shod. He also produced the information that Hugh had left Hazebrouck and incidentally his job as Liaison Officer between the IV Corps and Second Army Headquarters. He is now living in the charming white château with the ornamental water in front, at Oxeleare, at the foot of the hill on which Cassel stands. I have always wanted to see inside it, every time I have gone to Cassel.

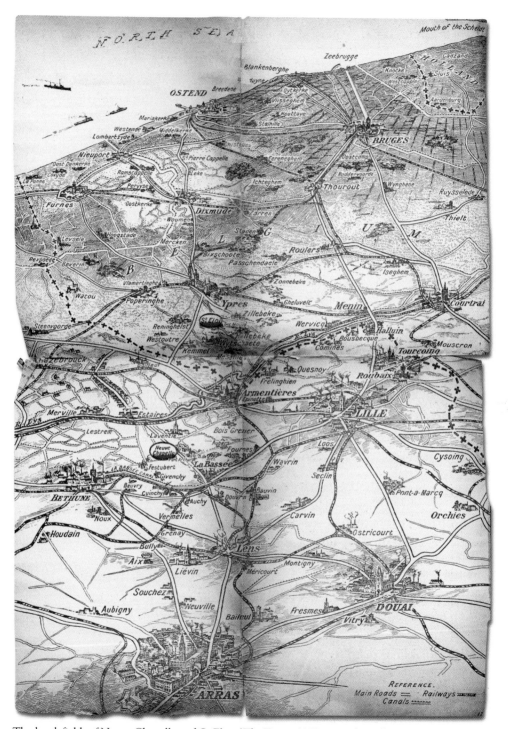

The battlefields of Neuve Chapelle and St Eloi. (*The Times, 1227, 1 April 1915*)

French, British and Belgian Battle Fronts Compared.

FRENCH BATTLE FRONT 543 MILES.

BRITISH FRONT 31 MILES.

BELGIAN FRONT 17 MILES.

The diagram, which is based on details published in the *Matin*, shows at a glance the great length of the front along which our French Allies are fighting as compared with the small fronts occupied by the British and Belgian armies.

French, British and Belgian battle fronts compared. (*Le Matin*)

The day cleared up a little after lunch, so I decided to ride over to see Hugh. Keith Menzies came with me and we reached the château about 3.30. I soon found Hugh at work in a very large room overlooking the garden. He is Chief Staff Officer to the South Midland Division which is now in the villages round Cassel, and this château is their Divisional Headquarters. He was very busy, so asked us to return about 5 o'clock and have tea.

To fill in the time we went on into Cassel, passing General Foch en route, whom we saluted with a great flourish. We returned at 5, and had tea in a sort of large smoking lounge, where the rest of the Divisional Staff had collected. Hugh was very pleased to see us.

He told us many titbits of news. He said he thought that three more divisions of Territorial Infantry were coming out now, and that the front we hold is about 32 miles long. We will shortly be taking over some more. We must have nearly 350,000 infantry at the front now.

The diagram above illustrates the respective fronts held by the Allies in the West.

Baikie said that he hoped a push would be made to get the Germans out of the present line of trenches before the hot weather and the flies come. Otherwise there will be a typhoid epidemic. The Germans are lying dead in thousands along our front and some of them have been there since October. He also told us that Kitchener, French, Joffre and Millerand* met together at Chantilly last Sunday and that we should soon begin to see the result of the conference.

---

* Alexandre Millerand (1859–1943) was Minister of War in Paris during 1914–15. Strong loyalty to Joffre caused his popularity to wane, and in October 1915 he was succeeded by Gallieni. Winston Churchill, *The World Crisis, 1911–1918*, p. 943.

MONDAY APRIL 5

Bitterly cold, and a pouring wet and very miserable day. What a contrast to yesterday!

Keith Menzies left us today for England to join the Welsh Guards, to which he has been transferred as a full lieutenant. I am very sorry he has gone as he is capital company and a very cheery person, of a kind that unfortunately is not too numerous out here. His departure leaves his brother, Stewart, the sole officer in the Regiment who came out on Oct 6 last, who has not been invalided home either for wounds, sickness or other causes.

We are now issued once a week with a green envelope. It is intended to be used for writing home private and domestic details. A certificate has to be signed on the flap at the back, to say that it deals with nothing but domestic matters. It may be censored at the base, and if any other matter is found in the envelope, the sender will be severely punished. The whole scheme seems to me very impractical, and is I suppose intended as a kind of sop for irregulars or Territorials.

We have today been served with a new censor stamp. This is the third that we have had in five months, the first round, the next square, and now triangular. If the war continues, what will they have this time next year?

About 5 o'clock during tea General Kavanagh arrived and told us that we had got to clear out of Staple as the area is required by the French. They are moving back one or two Corps from the trenches N and NE of Ypres as our Canadian Division is taking over that piece of the line. We are to be clear of Staple by midday tomorrow. This was a blow, but it can't be helped.

TUESDAY APRIL 6

At 9 o'clock Torrie, Walker the Vet and I rode off to Hondeghem to look for new billets for the next week, until we could return to Staple. We soon found some there, got our horses in and sat down to wait for the arrival of the Regiment. Luxmoore, Walker and I got a room with the local Curé after much discussion. It seems odd that our charms and merits are not at first apparent to these worthy people when we look for lodgings.

Several of the old ladies seem to agree with Madame de Pompadour* that the more they see of men, the more they like dogs. However, they succumb to

---

* This pungent remark was not made by Madame de Pompadour, but by the brilliant and cultured Madame Roland (1754–93). Her salon became a meeting place for the Girondins during the French Revolution. After the fall of the Girondins, she was arrested and sent to the guillotine by the radicals under Robespierre. See *The Life of Madame Roland*, Madeleine Clemenceau-Jacquemaire.

Lt F.N. Griffin (left) and Capt J.B. Walker outside Sir Morgan Crofton's new billet at Wallon-Cappel.

our fascinations in time (aided by the thought of the franc a night which they get as billet money) and really get to like us as time rolls on.

About 1.30, just as we were expecting the arrival of the Regiment, an orderly arrived to say that we were to clear out of the Hondeghem area as the 1st Cavalry Division required it. It is most unpleasant being harried from pillar to post like this. I can now experience what the feelings of a vagrant on the Embankment must be like when he is moved on by a policeman. We were ordered to a village called Wallon-Cappel, which is about 2 miles to the SE of Staple.

We arrived there about 2.30 and found the Colonel and the rest in the village street looking for billets. This was not an easy job, as a squadron of the 1st Life Guards was also in the town, and in addition the 7th Cavalry Field Ambulance had just short-headed us for the best billets. So the penalty that is always attached to being a latecomer is attached to us, and we must get in where we can. I am glad that it isn't for long.

Luxmoore, Walker and I got an attic in the Curé's house. The Curé's sister, a hardly human and most revolting creature of seventy summers and heaven knows how many winters, viewed us with marked suspicion. She said we must be in to bed by 8.30 at night, as the house was then locked up. We must be out of the house in the morning by 7.30 as that was when she went to Mass, and the house was again locked up.

However, I explained that what she suggested could not be, much as we desired it, and by much blandishment I succeed in extracting a latch key from her. It is about a foot long and very similar to those which pictures show the Burghers of Calais handing over to Edward III.*

We got for a living-room, a very smelly and dirty room in a filthy farm, where lived an equally dirty woman, with two squalling brats. Most unattractive the whole thing was. The husband was a bit of a lad, and had just lost his eye in battle somewhere in France. He had therefore returned to finish the war in his own house with *otium cum dignitate*.** He however didn't worry us much as his energies and interests were centred entirely on the village inn.

About 3 o'clock a regular wet afternoon set in, which did not greatly increase our hilarity.

WEDNESDAY APRIL 7

Very cold wind, sunny at intervals inclined to rain.

The losses of the German Officers seem very large. These losses have been most carefully compiled by the French Authorities. They have counted the names which have actually appeared on the German casualty lists. Many of the missing are probably killed.

German troops without officers are like sheep without shepherds. It is difficult to know how they will be replaced,† for it is impossible to make German officers from the ranks as the French and British armed services do. The German officer comes solely from the class which has always supplied officers, i.e. the upper and upper middle classes.

The French Authorities are making more and more stringent orders regarding the civilian population of France. Not only is every one registered,

---

* In 1347, Calais was besieged and racked by starvation. In order to end the siege, six senior citizens volunteered to be hostages to King Edward III. Queen Philippa of Hainault, who was known for her great compassion, interceded to save them from execution. The courage of the burghers is commemorated by Rodin in his monumental work, *Les Bourgeois de Calais*. A bronze casting of the group stands in the gardens adjoining The Houses of Parliament.
** Meaning 'dignity in retirement'. Crofton is fond of Latin tags. While a schoolboy at Rugby, he won a prize in 1896 for his attainments in the Humanities.
† According to figures published by the German General Staff, officer casualties up to 15 March totalled 31,276, of whom 9,925 had been killed. Only 25 per cent of the highly trained officers and NCOs could be replaced. Officer cadets or specially chosen NCOs from the reserve Landwehr and Landsturm had to fill the gaps and command platoons. David Lomas, *First Ypres, 1914*, p. 10.

but no one can go to visit anyone else in the neighbouring village without possessing a *Sauf-Conduit*. This generally has to be signed by the Maire and an officer.

THURSDAY APRIL 8

Still cold, but fine at intervals.

Our billets are still very uncomfortable. It is impossible to get any hot water, and the Curé's sister today has accused us of stealing two blankets. They were finally found on the Pill's bed. These people bore me to death. They regard life as one might have done in medieval times. They bar their houses as if thieves abound everywhere and as if they have many valuables. In reality there is nothing in the whole village worth two pence. It might not have been a good experience for these villages to have the Germans in them for a week or so, before we came in.

The French are making about 80,000 shells a week, and are firing about 50,000. So they now have 6–8 weeks' supply in hand. They have handed Calais over to us now as another base, and with it another railway through Abbeville. We are shortly taking over more of the line North of Ypres. Supply trains are now running every day into Armentières, and to within 2 miles of Ypres. The English South Eastern Railway has now taken over Calais. It has sent over 24 complete trains and more are to follow.

The English Authorities are very anxious to have Dunkirk as a base, but the French for some reason won't hand it over. I wonder if they think that we won't return it after the war?

SATURDAY APRIL 10

Fine day, but cold NW wind. Paraded at 9 o'clock for a regimental field day. The usual sort of thing – an attack on a line of trenches, this time through a wood. Went myself with the signallers to map out a line of trenches which were to be attacked. The attackers had to advance about a mile through brambles and thick undergrowth. Their cries and struggles made them plainly audible for half a mile, and they arrived at the trenches exhausted and worn out, and covered with thorns.

A pow-wow followed, in which Ferguson said that everything had gone wrong that possibly could. We returned to billets about 2 o'clock.

In the afternoon rode around C Squadron billets and went on into Hazebrouck, where we got a lot of new potatoes. The advent of vegetables like this will brighten our lives in this campaign. At 7 o'clock was inoculated for the third time since the war began, against typhoid. We expect an outbreak when the warm weather comes.

SUNDAY APRIL 11

A beautiful fine warm day at last. Hurrah!! What a difference it makes. Did not feel half so seedy this time over the inoculation as before.

We hear that we are not to return to Staple, as that area has been handed over to the 1st Cavalry Division. Our place there is to be taken by the new 9th Cavalry Brigade. This is being formed out of the 15th Hussars and the 19th Hussars and some Yeomanry Regiment. The addition of this new Cavalry Brigade now brings the strength of all three Cavalry divisions up to three brigades each.

One cannot help being sorry to leave Staple. We have been billeted there exactly 17 weeks. Nothing can exceed the kindness shown to all of us by the inhabitants, especially our friends, the Brewer and his family. It seems an age since we rode into the village, on a wet foggy and cold afternoon on December 7 last. The Regiment will leave behind many good friends.

We hear that we are to move across the railway, and take up a new area this side of the St Omer–Hazebrouck road, so we shall retain our headquarters in this village of Wallon-Cappel. This being the case I shall certainly look out for fresh lodgings, as I can't stand the Curé and his sister any longer.

At 10.30 Torrie came in and asked if I would like to come for a motor drive with him to St Omer. As the day was glorious, off we went. St Omer is a delightful old town, full of very old and interesting buildings, many dating from 1550. Being French's headquarters, it was of course crammed with English Staff Officers.

We got some very good maps there from the Map Office, which is established in a very old convent, and we also bought some tin tea cups for our mess, as we can't stand any longer the ridiculous thimbles which serve as tea cups in this country. We then motored back to Hazebrouck where we bought some papers, some more new potatoes and other vegetables, and then returned to Wallon-Cappel for lunch.

At 3 o'clock, the day still being hot and sunny I rode over to Cassel. Cassel was full of Canadian troops, chiefly Highlanders, belonging to the Canadian Division which now occupies that area of France. The men look extremely good, but we didn't think much of the officers. One Brigade of this Division is resting in the villages near about, the other two Brigades of the Canadian Division are in our trenches north and east of Ypres.

We hear that the 1st Cavalry Division Field Engineers are coming tomorrow to take over this billet. The proprietor, who was pleased at our departure, was depressed by the news of the arrival of the Engineers. He does not like soldiers, and raising his hands to heaven he exclaimed *Plus de misère!*

MONDAY APRIL 12

We spent the morning finding new quarters. We soon found two nice rooms in a house at the corner of the street, which had been occupied by the ambulance people. The house is kept by an old lady of about 75 and slightly balmy. It's a funny thing that every woman in Wallon-Cappel varies from 70–80 years of age, and looks exactly like a gargoyle. She has the most beautiful tiled kitchen which she keeps like a jeweller's shop. Everything shines like silver and gold. She is terrified that we shall want to use this model place, but we explained that it would not be required for the purposes of war.

She has now become as playful as a kitten. She asked if we were married, and said that we ought to be. She thinks that she would do for one of us. She goes to bed every day at 5 o'clock, I think in her clothes, for she appears looking exactly the same the following morning at about 7.30, generally when Walker is having his bath. I think she does it on purpose.

One of the farm billets occupied by C Squadron at Wallon–Cappel.

Our new landlady: '75 years of age and looks like a gargoyle'.

I have pinned all my maps up on the wall of our sleeping room. This is a great comfort, as it's much nicer to be able to mark up our daily progress in the various theatres of war.

We hear today that the German armed liner *Kronprinz Wilhelm*, a vessel of 14,000 tons, has reached Hampton Roads and will now probably be interned.* She is reported to have only 21 tons of coal on board and so little ammunition that she was unable to salute the American warships as she entered the harbour. The ship interests me particularly for it was the one on

---

* Hampton Roads, Virginia, an important naval and military base since colonial days, is formed by the deep-water estuary of the James River. Today, Hampton Roads remains the Headquarters of the Atlantic Fleet.

Wallon-Cappel, the village where 2nd Life Guards were based from 6 April until the battle of 2nd Ypres.

which I returned in November 1906 from America. She appears to be in a very different condition now as all her cabins and state rooms are filled with coal, and the paint has peeled off her stained and rusted sides. Her four funnels are bleached white, her plates battered in and badly dented, her rails smashed, and she has a bad list to port.

She reported that her coal bunkers were almost empty, and that she had food and fresh water for a few days only. Her boilers, condensers and engines badly need overhauling, and she has 63 cases of beri-beri or scurvy on board, caused by the rice diet.

The Germans are going through the farce of announcing that 'as soon as we are repaired, coaled and provisioned we shall return to the sea' (I don't think). With the disappearance of the last raiding German Cruiser, one can estimate the amount of damage done to British commerce. In all, there were seven German raiders patrolling the high seas, whose total catch in terms of sunken vessels is therefore 67 ships, representing with cargoes a value of £6,690,000. The *Scharnhorst* and *Gneisenau* were destroyed at the Battle of the Falkland Islands on December 8 last. This sum seems large, but it is trifling if we consider the values which have been afloat since the beginning of the war.

By contrast, the value of British ships and their cargoes for the eight months of the war is roughly £936,000,000, out of which shipping and cargoes to the value of £6,690,000 have been destroyed. This is less than 7 per cent.

Admiralty weekly returns based on arrivals and departures of ships in the ports of the United Kingdom average 1,373, so that about 44,000 voyages have been made. Of these 44,000, only 15 per cent have been abruptly terminated by German Cruisers. In addition, all hostile ships captured by us have been quickly employed in trade again, whereas the British ships sunk by the Germans are an absolute loss to the world.

TUESDAY APRIL 13

The Bishop of London seems to have enjoyed his trip over here at Easter. He held 60 services along the front and at the bases, and visited 22 hospitals ward by ward. On no occasion did he have a congregation of less than 1,000 men, and often it exceeded 4,000. He held services in the open air, cinema theatres, baths and warehouses. On Easter morning he celebrated Communion with 200 officers and men just behind the trenches in a barn which had had its roof destroyed by shellfire. When he had finished he found another 150 men waiting outside for him. As he held the service, aeroplanes circled about overhead to guard the attractive target of 4,000 kneeling officers and men with a Bishop in their midst.

Things are fairly quiescent here in this sector, and we watch with increasing interest the progress of the French at St Mihiel* and the Russians in the Carpathians. Last September the Germans succeeded in rushing a passage across the River Meuse at St Mihiel. There however their offensive was checked. Ever since they have attempted to widen the wedge and, with St Mihiel as the clasp, to buckle up the girdle which they have tried to throw round Verdun.

Had a fresh thrust here been successful, it would have obliged the French and the British to retire from our present line in Belgium and Northern France to concentrate against the hostile hordes which would pour into the heart of France through this door.

---

* St Mihiel dominates the Meuse Valley. It was not liberated until September 1918, when more than 200,000 American troops – many in action for the first time – achieved what the *Manchester Guardian* deemed 'as swift and neat an operation as any in the war'. Col George S. Patton, gaining early experience of tank warfare, and Col Douglas MacArthur, a brigade commander, were among the young officers taking part. Martin Gilbert, *First World War*, pp. 458–9.

No German troops can possibly be spared from the Eastern Front to make this attack through the gap of St Mihiel. As the French now have more troops to spare, it is essential that, before their new offensive in the coming summer, their line shall be straightened out. They are now endeavouring to close the gap here on the Meuse and are attacking vigorously along the Northern and Southern edges of the wedge.

WEDNESDAY APRIL 14

Not quite so cold, but a drizzling soaking day.

We again had to move our billets, as another horde of French troops are coming down from the North of Ypres, and our troops have to move out of Renescure this time. We are apparently taking over more of the front and I

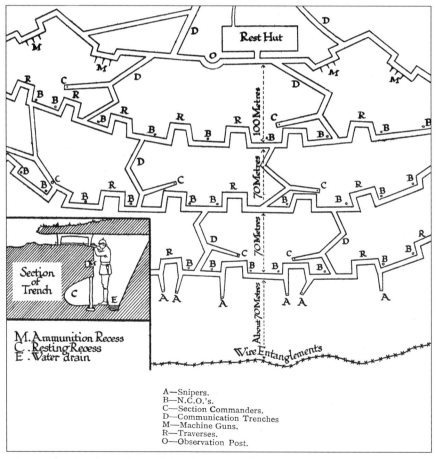

A—Snipers.
B—N.C.O.'s.
C—Section Commanders.
D—Communication Trenches
M—Machine Guns.
R—Traverses.
O—Observation Post.

Diagram showing the intricacy of the German trenches.

imagine we shall shortly take over the line to the Sea. The Belgian troops will remain on near Dixmude and we shall bolster them up.

The 7th Cavalry Field Ambulance whose billets we seized last Monday when they left, have now returned here again, and have had to take our beastly old billets amidst shouts of laughter.

No fresh news from St Mihiel. We have seen dozens of heavily laden trains going along towards the front for the last two or three days. I think that it is the West Riding Territorial Division going up.

This plan of the German trench will show how very complicated and detailed their system of trenches is.

VOLUME V

APRIL 15 – MAY 29, 1915

THURSDAY APRIL 15

A beautiful fine warm spring day. Went for a ride in the morning with the Pill round the D Squadron billets, and then on to our old friend Staple to see if the 124th Regiment of French Infantry, which had arrived there yesterday, was still there. We found that it had marched out at 5 o'clock this morning.

Our old friends MM Fovet and Balloy the Brewer and the Schoolmaster all came out to see us, and made anxious enquiries as to when we were returning. We had to break it gently to them that we were not coming back.

Sir John French's despatch on Neuve Chapelle and St Eloi came out today. He states that by 11 am on March 10 the whole of the village of Neuve Chapelle and the roads leading northward from it were in our hands. Also our artillery had completely cut off the village from any German reinforcements.

Considerable delay then occurred and Lieutenant General Sir Henry Rawlinson, GOC IV Corps, is deemed one of the culprits. French continues:

> I am of the opinion that this delay would not have occurred had the clearly expressed order of the General Officer Commanding First Army been more carefully observed. The difficulties might have been overcome at an earlier period of the day if the General Officer Commanding IV Corps had been able to bring his reserve brigades more speedily into action.
>
> As it was, the further advance did not commence before 3.30 pm.
>
> The 21st Brigade was able to form up in the open on the left without a shot being fired at it, thus showing that at the time the enemy's resistance had been paralysed. The Brigade pushed forward in the direction of Moulin Du Pietre.
>
> At first this made good progress, but was subsequently held up by the machine-gun fire from the houses and from a defended work in the line of the German entrenchments opposite the right of the 22nd Brigade. Further to the south the 24th Brigade, which had been directed on Pietre,

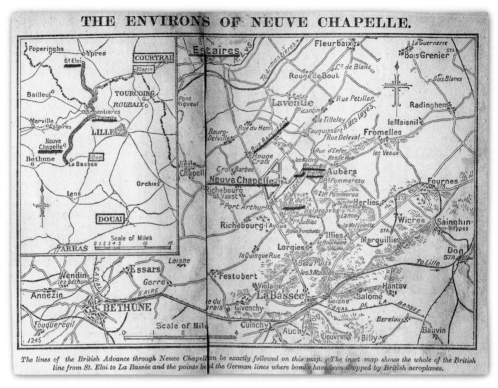

The lines of the British Advance through Neuve Chapelle can be exactly followed on this map. The inset map shows the whole of the British line from St. Eloi to La Bassée and the points behind the German lines where bombs have been dropped by British aeroplanes.

Environs of the village of Neuve Chapelle where a costly attack on 10 March failed to achieve a break-through. (*The Times*, 1245, 15 April 1915)

was similarly held up by machine guns in the houses and trenches at the road junction six hundred yards north-west of Pietre.

The despatch goes on to detail the heavy casualties sustained by both the British and Indian Corps:

THE CASUALTIES

The losses during these three days' fighting were, I regret to say, very severe, numbering –

190 officers and 2,337 other ranks killed
359 officers and 8,174 other ranks wounded
23 officers and 1,728 other ranks missing

But the results attained were, in my opinion, wide and far reaching. The enemy left several thousand dead on the battlefield who were seen and counted.

The casualties were nearly as great as those of the British, Belgian, Dutch and Hanoverian Armies at Waterloo combined and almost double the loss of the British Contingent alone, at that battle. Also the casualties at Neuve Chapelle, which lasted three days, were far greater than those of the Battle of the Aisne, which lasted two weeks.

FRIDAY APRIL 16

Another beautiful spring day. It rained last night, but only enough to benefit the crops. Made several signalling arrangements.

In the afternoon rode with Walker and Griffin to Staple where we found a lot of French soldiers. We heard that a brigade was probably coming in the village and its surroundings. My former host, M Balloy the Brewer, was full of pride because the Brigadier was going to lodge at his house.

On the night of April 12–13 two letters were tied round stones and thrown into the II Corps trenches by the Germans. The translations run as follows:

Dear Honoured Comrades,

As this war has now being going on for about nine months, and whole villages with their inhabitants have been devastated, it is now high time to put a stop to it.

We are all tired of this savage life, and you must be too. Our dear wives and children await and long for our return and yours must do the same. Hoping that we may do some good by this, we remain with friendly greetings.

The Germans Sapping Party
11 April 1915

The second ran:

Dear French and English Comrades,

It is now just about time that you stopped all this, for I think that you will soon have had enough of your war. Our losses are great, and yours must be three times as big. It would be better if we could be at home with our wives and children, who are waiting every day for us, as yours are waiting for you. Let us have Peace on Earth before the cherry blossom comes out, but the sooner the better, or do you want to go on for ever sitting in these damned trenches?

With friendly Greetings
The Germans

There are many signs that the Germans are becoming very homesick. As a race they are domestic and inclined to suffer from this sentiment.

In 1870, even when the war had only lasted six months, and the course of it had been practically a triumphal procession, the German forces suffered so greatly from homesickness, that in places they were with difficulty kept in the ranks. People who suffer from this sort of thing have no business to talk about 'World Power'.

SATURDAY APRIL 17

A fine bright day with a cold wind. We hear that several more Territorial Divisions are coming out. There is no reason now why all the remaining Territorial Divisions should not come out. The ones now arriving are the Lowland and West Riding.

General Kavanagh has today been promoted from the command of this Brigade to the command of the 2nd Cavalry Division, succeeding General Hubert Gough. The latter is transferred as Commander of the 7th Infantry Division in place of General Tom Capper* who has been sent elsewhere.

Is this an aftermath of Neuve Chapelle?

Ferguson temporarily commands this brigade, until Colonel Bridges has recovered from a wound. Bridges was first of all in the Royal Artillery, then transferred to the 4th Dragoon Guards, going from thence to the 4th Hussars to command. Previous to the war he was Military Attaché at Brussels, and when the war broke out, served on the staff of the King of the Belgians. He is entirely responsible for the re-creation of the Belgian Army, in fact he really is the Belgian Army. It is said that if anything happened to the King of the

---

* Maj Gen Sir Thompson Capper led the 7th Division which confronted the first German attacks on Ypres. When relieved on 7 November, its 14,000 infantry had been reduced to 4,000. *The Times* of 1 October 1915 stated: 'Nobody but Capper himself could, night after night, by the sheer force of his personality, have reconstituted from the shattered fragments of battalions a fighting line that could last through tomorrow.' A hand-grenade accident forced him to spend the summer of 1915 at home, but Capper returned to resume command of his old division and was so badly wounded on 26 September at the Battle of Loos that he died the next day.

Belgians, Bridges would become King!! He certainly is a first-class soldier and we are lucky to have him as our new Brigadier.*

A week ago, while visiting the Belgian trenches near Dixmude he was hit by the splinters of a shell on the head and arm. This will necessitate his lying up for some time. So in the meantime Ferguson will keep the place warm for him.

SUNDAY APRIL 18

Tiger Tim's birthday. 8 years old. How time flies, and what a lot has happened since April 18 1907.**

Another glorious day, with a cold wind. In the morning I drove into Aire with Torrie. As this town is the Headquarters of the First Army, it is crowded with soldiers. The Indian Cavalry Corps are also billeted in the villages around. The town looked very bright, quite different from the last time that I was in it, on the afternoon of Nov 26 last. I had just been inoculated for typhoid, and felt very seedy.

In the afternoon went for a ride to find some signalling positions round here. I found two very good ones, both on a ridge about a mile from here, of about 180 feet in height. Looking South from these stations one can see for miles right over the Forest of Nieppe, where we spent the first day of Neuve Chapelle.

On the way home from the ridge I rode into Morbecque, the small village in which I spent my first night at the Front. It is a small village with a very old church with the usual quaint steeple, and a most picturesque old Mairie dated 1757, with a delightful old roof and belfry, and a large sundial on the front wall.

The railhead for the whole of the Cavalry is Steenbecque Station which is a mile off Morbecque. Two trains filled with oats, hay, groceries, meat and bread come every day to this station. The Infantry are supplied by other

---

* A nephew of Robert Bridges, the Poet Laureate, Lt Gen Sir George Bridges (1871–1939) had twice been severely wounded in South Africa. But it was with the Belgian Army that he established the reputation here described. Following his wound at Dixmude, Bridges lost a leg at Passchendaele in 1917, soon after being promoted Major-General. Nothing daunted, he was back in action at Smyrna with the Greeks in 1922. See *The Times*, 27 November 1939.
** Tiger Tim is the diarist's son, Maj M.G. Crofton. He was commissioned into the Hampshire Regiment and served with the Fourteenth Army in Burma (the 'Forgotten Army') in the Second World War. In 1935 he stood as the National Party candidate for the Colne Valley constituency, against E.L. Mallalieu QC. He died on 31 March 1947.

railheads, namely Hazebrouck, Poperinghe, Bailleul, Bethune and others. The railhead for ammunition is, I believe, St Venant.

The flying ground for this area lies just east of Morbecque. The Flying Corps have made quite a large plain for landing purposes, and there are now four hangars built on it, one entirely of wood, and three others of tarpaulin. The four aeroplanes which live there are responsible for the aerial protection of this area.

MONDAY APRIL 19

A most important paragraph in the *The Times* today. When Archangel is open, the Russians will have no difficulty in completing their equipment, and then their general advance may be expected.

Ice-Breaking at Archangel

A Lloyd's telegram from Archangel states that, if the present warm weather continues, ice-breaking and the re-opening of the river there may be expected in two weeks' time. According to another message, an ice-breaker has already forced her way through to the port of Archangel.

The Russians have been greatly handicapped all winter by the closing of Archangel, Vladivostock and the Dardanelles. This has prevented them equipping the vast number of men that they have.

During the winter the Russians have doubled the single, narrow gauge line from Petrograd to Archangel,* so we may soon expect supplies to flow in to Russia from this new lifeline.

Rode into Morbecque in the afternoon. The village is crowded now, as it has been for seven months, with the supply columns which feed the Cavalry Corps. The organisation is splendid and there are nearly 250 large lorries in this column. Repair shops are situated round the Mairie, in which every sort of repair can be carried out. Later I went on to Steenbecque Station.

TUESDAY APRIL 20

This country dries extraordinarily quickly. One would hardly know that we have had such a wet winter. The question of water for our horses will become very serious later on.

---

* Just over six weeks later, Archangel was Lord Kitchener's last destination when he set out from Scapa Flow in HMS *Hampshire*.

A most excellent account of Neuve Chapelle is published today. It is a narrative that is written by an independent individual, Sir Arthur Conan Doyle,* and coincides with Sir John French's despatch of April 5th. The great advantage of this report is that individual Regiments are mentioned. It is inconceivable why this sort of report has not been written before. The relating of these gallant performances is the greatest incentive to recruiting.

I do not believe that there is such a shortage of men as is made out. The recruiting figures are kept very confidential, and nowhere can one get any labour. The young and able-bodied man seems to have disappeared, and every other man in the street is in khaki. The numbers of men fit for army purposes who are now seen loafing, playing games or going to race meetings are greatly exaggerated.

WEDNESDAY APRIL 21

An extract from the *Cologne Gazette* of April 18** gives us some interesting information regarding the distribution of the Iron Cross. More than 2,500 have been given to Austrians and Turks.

In the war of 1813–15, when the Cross was instituted, only 568 officers and 64 men received the 1st Class of this Order. In the present war it adorns the breasts of 47 Princes, 210 Generals, 5 Ministers and State Officials, and 1,792 Officers. Besides these, 168 NCOs and 97 men are in possession of this order.

THURSDAY APRIL 22

Arranged a signalling scheme. Tried to get a line through from Cassel to La Belle Hôtesse, via a hill above Morbecque, where we had our transmitting station. Total distance about 13 miles. The Stations were all in position by 9.30, but owing to the mist, the helios couldn't be used, and the distance was too far for the use of flags. About 11 o'clock the mist departed and we were able to send and receive the prepared messages.

After lunch Torrie, Griffin and I visited Staple, and found it like a place of the dead. Not a living creature was visible. However, we found our worthy friend

---

* A household name since 1887, when he introduced Sherlock Holmes to the public in *A Study in Scarlet*, Conan Doyle also wrote about aspects of the South African War and the First World War. See his six-volume *History of the British Campaign in France and Flanders* and *A Visit to Three Fronts, 1916.*
** Extracts from this German newspaper were regularly reprinted in *The Times.*

M Balloy, who told us that life was very quiet there now and they all wished that we were back. He said that sometimes French troops came in for one night, in which case the Colonel and the *porte-drapeau** generally stayed with him.

We rode on to Cassel, stopping to look at the château at Oxeleare which we found being prepared for General Smith-Dorrien. He is moving there from Hazebrouck tomorrow with the Headquarters of Second Army. We went on into Cassel and had tea at the Hôtel du Sauvage. On the way back about 6.15 we heard gunfire towards Hazebrouck. The people in the fields called out that they had seen three Zeppelins. Luxmoore also said on our return that he had seen one.

At 8.30 we went to Renescure to an amusing show, which was given by the 1st Life Guards.

FRIDAY APRIL 23

A fine day with cold wind, light rain later.

During breakfast O'Malley,** who is Stewart Menzies' servant, rushed in, in a state of great excitement. News had just arrived that the Germans had overpowered the French near Bixschoote with gases during the night. They were now advancing *en masse*, as they had broken through our line.†

This was jolly, and we at once sallied out to see if there was any authentic news of this affair. I went to our signaller's office where I found a message which had been sent off at 1 am. This said that the Germans had overpowered the French on this line with gases, and were now advancing towards the canal.†† This looks like the long expected German boost coming off at last.

---

* A standard-bearer. He marched at the head of the infantry column, bearing his regimental flag aloft.
** Tpr Charles O'Malley, from Limerick, had perhaps found peacetime soldiering dull. Absent without leave in October 1903, he was discharged from the 2nd Life Guards for desertion, but rejoined them on the outbreak of war at the age of forty. He served in the Regiment (without a further blot on his escutcheon) until 1920. *Household Cavalry Museum Service Records*, Windsor.
† The gas attack signalled the start of the Battle of 2nd Ypres and is the first recorded instance of organised chemical warfare.
†† 'The [gas] attack came north of Ypres . . . and it fell in an awkward place, on the shoulder of the line where the Canadians joined hands with the French in front of Poelcapelle. The [French] 45th Regiment had just moved into the line and had barely settled down. It was a Regiment composed of French Colonials – native troops from North Africa – and it was on them that the full force of the gas cloud descended. The unfortunate Algerians had no chance.' Lyn Macdonald, *1915 – The Death of Innocence*, p. 192.

The Regiment had already gone out for a field day. I was just setting out with my signallers for a scheme, but these movements were all cancelled. We were advised at once to return to billets and stand to, ready to move in half an hour. We packed up, our old landlady hovering round our valises like a dilapidated bird of Paradise. We were soon ready and merely had to wait for orders. About 10.30 they arrived.

We were to rendez-vous at La Bréarde, the crossroads 2 miles north of Hazebrouck, at 12 o'clock. Our heavy baggage was to be left behind, and our light carts only were to accompany us.

At 12 o'clock we were at the rendez-vous and shortly after we marched off, NE to Caestre and from there we marched still NE to Godewaersvelde, about 3 miles further on. It was a beastly march, the marching columns raised clouds of chalky dust which was driven into our faces by a biting North wind. Our eyes, ears and mouths were filled with this filthy material and the day began also to get very cold.

From Godewaersvelde we proceeded to Abeele 2 miles off, where we halted. The whole Cavalry Corps was evidently on the move too, for every road, as far as we could see, had columns of cavalry marching on it, and the haze of dust which rose behind the hills showed where the supply and ammunition columns were moving. Everything was going in a NE direction, where there was heavy gunfire.

At Abeele we formed mass on a bleak hillside and stood shivering about the streets, or round the camp fires which the men soon set alight on the edge of the road. All sorts of rumours were flying round. We heard definitely that the Germans had not yet been checked and that they were advancing in great numbers.

About 4.30 a long column of French motor buses appeared, crammed with Senegalese soldiers and Zouaves. I should think about 200 passed us and proceeded at a steady pace up the road to Poperinghe, near which a considerable cannonade seemed to be taking place. These buses contained about 20 men each, so it was about a Brigade being marched up.

About 6 o'clock our familiar General Omnibus Co. buses began also to make their appearance. They contained about 30–35 men, as they were packed inside and out. The men belonged to one of the Territorial Battalions of the Durham Light Infantry and were mad keen to get up to the front. The Regiments going up like this belonged to the Northumbrian Division. About a Brigade went up in the buses, and they were followed by several battalions marching. The men were chiefly miners and colliers, very useful looking men and in splendid condition. They created a very good impression. Everyone seemed very cheerful at the prospect of a fight at last and it was a most inspiring sight to see these cheering, laughing battalions marching up the road.

The night began to come on. It looked as if we were going to spend the night in our chilly uninteresting field, when a shout was raised for billeting parties. I was sent off with one officer from each squadron, to go back to Godewaersvelde and take over billets where the Regiment could spend the night.

It was a beautiful night, by now, with a brilliant moon, and our party trotted down the road to our town, which was 3 miles off. On our arrival, we collected in the *Place*, and waited an interminable time. Meanwhile, the Staff Captain sorted out the Maire, who seemed partially an imbecile, to allot the quarters. After some time the Regiment secured the West side of the *Place*, which was filled with motor lorries belonging to the Canadian Division.

We managed to cram in somehow, and secured quarters at the Bank, which was a fine stone building and well furnished. The caretaker seemed very glad to see us and we got quite a decent dinner of eggs, cocoa and jam, and then bedded down three in a room. Slept like a log.

SATURDAY APRIL 24

A fine bright morning. Considerable cannonade going on to NE. Breakfasted at 6 o'clock. Got ready to move at half an hour's notice.

About 7.30 we all lay down and pinched another two hours' sleep. At 11 orders came to saddle up and march. We set out about 11.20 in a NE direction to Boeschepe, from which we marched to Westoutre and passed on, still NE, to Reninghelst, where we received orders to proceed to Point 35, 2 miles SE of Poperinghe, and then dismount and wait. This point was reached about 3.30.

The wind was very cold, and the dust beastly. We off saddled and found a barn full of hay into which we climbed and remained until the order came to saddle up. There was a good deal of firing going on in the direction of Poperinghe, away to our left. To our right lay the village of Vlamertinghe with the tall church spire. Away to the far right we could dimly see the towers of Ypres. We could not get any definite news, except that the Germans seem to be attacking with three Corps, on a front of about two miles.

At about 6 o'clock orders came that we were to go back towards Westoutre to billet for the night. I went on there with the billeting party, and allotted the area to the three squadrons, keeping the village of Westoutre for our Headquarters. When we arrived at Westoutre we found that the Headquarters of the Cavalry Corps from La Motte had already taken up most of the accommodation. The village was full of their motors. The Headquarters of the 3rd Cavalry Division also arrived, making the crush greater still.

Brigade Headquarters were turned out of various houses and our chance of getting a house looked very thin. We finally found a room at the back of a general shop in the village. It was very uncomfortable, and the floor was stone, but it was better than nothing. We had succeeded in buying some food, so we had a fair dinner.

Our rugs were spread out and we turned in about 10.

SUNDAY APRIL 25

We got up at 5 o'clock. It was raining hard and very cold. Our orders were to stand to, ready to move in half an hour.

We got a good breakfast, cooked by a servant of a sick officer of the Middlesex Regiment who was in hospital in the school. We heard little news, except that the Germans had reached the Dixmude–Ypres Canal, and were throwing pontoon bridges across it.

About 10 o'clock several Regiments of the Lahore Infantry Division began to march through on their way to Vlamertinghe. This was the first time that I had seen the Indian Corps. They looked rather tucked up, for it was very cold, and they had had a long march of 19 miles the day before. The English Regiments with them looked very fit.

At 12.30 orders arrived for billeting parties to go and take up an area, north of Poperinghe. Poperinghe was full of troops, and all the shops were open, which was surprising as the town has been well shelled for the last few days.

We were then told that our new area was near Watou. I went on with Walker. The road from Poperinghe to Watou was crowded with all sorts of troops, Cavalry, Medical Corps and Engineers. On the road we passed about 200 French motor buses filled with troops going up to the front. We got to Watou about 7 o'clock, and found the billeting party standing about. They had done nothing owing to the Staff Captain being very vague as to our exact area. We found that the North Somerset Yeomanry had taken some of our farms and there was an officer of the Royal Dragoons trying to take another. We soon expelled him, and finally managed to get all our squadrons billeted by taking a farm off the 1st Life Guards.

Walker went into Houtkerque and bought some eggs. The people on our farm seemed really pleased to see us. Our area lay just over the Belgian border in France. There is an extraordinary difference between billets in France and Belgium. The idea current in England about 'Brave Little

Belgium' is entirely wrong. It is their Government who is fighting Germany, not the people, who really prefer the Germans to us. They don't mind who conquers them as long as they don't have to fight.[*]

MONDAY APRIL 26

Breakfasted at 6, saddled up and moved out at 6.30. We marched to Watou where we off-saddled and waited. The day soon became very hot.

We heard that French reinforcements are moving up fast and that they are making strenuous efforts to recapture Lizerne and Boesinghe. We hear also that the left of the British line was left in the air on Thursday last, when the Algerians retreated, and was attacked by the whole available German Force. This line was held by the Canadian Division, who behaved most gallantly. Although they had to fall back to conform to the French line, near St Julien, yet they were never broken and undoubtedly their steadfastness saved the day.

Special Order of the Day
The Field Marshal Commanding-in-Chief has received the following telegram from Field Marshal HRH the Duke of Connaught, Governor General and Commander-in-Chief of the Dominion of Canada:

Sir John French,
Headquarters, British Expeditionary Force, France

Ottawa,
25th April

I am deeply gratified with your telegram and the splendid behaviour of Canadians at Langemarck.

Arthur

The following message has also been received by the Field Marshal, Commanding-in-Chief, from Sir E. Borden and Major General Hughes:

Please convey to Canadians the pride and joy of their comrades in Canada for the part they have so nobly played. Canadians are justly proud that there was no surrender and also that the guns lost were not allowed to remain in possession of the enemy.

---

[*] 'No wonder the burghers [of Ypres] hated all the larger nations equally, always at war through the centuries across their peaceful fields.' Geoffrey Winthrop Young, *Grace of Forgetting*, p. 193.

From 11 o'clock onwards the most terrific cannonade had begun. As time went on the roar increased in intensity until about 2 o'clock when the whole ground shook with the thunder of this gunfire. As far as we could make out from the map, the sound came from the direction of Lizerne. I have never heard such a terrific cannonade.

The sun was sweltering and the dust awful. We stood in this field all day, and watched from time to time aeroplanes of both sides being shelled. Towards 5 o'clock we heard terrific explosions from the direction of Poperinghe, which was 3 miles away to our NE. The Germans were putting high-explosive shells into the town. Altogether I think 19 were put into it.

Towards 6 o'clock orders came for every man to have an additional 100 rounds of ammunition. Probably we were to leave our horses, and go up to the trenches that night. The spare ammunition came up on a limber shortly afterwards and was at once issued.

At 7.30 we got orders to saddle up, and march to a farm about 1½ miles off, to leave our horses. Each of the three squadrons was to supply about 80 rifles for the trenches. So the whole Cavalry Brigade could produce about 750 men altogether. At the farm we collected our kit. We left our spurs, and at about 8.30 fell in to march to Vlamertinghe, where we were to spend the night. We stopped in Poperinghe to await the 6th Cavalry Brigade.

About 10 o'clock the Germans started shelling Poperinghe. The explosion of these shells resounded all over the town. The first reports brought all the Belgian soldiers out in the street, running like mad, and they poured along the street out over the fields. A small stream of refugees followed, with their belongings in carts. But there were not many of these, as most of the population had already gone.

The 6th Cavalry Brigade was very late, and we sat on the pavement with our backs against the wall for over an hour and a half. From time to time shells exploded in and about the town, making a terrific noise, but not doing a great deal of damage. About 11.15 pm the head of the Brigade arrived and walked slowly up the street. It took some little time for them to pass as they were marching in half-sections. We followed on, as soon as the road was clear.

Our way lay through the *Grande Place*, which was now full of supply and ammunition waggons. We passed out of the town about midnight, and took the road beyond to Vlamertinghe. The night march became most tedious; the long columns trailed slowly along, stumbling over the uneven road in the dark, for there was no moon, though the night was otherwise clear. A constant stream of vehicles kept passing us. Chief amongst these were long strings of ambulance cars.

The whole horizon on both sides of the road was lit up at times most brilliantly by the incessant discharge of star shells by both sides. The balls of magnesium kept rising in the air, ten or twenty at a time, and, bursting into a white flare, sank slowly down out of view. The gunning was very strenuous at times, and sometimes a random shell pitched very close to the crowded pavé.

Owing to the proximity of the German artillery, no lights were allowed on the cars or carts. The many close shaves we had from rapidly moving ambulances added a further irritation to the march. The trek seemed endless, although the whole distance to Vlamertinghe is only about 5½ miles. When we were about 2 miles off the village, Torrie sent me on to billet in the hutments, which were behind Vlamertinghe, and in which we were to spend the rest of the night.

I collected our party, an officer and man from each squadron, and walked on ahead. I thought we should never reach this infernal place, we were all very tired and cross. We reached the village about two in the morning.

TUESDAY APRIL 27

We had considerable difficulty in finding the point where we were to meet the staff officer who was to give us our billets. It was by a railway crossing just through the village. The street of the village was full of French and Canadian ambulance motors. Every house seemed to be used as a hospital. A ceaseless flow of wounded kept coming back from the district N and NE of the road, where the firing showed that considerable fighting was still going on.

At the railway crossing we met the billeting party of the 1st Life Guards, but the Leicester Yeomanry one had not yet arrived, so had to wait. About 3 o'clock we set out for the hutments which were situated about a mile S of the village. These hutments consisted of huts made of planks leaning together, the apex forming the roof. They held about 25 men each, and there were enough to hold about 1,500 men. We were allotted Nos 32–40 for the men, and one hut, about 10 feet square, currently being used by the Canadians who occupied most of the huts, as an orderly room. The room was full of boxes and other bulky baggage, and the floor was six inches deep in straw and old paper.

The 1st Life Guards officers lived in the next hut to ours. We were all dog tired, so we crowded in, put down our blankets on the floor and dropped into a heavy unrefreshing sleep. We received orders the last moment before we bedded down to say that we were to remain ready to move at a moment's notice, and that on the following day we should probably have to go into the trenches.

We woke about 7 o'clock and at once set about getting some food. We discovered in a neighbouring field four Canadian Cookers, and from the NCO in charge we managed to get some hot coffee. We felt better after that, but we still felt very stiff and sore from the effects of our plank bed. We couldn't get much news.

The hutments were full of the details* for the Canadian troops who were in the trenches, and in addition there were odds and ends of Artillery and various supply and ammunition columns. Firing going on all round.

During the morning we cleaned out our hut and wrote some letters. These huts were put up last January to act as a rest camp for those Regiments who were in the trenches. When relieved, these men were brought back here to rest for two or three days. It saved them the trouble of marching back to Poperinghe or other places large enough to hold a battalion or brigade.

We had a scratch lunch at 12.30 of tinned tongue and the foulest tasting tea. About 4 o'clock the first shell arrived. It came with a whoof and a crash bang into Vlamertinghe. This was followed by a regular shower of them.

We all crowded out to watch. About 50 per cent didn't burst, but those that did, threw up tall columns of dust and bricks. They seemed to fall right amongst the hospitals in the village. The Germans soon began to lengthen their fuzes. We could see the shells coming nearer and nearer, pitching and bursting on the field and road which lay between us and the village.

We had just decided that the shelling wasn't going to amount to much, when there was a roar and a crash. Hut No. 29, which was three from ours and which was occupied by the 1st Life Guards, flew into the air, in the midst of a column of black greasy smoke. There was no mistaking this portent. We were being shelled with high-explosive shells fired by an eleven inch howitzer. Considerable confusion ensued, increased by the arrival of two more of these tokens of regard. Hut 29 had entirely disappeared. In its place lay two dead men and another with both his legs blown off.

The order was given to fall in at once and march to a point previously fixed (a tree with a bushy top) where we were to lie down in extended order. Torrie told me to go on and act as a directing point. There was a great rush to collect kits, belts, glasses, etc., and in the rush many went out without bothering to collect anything.

The shells now began to fall fairly fast all over the whole camp. Two or three pitched into Vlamertinghe, blowing up huge pillars of dust, black smoke and pink fluff from the pulverised bricks. Outside amongst the

* Men detailed for special duties behind the lines.

waggons and the men of the ammunition and supply columns, the panic was considerable. This was natural owing to the fact that most of these men were very young and hadn't been under shellfire before. The fields were covered with loose horses galloping in all directions and dozens of little parties of men riding half-saddled or harnessed horses, all galloping.

I proceeded over the fields to the S, to take a position where I could be seen so that the Regiment could march on me. When I reached the rising ground which I had selected for my point, I turned to watch the excitement. A shell burst with a terrific report about 10 yards behind two men who were running towards me; they both fell like dead men, and remained motionless. Then they started rolling away like mad, to what they considered a safe distance before they resumed their upright flight.

There was a four-wheeled waggon, packed very high with chairs, tables and cooking pots. This was drawn at full gallop by four horses which were urged to greater efforts by their drivers. By way of taking a short cut, it dashed across a field in front of me. About half way across the intrepid drivers were confronted by a gully, five feet deep and nine across. In they plunged, the waggon rocking and clattering, over it went as it attempted to ascend the opposite side. Off the drivers flung themselves, unhooked the team, mounted and disappeared towards the setting sun in clouds of dust. A field-kitchen, belching smoke like a fire engine, and streams of soup pouring from it in cascades, rumbled past, also *ventre à terre*,* the driver applying his whip like a threshing flail. Into the gully it plunged like its *confrère* of the four wheels, over went the kitchen, the mingled fumes of wood fire and soup rising into the evening air. Off sprang the driver, the horses were unhooked and off quicker than I can write this.

About 50 shells in all were put into the hutments, surrounding fields, and onto the Poperinghe–Vlamertinghe road. Every road leading from this area was now packed with long straggling columns of marching men, ambulances, and supply waggons moving back. Shortly after 5.30 the shelling ceased.

We took up our position about a mile and a half to the south and lay down in extended order in the fields round a large farm, in which, later in the evening, we fixed our headquarters. Towards 7 o'clock parties were sent back to the hutments to remove any kit or belongings left behind in the haste of the departure. The evening was delightful, very clear and cool, after a blazing day.

About 10 o'clock we heard the ominous sound of a motor cycle approaching us. Our worst fears were realised when its cessation was followed

* Flat out, going hell for leather.

by a cry of Turn Out. We collected in the field outside, and heard that the Turcos* were falling back in some disorder on Brielen, and we were ordered to go in as supports, and fill any gap which they might leave.

The moon was most brilliant, the night was as bright as day. We sat, awaiting the order to move. I was very tired, and dozed pleasantly off. At about 11.30 I was awoken and told that counter orders had arrived. We were to stay where we were for the night.

WEDNESDAY APRIL 28

Many alarms during the night, chief one at 2.30 am when a message from our aircraft arrived to say that our bivouac fires were very conspicuous. They formed likely marks for hostile aeroplanes, and were to be extinguished at once. Torrie and Stewart Menzies in a state of coma, so I went round to the offending fires.

At 6.30 we made a frugal breakfast of coffee and partially raw bacon. We then snoozed on and off until 9. Borrowed Bethell's safety razor and Luxmoore's sponge, and had a splendid wash and shave, the first since Monday.

At 10.30 orders arrived that we were to return to our horses, which we had left on Monday night, in a farm 2 miles to the SW of Poperinghe. The sun was blazing and the dust very irritating, the progress of our column was very slow, weighed down as the men were with 200 rounds of ammunition, rifle, cloak and blanket and all their other equipment. We slowly trailed along the country lanes and over the hop fields, to the South of the Poperinghe–Vlamertinghe main road, to avoid the shelling. The Germans began their old trick of shelling the main road again, but they didn't reach us.

It appeared that the Turcos had been very unsteady yesterday, and General Joffre had been up to Brielen and had harangued them. Order had however by now been completely restored, and we were considered to be more valuable with our horses. The men are not trained, nor used to walking far, and our columns were straggling in the hot sun. We arrived about 2 o'clock, our horses in an exhausted condition. I like horses better than ever now.

At 3.30 orders arrived to send on billeting parties to Watou to await there the Staff Captain. I proceeded there with my usual crowd, arriving about

* French Colonial troops.

5 o'clock. The square of the town was full of Staff motors, as the Headquarters Cavalry Corps had arrived.

We went and sat in someone's motor to await events. Had a chat with George Meyrick. He was billeting for the Blues. No Staff Captain arrived, but at 6 o'clock a note arrived to say that we were to meet him in Rattekot, 1½ miles S of Watou. Off we went, getting there very shortly, and on dismounting we lay on the grass at the roadside.

7 o'clock came, but no Staff Captain. At 7.30, just as I proposed to go back to where we had started from, a note arrived vaguely addressed to the 'Senior Officer Billeting Party' saying that we were to return to our Regiments, near Forge, 2 miles SE of Watou. We jogged off thither, meeting the 8th Cavalry Brigade billeting on the way. The whole country crawls with Cavalry.

The Indian Cavalry Corps pervades Watou, and has taken up the billets which we occupied last Monday. About 8 o'clock we found our Headquarters, which for the moment were in a farm which was full of enteric. We unanimously decided to spend the night in the fields, but we finally discovered a small and very dirty estaminet, with a good barn at the back, into which we moved. The Hostess cooked us a most attractive omelette, and Torrie produced some port, so we didn't do too badly.

Indian Cavalry Corps moving up to the Front.

Evening grooming, after standing by all day, in sweltering heat.

FRIDAY APRIL 30

A very hot day again. Breakfasted at 7.30, and moved out to our spot of yesterday to wait in support. We occupied our old Headquarters in the Estaminet.

The Canadians have done extremely well. They certainly saved the situation at one moment. The defensive powers of these comparatively new troops must have come as a nasty surprise to the Germans. They waited until the French had removed their two good corps, the IX and XX, and then they struck at the weakest point in the line, the point where the two nationalities joined. The French troops were very moderate ones, being Composite Corps, consisting of Colonials, Zouaves, and some Belgians and Marines. The Imperial troops were Canadians, which the Germans did not think much of, as they considered them undisciplined and untrained.

The Germans thought, here is a heaven-sent opportunity. Their asphyxiating gases came as a complete surprise to the French Colonials, who retired in the utmost disorder. The Germans poured troops through the gap, and advanced right up to the canal, which they at once proceeded to try and cross.

The Canadian left,* which joined the French near Langemarck, was by now completely in the air. Had they been involved in the débâcle, nothing

---

* The crucial Canadian left was held by 3rd Canadian Brigade, commanded by Brig Gen, later Lt Gen Sir Richard Turner VC. See 6 May. He had won his VC at Komati River in South Africa in November 1900, when he saved guns by driving off the Boers at close quarters, despite being twice wounded.

could have saved the line, the Germans could have marched on Hazebrouck, and the remainder of Belgium would have gone. The Germans were working with 3 Corps (120,000 men) on a front of 2 miles. This was the situation about 8 o'clock on the evening of Thursday April 22.

The following day the Germans made desperate efforts to bridge the canal, and eventually succeeded in doing so and capturing Lizerne. They also fiercely attacked the British at Passchendaele and Broodseinde, but were driven off with great loss. During the 23rd (St George's Day) the Canadians fell back slowly, so as to conform with the French line. It is significant that the only ground gained by the Germans in this attack was gained in the first two hours.

SATURDAY MAY 1

Breakfast at 7.30. Proceeded to our rendez-vous, the wheat field, where we dismounted and off saddled as usual.

We hear considerable gunning still going on. The French are trying finally to expel the enemy from the west side of the canal. They have everywhere been pushed back except at Lizerne and Steenstraate, where they have bridgeheads. The French shell these bridgeheads and from time to time kill everyone in them. They are then refilled with German reinforcements. These reinforcements are shot at with Maxims all the way across on the bridges, and German officers stand on the other side and shoot all who decline to cross. This should raise their morale.

The Germans had made every arrangement for pushing ahead had they got through last week. Snipers were to have been pushed along the roads on bicycles. Dozens of these gentry were shot, as they pushed their bicycles along over the ploughed fields, as they attacked. After all, this attack, strenuous as it has been to all of us here, is but one episode of the whole front.

From the location chart issued by our Intelligence Corps today, we can see what units the Germans have produced against us in this recent attack. It will be noted that most of the formations are regular ones.

About 3, the day clouded over and became very dull and rather chilly. Rain seems blowing up. We returned to our previous billets about 6.30 pm.

SUNDAY MAY 2

A cooler day, but fine. Breakfast at 7.30, and the usual trek afterwards to our field, which has been trodden into a sort of macadamised road. There is not a vestige of green left, not a blade of corn, and the owner, a Belgian who

Getting the belts ready: Lt F.N. Griffin's machine gun section load up.

should be in the ranks fighting for his country, hovers round like a disturbed spirit whining and bleating. He refuses to be comforted by the assurance that the Germans wouldn't have left him his field at all.

Belgian womenfolk follow us everywhere on the march and try to sell us cigars and chocolate. They are exactly like the people on manoeuvres in England. The odd thing is that these people sell us objects that contain letters from people in England. They are obviously gifts to the troops from home, which have been stolen from the base here.

The Aerodrome at Poperinghe has been under shellfire for some days now, so it was decided to move it back. The point selected by the Flight

Commander was a large field to the South of our rendez-vous. Here two aeroplanes arrived yesterday. The Pilots seemed very dissatisfied with their landing ground. One side is too much downhill, and the other end is spoilt by a tall line of trees, which made rising a very difficult and dangerous matter.

About 11 o'clock today, one of these aeroplanes attempted to go up. The machine was a Bristol, which is underpowered.* As a result it took a long space to climb high. The machine started off with Monckton in the Royal Artillery as pilot, and Arkwright** in the 11th Hussars as observer, to go on a reconnaissance to Ostend. They rose very slowly and it was evident to us that they couldn't clear the trees. They wobbled to avoid a house and then rising still further, crashed into the very top of a tree. The engine stuck head downwards, the tail rose and looked as if the whole machine would turn over and fall to the ground. The two aviators hung out over the tree 40 feet from the ground. Great excitement followed. Crowds of men ran off over the fields and a great mob collected. The petrol from the tanks was pouring down in a shower and everyone smoking had to depart or put out their pipes, etc.

Every second we expected the machine to crash to the ground, for it was standing on its nose on the very topmost branches of the tree.

The difficulty now was to get the two aviators safely down without an accident or shifting the machine. Two Canadians tried to climb up with ropes, but only got half way and then stuck. At last a man appeared with climbing irons on, who soon succeeded in reaching the machine with a rope. After much difficulty the rope was fixed up, and the aviators climbed out and down it and escaped.

The machine remained on its nose, until the tree was cut down. The whole line of trees was removed later in the day, thus making the landing ground more satisfactory.

The aeroplane itself was badly smashed when the tree fell to the ground, though the engine and all the instruments were saved. I took several photographs which I hope will come out. I promised the Aviators a set if they were satisfactory.

---

* The vivid photographs of this episode reveal that the aeroplane which crashed into the trees was not a Bristol. It was probably a BE (Blériot Experimental) 2C retro-fitted with skids, produced by the Royal Aircraft Factory at Farnborough in the spring of 1914 (letter from Gp Capt David Baker to the editor, 11 January 2004).

** Capt F.G.A. Arkwright had been a troop leader with A Squadron, 11th Hussars, then transferred to the Royal Flying Corps as an observer. He survived in spectacular fashion the crash described above, but died, ironically in Scotland, at Forfar, on 14 October 1915 in another flying accident.

The Aeroplane.

Crowds gather on the impromptu aerodrome near Poperinghe.

The intended flight to Ostend ends in the trees.

Rescuing the occupants, Capt F.G. Arkwright and 2/Lt W.H. Monckton, who can be seen clambering out of the aeroplane.

MONDAY MAY 3

A fine day. Orders today were to stay in billets until fresh orders came. A good deal of gunning was going on all round, and a few shells were dropped into Poperinghe.

About 2.30 billeting parties were ordered, and I was sent on to meet the Staff Captain at Forge. He marked an area on my map near a small town called Herzeele about six miles to the West of Watou. We rode off there, reaching it about 5 o'clock, when I divided up the area, and took over, as our Headquarters, a farm with a large barn, and well shaded field around. I then settled down to await the advent of the Regiment.

About 7.30 an orderly arrived to say that we were to rejoin the Regiment at once, as it had been ordered to march to Vlamertinghe. This was jolly, for this village was 16 miles off and it was by now very nearly dark. The message further added that we were to march via Poperinghe and Point 35. We collected our billeting party after some difficulty and set out about 8 o'clock towards our new place, along the Watou–Poperinghe road.

It was soon quite dark, and on the way we passed long columns of the Northumbrian Division coming back from the trenches. We reached Poperinghe towards 10 o'clock. The town looked very like Ypres on the night of Nov 13 last, when I was riding out to join the Regiment. It was absolutely deserted, and in pitch darkness. The only moving things in the streets being a few of our supply waggons. Here and there we could see a wrecked house which had been hit by a shell.

The night was lit up by the dozens of flares and star shells, which both sides fired. Towards the German lines we could see a searchlight aimlessly sweeping the heavens. It was now getting towards midnight and we were still far from the farm where the Regiment was supposed to be, near the crossroads 1 mile south of the V in Vlamertinghe. The roads were little better than tracks, and very hard to find on a dark night helped only by the star shells fired into the sky and by vigorously striking matches.

We found Smith-Cuninghame asleep on the floor of a filthy inn. He told us, when he was shaken into a state of wakefulness, that everyone had gone to the trenches except himself, who was looking after the horses which had been left behind. There was no room in with him so we decided to cast round to find quarters in which to spend the remains of the night.

TUESDAY MAY 4

After hunting about in the mud and darkness for nearly an hour, we discovered an empty house about 200 yards from the road. We at once proceeded to investigate. The barn was found to be filled with Gendarmes, all lying like logs. The farm house itself promised better. We found the house completely locked up, but we soon forced a window and pushing Walker in through it, we very soon got in after he had opened the door. There was one fair-sized room which was empty, so we decided to sleep there. For the purposes of our bed, we annexed all the Gendarmes' supply of hay, which was close to the barn, and made a thick mattress of it. We spread our blankets on the top, and soon slept the sleep of the just.

Most of us woke at 5 o'clock and found a dull and drizzly morning. The little kitchen in the next room to ours was soon full of men of all Regiments trying to boil water for tea or coffee.

The loss of the ground North of our Ypres line on April 23 by the French, owing to asphyxiating gases, had caused a very serious situation, forcing us to retire in order to conform to the new French line. The result was that the Ypres Salient as held by us now became almost untenable, owing to the opportunity given to shell it from all quarters.

It soon became evident that the extreme apex would have to be given up, and it was decided to evacuate the area Grafenstafel–St Julien–Gheluvelt. This movement was carried out last night with complete success, and it was to act as a support during the operation that our Cavalry Division had been required.

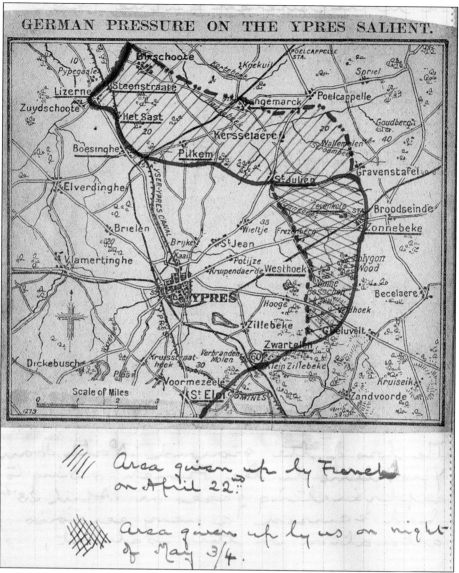

GERMAN PRESSURE ON THE YPRES SALIENT.

||||| Area given up by French on April 22nd

XXXX Area given up by us on night of May 3/4.

German pressure on the Ypres Salient. (*The Times*, 1273, 5 May 1915)

The movement completed, we were sent back to our rendez-vous, with orders to return to the billets which we had taken over last night at Herzeele.

It was amusing to ride into Poperinghe. The road was full of troops, French, Belgian and ours, and dozens of supply motors and guns continually passed me. Hundreds of Belgians were hard at work on two lines of trenches, and putting up long and broad patches of wire entanglements. These lines which are situated about midway between Poperinghe and Vlamertinghe are extremely strong and well sited, and if we should ever have to retire, they would be of the greatest help to us.

By 9 o'clock the rain had completely stopped and a glorious hot day began. I reached Poperinghe about 9 o'clock and bought some papers in the main square. There were a certain number of the inhabitants walking about the street but the place was mostly full of soldiers.

The day was turning out sweltering hot and I took it very easy, having nobody with me except Winder my groom. I reached Watou about 10, where I found the 8th Cavalry Brigade crawling along the roads. I at length reached our farm at Herzeele about 11.15. Winder settled in with my horses, and I sat down to await the Regiment's arrival.

The Regiment came in about 4.30 after a very long and dusty march. Owing to the several columns on the road, they had had to go a long way round.

WEDNESDAY MAY 5

A fine summer morning. The farm looked very pretty with all its fruit trees out, and the willow-fringed moat. Spent the morning cleaning up.

The news we had during the morning was not particularly good. We heard that Dunkirk had been shelled by a big German gun. This was certainly a surprise. The weapon is supposed to be either an Austrian 38cm howitzer or a naval gun. The shells came from near Dixmude. These guns should be easy to locate as they must be fired off a solid concrete bed to which they are bolted, and therefore they cannot be easily moved. Several buildings in Dunkirk were wrecked, one shell falling in the Square killing several civilians. The Hôtel de Ville, the Mairie, the Railway Station and the barracks were struck. The range must have been about 23½ miles. This causes great consternation amongst civilians, but will not have made much effect on military opinion.

The second bit of news is much worse. It tells of the tremendous advance by the German and Austrian Army on the Dunajec and Biala Rivers. We have reason to believe that the Russians have fallen back a considerable distance.* Of course they have often done so before. We must wait for more news from Russia. It seems to have been a big affair, and may set the show back a bit if it is serious.

---

* They had. This was the Gorlice Offensive, launched on 1 May 1915 and led by Gen von Mackensen, which effectively won back Galicia for the Austrians. Thousands of Russians were either killed or taken prisoner. In his *First World War*, pp. 154–5, Martin Gilbert describes the heartrending experiences of a British nurse, Florence Farmborough, who witnessed the suffering of the Russians and felt the torment of having to leave so many of the wounded behind.

We thought that our room was a bit crowded at night, so Torrie and Griffin got beds in the town of Herzeele close by. Ferguson turned up too, as the new Brigadier, Kennedy, had arrived. There were vague rumours as to what was to happen to us.

THURSDAY MAY 6

Another fine bright day. Went for a ride in the morning, the roads and lanes round here are lovely. Had a great bath today, the first time I have taken my clothes off since Friday April 23. Torrie found a bedroom in the village and got me a billeting ticket, but I thought it less trouble to stay on the farm.

We are at last beginning to hear the real story of the German attack, after the début of the asphyxiating gas. It appears that the Canadian Division held a line of roughly 5,000 yards on April 22 extending in a north-westerly direction from the Ypres–Roulers railway to the Ypres–Poelcapelle road, and connecting at its terminus with the French troops. At 5 o'clock in the afternoon, a plan, carefully prepared, was put into execution against our French Allies on the left.

Asphyxiating Gas of great intensity was projected into their trenches,* probably by means of a force pump and pipes laid out under the parapets. The result was that the French were compelled to give ground for a considerable distance. The immediate consequences were extremely grave. The 3rd Brigade of the Canadian Division had its left flank in the air. The enemy being aware of this breach in the line, immediately began to push a formidable series of attacks upon the whole of the newly formed Canadian salient.

The attack was everywhere very fierce, but it was especially so at this moment, upon the apex of the new line, running in the direction of St Julien. Four British guns had already been captured in the wood early in the evening of April 22. In the course of the night, under very heavy machine-gun fire, this wood was assaulted by the Canadian Scottish 16th Battalion of the 3rd Brigade, and the 10th Battalion of the 2nd Brigade. The attack was carried out with the greatest dash. The German garrison in the wood was completely overwhelmed, and the far edge of the wood was gained and there the position was entrenched.

---

* This was the first of six chlorine gas attacks between 22 April and 24 May. The valves on 6,000 gas cylinders were opened along front lines which at one point were only 50m apart. 'Within minutes Zouaves in the front and support lines were engulfed and choking. Those who were not suffocating from spasms broke and ran, but the gas followed. The Front collapsed.' L.F. Haber, *The Poisonous Cloud*, p. 34.

The four guns however were discovered blown up by the Germans. Later on a concentrated fire on the wood made the position impossible, and it had to be sacrificed. At 6 am on Friday April 23 it became apparent that the left was becoming more and more involved, and a powerful German attempt to outflank it developed rapidly. A counter attack was carried out by the Ontario 1st and 4th Battalions of the 1st Brigade under Brigadier General Mercer,* acting in combination with a British Brigade. After a terrific struggle, the attack was carried to the first line of the German trenches. The 3rd Canadian Brigade commanded by Brigadier General Turner was at 5 o'clock on Thursday holding the Canadian left.

At 4 am on Friday morning a fresh emission of gas was made upon both the 2nd and 3rd Brigades. The Royal Highlanders of Montreal remained firm on their ground. The 48th Highlanders, who received the brunt of the gas, had to retire for a short time, after which they re-occupied their trenches. Several German Divisions were now attempting to rush this 3rd Brigade, and to sweep round and overwhelm its left wing. The last attempt partially succeeded, and considerable bodies of German troops slipped in between the wood and St Julien. On Friday afternoon the left of the Canadians was strengthened by the arrival of seven battalions of British troops. A tremendous artillery fire was now directed on this salient and it soon became evident that even St Julien was no longer tenable.

General Currie,** commanding the 2nd Brigade, now flung his left flank south and held his line of trenches from Thursday at 5 o'clock to Sunday afternoon. But on Sunday the Germans succeeded in capturing St Julien, a success which opened up a new and formidable line of advance. By now further reinforcements had arrived under General Alderson,† and an advance was made by a British Brigade through the Canadian left and centre.

---

* Maj Gen M.S. Mercer CB later commanded the 3rd Canadian Division. The most senior Canadian officer to die in the Salient, he was killed in the fierce fighting at Hill 62 on 3 June 1916 and was buried in the vast Lijssenthoek Military Cemetery, near Poperinghe, where there are 10,802 graves.

** Gen Sir Arthur Currie later commanded the Canadian Corps. In the final stages of 3rd Ypres (Passchendaele) in October 1917, he tried to dissuade Haig from launching yet one more assault. He predicted it would cost his Corps 16,000 casualties. In the event he lost 15,634 killed and wounded. Three of his soldiers won the Victoria Cross. John Keegan, *First World War*, pp. 393–4.

† Lt Gen Sir Edwin Alderson (1859–1927) had taken part in the unsuccessful attempt to relieve Gen Gordon at Khartoum. He was ADC to Queen Victoria and King Edward VII, and in August 1915 the first Commander of the Canadian Corps in France. In 1921, he became Colonel Commandant of the Royal West Kents. *The Times*, 15 December 1927.

The two Canadian Brigades were at length relieved and our line fell back on trenches running roughly from Fortuin, South of St Julien, in a north-easterly direction towards Passchendaele.

FRIDAY MAY 7

A showery spring morning. Another hot bath. The weather is topping now. For the last two nights we have dined out of doors in the orchard, to the accompaniment of the croaking of myriads of frogs.

About 1 o'clock orders came for us to go back to our old billets in Wallon-Cappel, a most welcome order. I was sent on to take over, which pleased me, for I like being on my own, and not tied down to the tedious march of Brigades, which are always slow when great numbers are moving. Before leaving I bought two fine old pewter jugs from the owner of the farm as souvenirs of a very nice billet.

Started off at 2.30 with Wallace, Gale and a few others as billeting party. Ride was delightful. We went via old friend Cassel, through which we found the 6th Cavalry Brigade marching. We reached Wallon at 5.30. The Second Army Headquarters were in Cassel and the surrounding villages. Wallon looked very pretty and quite different to what it looked like a fortnight ago when we left, for now all the trees and flowers are out. Everyone seemed very pleased to see us, and our old landlady was most overwhelming.

The Regiment didn't arrive until 9 o'clock in the pitch dark, and they all seemed very tired and cross as they had had to go on a long detour. Very good to get pyjamas on again.

SATURDAY MAY 8

Showery and dull, but warm. Good to be back in billets again.

Intelligence today issued a description of the gas apparatus used by the Germans in their attack on April 22. The authorities at home have sent out hastily-improvised respirators. We have already been issued with two kinds, and a third is just ready. The best kind is the sort taken off some captured Germans, and consists of a handful of cotton waste placed in a yard of black gauze, the whole thing dipped in hyposulphate of soda and tied over the nose and mouth. When not in use it is carried in a neat waterproof bag, which is attached round the neck by a tape.

Several kinds of masks with talc eye pieces are being sent out from England by anxious friends. The best kind I have seen is one made by Allen and Hanbury.

Officers try on makeshift gas respirators at Brielen Camp. The Medical Officer, Surgeon Capt E.J. Luxmoore, has his back to the camera.

Torrie went off to St Omer for news, and returned full of rumours of a great French move down near Arras. He thought that we shouldn't remain long quiet in billets.

About tea-time, we got news of the sinking of the *Lusitania* yesterday off the SE coast of Ireland. This sort of thing is part of the supreme effort that they are now making, and will make no difference to the course of the war.[*] The *Lusitania* was the ship on which I went to America in November 1909.

SUNDAY MAY 9

A fine morning, very warm.

At 9 o'clock church began, and we had got about half way through the service when the Regimental Corporal Major suddenly left the barn where the service was being held, and went up the street. The Adjutant came in a few minutes after and spoke to the Colonel, who made signs to the parson to close the service.

---

[*] Not in the short term. But the sinking of the *Lusitania* outraged American opinion, since 128 Americans were among the 1,198 civilians drowned. It focused attention on American neutrality, in the light of Germany's unrestricted war on shipping. In *First World War*, pp. 157–8, Martin Gilbert shows how the Captain of the vessel, William Turner, might have averted the disaster had he heeded Admiralty warnings.

We all went out into the village square, where we were told that an order had come for the Regiment to go up to the front at once in motor buses. Great excitement followed as to what the reason was. Arrangements were made for the Regiment to parade, 80 a squadron, with machine guns and signallers. The motor buses were due at any moment.

Shortly after 9.30 the Colonel told me that I was to be in charge of the Brigade pack horses, and to go off to the General's billet for orders. I trotted off there and got my instructions, which were to lead all the pack horses via Poperinghe and Point 35 to a point near Vlamertinghe. Each regiment of the Brigade was about 250 strong. The remainder of each regiment was left behind to look after the horses. There was about one man to seven horses.

As soon as the Regiment had filled its buses, and had been joined by the ones containing the 1st Life Guards from Ebblinghem, they moved off and at 11.15 I followed with the 36 pack horses for the machine guns and entrenching tools.

We rode easily along through La Bréard and St Silvestre, where we took the road to Steenvoorde, which we reached about 1 o'clock. On the way we were caught up by a motor cyclist with orders for the wheeled transport to proceed to Vlamertinghe with the pack horses, and not to stay at Poperinghe.

About a mile out of Steenvoorde we met a long string of motor ambulances, full of wounded. A short way further one of our returning buses, having dumped the Regiment, passed us also full of wounded.

The cannonade was considerable and there was a large battle going on. We watered and fed about half way to Poperinghe and then pushed on through Abeele to Poperinghe, which we reached at 3.30. The paved streets were frightfully slippery; about half way down the main street one of the 1st Life Guards pack horses fell and badly hurt his rider. This delayed us and it was nearly 5 o'clock before we were clear of the town.

As we passed the railway station, battalion after battalion was marching out of the station yard. They were new troops and they looked very fit and well equipped. They were the Welch Division which had landed from England only two days before. Further on I passed sections of the Northumbrian Division, also moving up.

The main road was choked with troops and lorries. It was with the greatest difficulty that the pack horses threaded their way through the tangle. We arrived quite safely at our point, one mile west of Vlamertinghe, at about 5.45, where I reported my arrival to a Staff Officer of our Cavalry Division. He pointed out a side-road down which I was to take the pack horses and pick up our machine guns and ammunition. I found our guns and Griffin

Lt Wilson (left) and Capt Penn in their dugout at Brielen.

there, also the Machine Gun officers of the 1st Life Guards and Leicester Yeomanry, to whom I handed over their pack horses.

Having loaded up our belongings, Griffin and I walked to some hutments near Brielen. Here we discovered the Regiment. The huts were rather ramshackle, being made of boards with a tarpaulin or tarred canvas stretched over them.

One small hut was allotted to the officers of each Regiment. We found the Regiment getting ready to go out to dig trenches. The signallers and machine guns were not required, so we dined quietly and settled down on some straw for the night. As the Warwicks had been shelled out of these huts two nights before, we decided to move into some dugouts in a field adjoining the farm. The farm had French artillerymen and horses in the yard and field round it. The building itself was full of Canadian Engineers and Canadian rifles and blankets, to which we helped ourselves.

We found our line of dugouts which were not at all bad. There were enough to hold about 200 men. Griffin and I chose one which had good head cover, which was about 5 feet square. We put some straw into it and soon made it habitable.

The firing which was going on seemed very near and we could easily distinguish rifle fire. As night came on flares rose from three sides, showing very plainly the line of the Ypres Salient. Incendiary shells had been put into

Le comte de Rougé, interpreter to the Staff of 7th Cavalry Brigade.

Sir Morgan Crofton's dugout at Brielen. This was the 'rabbit warren' which he occupied with Lt F.N. Griffin from 9 to 14 May 1915.

Ypres, and our engineers were engaged in burning houses to clear passages from gunfire. The sight was magnificent to watch and we sat for some time on the roof of our dugout to watch the conflagration.

The wind was from the NW now and the smoke and flames were blown across, forming a very effective background against which stood out the ruined wrecks of the Cathedral spire and the Cloth Hall tower. Every now and then a roof or floor would fall in with a crash, a column of sparks rising into the sky.

After watching this spectacle for about an hour we turned in to our rabbit warren and plunged into our straw and blankets.

MONDAY MAY 10

Woke at 5.30. Lovely morning. Slept very well, but had awoken about 2.30 feeling very cramped, as our dugout was not long enough for us to stretch out our legs. Griffin and I decided to rectify this, so we seized spades and added another foot to the length of our hole. Ypres was still burning fiercely. A good deal of shooting was going on.

We had a splendid breakfast at 7 o'clock when we met the Colonel and Stewart Menzies who had returned about 2 o'clock from the digging. We had got a good dugout ready for them, and marked it with a rum jar on the top, as a dugout in a labyrinth of this kind is not easy to find.

Life outside the dugouts at Brielen. Troopers in C Squadron use the break from the heavy shelling to brew up tea.

In the field near the farm we found a French 75mm gun, one of the famous 'Soixante Quinze'. The Sergeant in charge was very obliging. He explained a great deal of it to us, in fact he took us as far as he could before he stopped. He wasn't allowed to show us any more without a French officer being present.

The secret lies in the recoil chamber in the strength of a certain metal plate which divides the air from the oil in the recoil box. It is practically the only true quick firer in Europe. It can easily fire 18 shots a minute and experts can get 22–24 out of it. There are two spiked shoes for the wheels to stand on. Thus when firing the gun is firmly stuck into the ground and is so fast that if a glass of water is stood on each wheel, the water is not spilt by the discharges of the gun. In the recoil the band of the gun slides slowly back about a yard, and returns quietly to its original place.

Underneath the breech of the gun is a small bolt which can be withdrawn if the gun has to be abandoned. If when the bolt has been withdrawn a shell is fired from the gun, the barrel recoils, shoots out backwards and falls 20–25 yards away. The barrel thus flung off cannot be replaced except by hydraulic pressure in an arsenal. I took some photos of the gun and its crew.

We hear that we are to go up into the trenches tomorrow night. We spent most of the day sleeping in the dugouts and watching Ypres burning.

TUESDAY MAY 11

A beautiful warm day. I spent the morning sitting on the top of our dugout watching Ypres being shelled. The French offensive which began on May 9 near Arras is doing very well. Their infantry seems to have gone through the German trenches like a knife through butter. Very many prisoners were captured and a great number of Germans bayoneted.

The new French method of attack is to attack on the two extremities of a broad front. Then, having pierced the line, the two extremities circle round towards each other and should they succeed in uniting, the whole of the contents of the circle thus formed falls into their hands.

The First Army under Sir Douglas Haig attacked on Monday last in accordance with the general plan in support of the French. Its success however was not so marked, owing chiefly to a shortage of high-explosive shells. It seems ridiculous to have attacked if there was such a shortage. Rumour has it that it was the damned idiocy of the officer commanding the Artillery, who imagined during a moment of mental aberration that wire entanglements could be destroyed by shrapnel. Hence when the infantry emerged from their trenches they found the wire still intact and were therefore checked with considerable loss.

We gained some ground, though nothing like what we ought to have done. To rectify this, the Intelligence have shown our gain on a very large scale map,

The French gun crew heave their Soixante Quinze into position – 'the only true quickfirer in Europe'.

6¼ inches to a mile. Thus the uninitiated are deluded into the idea that our gain is as large as that of the French which is shown on a map on a scale six times smaller. There is a certain amount of low cunning about our Intelligence Corps.

WEDNESDAY MAY 12

Another fine day. Orders were received that we were to go into the trenches tonight, to relieve part of the 27th Infantry Division.

The three Regiments of our Brigade are each to supply 260 men. The whole Division of three Brigades is to go in, making a total of 2,300 rifles at the most. Most of today was spent in preparing for this event.

We dined at 7 o'clock, and got ready to go up to the trenches. During dinner the Colonel said that a signalling officer was not wanted in the trenches. So I was to take charge of the machine guns and pack horses, and after the guns had been dumped to bring back the horses.

About 8 o'clock we marched off, about 250 strong headed by the Colonel and Stewart Menzies. Ypres lay about 2 miles off down the road. We marched down the lane to the level crossing and on to the main Ypres–Vlamertinghe road, beyond where we turned to our left and made for Ypres.

As we approached the town, we could see even on the outskirts the damage done by shellfire since we were there in February last. A large convent on our left as we reached the town, was in utter ruins, the wooden domes off the roof lying like enormous extinguishers in the roadway, on the top of piles of bricks and rubbish. The moat and canal at the entrance to the town were filled in with rubbish.

As we passed the canal crossing by the station, word was passed back that we were to keep in sections, but that 1½ yards was to be kept between sections. A precautionary measure, in case we were shelled going through.

We marched noisily on the stone pavé down what was once one of the main streets towards the Cathedral and *Grande Place*. Not a moving creature, not a light, not a house that was not a wreck, and only with difficulty could we find a clear path between the piles of rubbish. At the end of the street we turned to our right and crossed in front of the Cathedral and the SW end of the Cloth Hall.

The little column with the gilt figure on the top, which up to February last had escaped all damage, now lay in fifty bits. Likewise the statue of a celebrated resident of Ypres, who on our last visit to the town in February proudly surveyed the town from his stone pedestal, now lay in many pieces, legs in the air on the rubble below.

In the roadway two caverns, 20 feet deep and 60 feet long, showed where high-explosive shells had burst into the sewers. In the twilight the gaunt relics of the Cathedral and Cloth Hall stood silent witnesses to this organised holocaust.

The spirits of the men became more depressed as we progressed in the silent deserted town. The ripple of laughter, songs, whistling and badinage, which had risen as we marched in, had now completely ceased and one heard only the eternal clatter of hobnailed boots on the hard stones of the road.

Having passed the end of the Cloth Hall we turned to our left, and gained the square. Our engineers had been busy most of the day burning any house which might impede the aim of our guns; as we passed the corner house, a fire, which had been for some time internally combusting in the cellar, burst out and engulfed with a roar the whole structure in its inflammatory embrace. By the light of this house we wended our way across the square.

Here the change from our previous visit was even more marked. The burnt-out shells of houses, roofless and windowless, surrounded the square, houses which before had been full of buyers and sellers, and doing good trade.

The smell of dead horses was disgusting. Dotted about the square were heaps of these unfortunate animals each smouldering and pointing to the abortive attempts of scavengers to clear up by burning. A few wrecked waggons added to the gaiety of the scene. As we crossed the Eastern end of the square, a few random shrapnel came with a whine and a shriek over our heads and burst in the battered and mutilated Cloth Hall.

We marched rapidly on, and reached the road that led out to Zonnebeke, through the Menin Gate. The streets here were merely heaps of ruins, in many places burning fiercely. The Menin Gate itself is now non-existent, and the old solid masonry walls built by Vauban* had yawning gaps in them as big as houses from the recent shelling.

The glare from burning Ypres was now considerable, and in the light of which we marched on up the road. Dead horses and broken waggons marked most of the way, relics of the supply columns which had been caught on the road when the Germans opened their last bombardment. The stink was awful.**

* Sebastien, Seigneur de Vauban (1633–1707), Marshal of France, was Louis XIV's great military engineer. Many of the fortresses he built to defend the French frontier are still in place today, including the solid walls at Ypres. Once intended to keep out incursions from the Spanish Netherlands (modern Belgium), in 1915 they still provided a useful defensive barrier. 'A town besieged by Vauban was a town captured – a town defended by Vauban was impregnable', Maurice Ashley, Louis XIV and the Greatness of France, pp. 87–91.
** 'The stench of the horse carcasses being burnt in the square was such that it remained in one's nostrils for months.' Tpr Stanley Down of the North Somerset Yeomanry, quoted in Max Arthur, Forgotten Voices of the Great War, p. 86.

On either side of the road away in the fields odd shells were bursting and heavy firing was going on. It was now about 10 o'clock, and we reached the crossroads at the entrance to Potijze, where we halted. As spent bullets were beginning to hum over, we lay down at the side of the road, on which a ceaseless stream of wounded men, ambulance motors and supply waggons were passing up and down.

About 10.30 we moved on, following the Leicester Yeomanry who were immediately in front of us. 200 yards further on we passed a large white château on our left which was a dressing station, and also the headquarters of some General. It was humming like a bee hive. Dozens of white flares were rising into the sky on the right and left of us, and made a striking contrast behind the angry glow of Ypres.

After we had gone a quarter of a mile down this road a messenger soon reached us to say we had taken the wrong road, so we retraced our steps. The magnesium flares lit up the night continuously, by which we saw that in front of us was Frezenberg Ridge, on the top of which we could see the silhouettes of long lines of men getting into their trenches. We came right back to where the lane joined the main road, and at its junction we found the Colonel and Griffin with his machine guns which he had just dumped.

Our trenches were a few yards further up the road, and all pack horses were now ordered back. I therefore proceeded back along the road towards the molten crucible of Ypres. More troops were coming up. I passed the 19th Hussars and the Royals. The clatter of the timber waggons on the pavé was deafening. The way back seemed very long. A few shells burst over Ypres as we left the square, but the town was now empty save for a few parties of engineers completing their work.

The square was very hot, and the clouds of smoke and showers of sparks made our journey very unpleasant. We trudged along and at last got out into the open country beyond, and turned off to our huts and dugouts at Brielen.

At midnight I burrowed into my dugout in the straw feeling very tired.

THURSDAY MAY 13

At 7.30 I was going through the farm on my way to breakfast when I was stopped by a trooper, whom I did not know by sight, who told me that he had just seen some stragglers from the 1st Life Guards. He said that we had all been shelled out of our trenches during the night, and that we were all retreating as our line had been broken. This was nice, so, telling the man that it probably wasn't true, I decided to go and breakfast and wait for confirmation which would most certainly follow. At the same time I left word that all stragglers of whatever regiment were to be brought to me.

Ten minutes after having breakfast a wild eyed and dishevelled man called Hills in D Squadron appeared. He said that he was the only survivor of the Regiment, which had been badly shelled, and had had frightful losses. He understood that the Germans were now entering Ypres. I told him to go to the pack horses and stay there and I decided to go and see Staff Captain Balfour, who had been left behind in the camp.

Balfour turned up about 8.30 and showed me a message from Kennedy the Brigadier* from the dugout at Potijze saying that the Brigade had been shelled out of the front trenches with considerable losses. Balfour and I decided to collect every officer and man we could as a reinforcement, and towards dark take them up to where I had dumped the guns the night before.

More and more 1st Life Guards and Leicester Yeomanry kept coming in, but up to midday only three of ours had turned up. About 12.30 Wallace appeared in our motor, having come over with letters, parcels, etc. from Wallon-Cappel, and he decided to stay and help. Four of the officers of the 1st Life Guards and two Leicester Yeomen also turned up, and we collected about 40 men from stragglers of all regiments. We also sent back a message to Wallon-Cappel for more men, and extra rifles and bandoliers.**

Balfour went off to Divisional Headquarters about 3 o'clock, leaving me in charge as Staff Captain. About 3.30 another message from Kennedy arrived, enclosing our list of casualties, saying that Balfour and all available officers and men were to go up to the trenches as soon as it was dark, and that I was to be left in Balfour's place to take charge of the camp and do his job of Staff Captain.

Balfour arranged with me about forming up the supply column and getting more ammunition. I went over to the ammunition column and arranged for 100,000 rounds to be dumped in our camp. At 7 o'clock I saw to the rations.

About 6.30 Wallace and Balfour and their motley crowd of Life Guards and Yeomanry marched off and I was left to attend to my duties. The new rifles and bandoliers arrived, so I at once armed all stragglers I could find. These duties and the supplies occupied me until dark. The news from the Front seemed better, and I heard counter attacks had been organised. Burkett, the doctor of the Leicester Yeomanry,† came in about 7.30, almost in a state of collapse.

---

* Brig Gen Alfred Kennedy, 'a keen and skilful officer of the Third Hussars', had taken over command of the 7th Cavalry Brigade from Maj Gen Sir Charles Kavanagh in March.
** Bandoliers were shoulder-belts with pockets or loops for rifle ammunition.
† Maj J.C.S. Burkett, North Midland Field Ambulance, Royal Army Medical Corps.

I fed him and gave him brandy and he seemed better. He said that his regiment had lost very heavily, 7 officers killed including the Colonel, Evans-Freke, 4 wounded and about 180 men killed, wounded or missing.*

Menzies' memo in the afternoon stated that our officer losses at Frezenberg Ridge were:

Killed	Wounded
Blofeld	The Colonel
Hobson	Bethell
Townsend	Cuninghame

and about 120 Other Ranks. Later in the evening it transpired that Blofeld had been killed the day before, by a shell bursting in a dugout, in a line of trenches he had been sent up to take over for us on Tuesday evening. Two Leicester Yeomanry officers had been killed at the same time. I couldn't hear what the 1st Life Guards had lost, but judging from the stragglers they must have lost heavily.

At 8 o'clock I had a scratch meal of some tea and eggs. Afterwards settled down on some straw in a corner of the hut to sleep after leaving word where I was to be found.

A tiring, depressing day, very dull, and pouring with fine cold rain all day. The mud began to be beastly.

FRIDAY MAY 14

Another cold and drizzly day. Spent the morning getting more rifles and ammunition. About 12 o'clock Bonham in the Greys turned up, and asked if anyone knew where the Headquarters of the 8th Brigade was. I told him, I thought that it was in the château near Potijze, and offered to show him where it was. We started off in his car, and took the same road through Ypres that I had done two nights before. If possible, Ypres looked more awful in the daylight than it did at night.

The sunshine on Ypres only accentuated the utter desolation of the scene. We rapidly passed through the town and out through what was once the

---

* The Regimental History confirms these heavy casualties. The final death toll was 96 all ranks, out of 282 men of the Leicestershire Yeomanry who had left their billets at Brielen the previous day. Of these, 83 have their names recorded on the Menin Gate. No other Cavalry Regiment which took part in the Battle that day paid such a price.

Menin Gate to the country beyond. On the right and left of the road the little châteaux and farms half-hidden in masses of mauve lilac and laburnum looked the very opposite of war. At this distance we could not see the individual havoc of each dwelling, which was mercifully hidden behind natural screens of this highly coloured foliage.

We left the car under the shelter of the ruined wall of the cemetery about a mile from Ypres. It is unsafe to use the road further by day for motors, so we proceeded on foot to the corner of the lane leading to the village of St Jean, where I stopped, for it was then 2.15 pm. I was due at Divisional Headquarters at 2.45. I pointed out the white château which was the Headquarters of the 8th Brigade, which could now be partially seen through the trees.

The house I stopped at was an estaminet and is now totally wrecked. In November when I was journeying down this road to join my Regiment, it was the centre of conviviality and full of people.

Dead horses lay thickly in all the fields round. The smell was disgusting so I decided to walk back to the car. On the way I passed a field in which there were rows and rows of little wooden crosses. These mark the burial places of hundreds of our men who have fallen nearby since October.

On reaching the car I told the driver to take me back to the Divisional Headquarters, which was about a mile outside Ypres on the western side. Here I was to meet the DAAG who was arranging for a motor lorry to remove our surplus ammunition, which amounted to over 100,000 rounds.

About 5 o'clock the chaplain of our Brigade came along to bury the body of Evans-Freke, the Colonel of the Leicester Yeomanry, who had been killed the day before.* The ground chosen was a corner of a pretty little farm, just off the road, where several others who had died in the adjacent dressing station were also buried.

The lorry was very late, not turning up until 5.30, when I returned to the huts at Brielen, and got the ammunition loaded on. Orders then arrived to say that all the regiments of our brigade were coming out at night, and that we were to move back to Vlamertinghe. So collecting all my stragglers, horses, baggage, spare rifles, etc., I marched back across the fields to Vlamertinghe, the village where we had spent April 26–28. We were given

---

* The trenches occupied by A Squadron of the Leicestershire Yeomanry had been in poor condition with little shelter from shellfire. On 13 May this was incessant from 3.30 a.m. until 1 p.m. According to the Regimental Diary, Lt Col the Hon. P.C. Evans-Freke placed a detachment about 150 yards in front of A Squadron, and it was while returning from overseeing this that he was killed.

huts on the left of the road crossing the railway, and there we settled in to wait for the Regiment. Had a supper of cold ham and biscuits, and the remains of a bottle of brandy.

At 9 o'clock Wallace and Griffin arrived, having been sent on ahead of Torrie from the trenches to prepare the way. The Regiment soon followed. Everyone soon settled down to their billets, the officers, all fourteen of us, crowding into a hut ten feet square. Notwithstanding the discomfort, we all slept soundly.

SATURDAY MAY 15

A dull day, inclined to rain. Spent the morning cleaning up and seeing what casualties we had. During the morning we heard that the Royal Dragoons had buried Hobson, and the 12th Lancers, Townsend.

Am so sorry about Townsend; he and Blofeld had both come out with me on Nov 5, and we had all joined together. Of the little party that joined on that date I am now the sole survivor. Mathey of the 1st Life Guards went home sick in December; Goodliffe fell out of a loft, had concussion and went home in November, and now Townsend and Blofeld have been killed.

The Canadian casualty list in the terrific fighting from April 22–26 now amounts to

Killed	709
Wounded	3,275
Missing	1,091
Total	5,075

SUNDAY MAY 16

Brighter. Sun threatens to come out. The camp is getting beastly from the mud. Our hut is too crowded, so this morning we found a semi-wrecked house with a good room and kitchen which will serve us for meals.

About 11 o'clock the enemy dropped 8 shells into the village. They all fell in the same field, and some did not burst. Poperinghe has also been shelled and has now been put under the rigours of Martial Law. A kind of Military Governor has been appointed. Both Poperinghe and Vlamertinghe are shelled from time to time, we imagine by a gun brought up by an armoured train.

At 6 in the evening, we had an open-air service, which was most impressive. The 1st Life Guards and Leicesters attended as well. The service was held in the field just behind our huts, amongst the dugouts, and the words of the chaplain were punctuated by roars of artillery and bursting shells. Overhead several skirmishes between Taubes and our aeroplanes were taking place. Holy Communion followed and was partaken standing up.

No news of our return to our horses. We hear that we are to stay in this village until the situation becomes normal again.

MONDAY MAY 17

Fine but dull: much warmer again. Camp drying by degrees. We secured another hut today for sleep purposes, so we turned seven into it. Motorcars arrived from Wallon-Cappel bringing mails, food, and luxuries of all sorts, including 3 small barrels of beer.

The regimental strength here is largely reduced and since the number of officers left is out of proportion we asked if some of us could go back to Wallon-Cappel for a bath.

Torrie allowed Penn, Walker and myself to do this, so about 3.30 we got into the motor and returned via Poperinghe, Abeele and Steenvoorde, arriving at Wallon about 5.30. Village looked very nice, it was a great comfort to be back even for one night. Had the grandest of hot baths. After tea Walker and I walked over to Staple to look up M and Mme Balloy.

Staple looked very pretty, all the trees and flowers are now out, a great difference to a fortnight ago. Staple was very 'calm' and a regular backwater now. M Balloy was out, but Madame was very pleased to see us.* Walker had a great banquet ready at 7.30. New potatoes!!!

TUESDAY MAY 18

Dull but warm and fine. Breakfast at 8.30.

At 10 o'clock the motor arrived to take us back to Vlamertinghe. I picked up Penn and Joicey en route from their farms. Took out good supply of daily papers, food, etc. We had moved into a better house at Vlamertinghe, which we used in conjunction with C Squadron. There was a piano there which we

---

* The tiny village of Staple lost forty men in the war. Among their names, carved on the War Memorial in the market square, is that of Sgt Raymond Balloy, the son of Crofton's brewery friends.

Getting dug in at Vlamertinghe, where shelling had already caused carnage among 1st and 2nd Life Guards on 27 April.

made good use of. Farquhar of ours and Benson of the 9th Lancers playing very well on it.* We all sang.

The General sent in to say that the noise we were making would probably get the village shelled. The house belonged to the Station Master of Vlamertinghe, who was now working at Bailleul, as there isn't much railway traffic at Vlamertinghe. He turned up this evening and viewed us with doubtful pleasure. He however condescended to borrow some fresh meat from us, and so left in a better frame of mind. We are to stay there a few more days, while the 27th and 28th Divisions are resting and refitting.

In the middle of dinner the first shell arrived; at the second we departed to our dugouts on the hill in front of our huts. After the usual eight the firing stopped, and we returned to finish the meal and have more music.

WEDNESDAY MAY 19

A fine day at last. Camp completely dried out. Not much to do but sit about, as we are now acting as a mobile reserve. We and the 1st Life Guards have to

---

* Capt Sir Reginald (Rex) Benson (1889–1968) not only played the piano, but formed a regimental orchestra. On 25 May he was gassed (see 28 May) but survived. In hospital, at Boulogne, he was in the next room to the poet Julian Grenfell when he died. After service in Ireland during the Easter Rising in 1916, Benson was liaison officer at French Headquarters with Marshal Pétain. In peacetime he was a proprietor of the merchant bank which merged with Kleinworts to become Kleinwort Benson. (Letter from David Benson to Dominiek Dendooven.)

Capt Stewart Menzies, Adjutant, 2nd Life Guards, stands in the entrance to RHQ at Vlamertinghe Camp.

Strangling the 'Pill'. 2nd Life Guard officers get their own back on the Medical Officer, Pill Luxmoore, outside A Squadron hut.

supply one squadron each, 80 men strong, and a Territorial Battalion has been added. This combined force is to act as a reserve to the 2nd Cavalry Division, which is in the trenches.

Officer casualties of Thursday last are beginning to filter through at last. Some Regiments suffered very heavily.

	Killed	Wounded
Leicester Yeomanry	7	5
10th Hussars	4	6
North Somerset Yeomanry	3	8
1st Royal Dragoons	5	7
Blues	6	3
3rd Dragoon Guards	2	5
2nd Life Guards	3	3
Essex Yeomanry	4	5

These are up to date, there probably will be more to come. The 3rd Cavalry Division won't get out of it under 100 officers and 1,300 men.

We were again shelled during dinner, but very few shells burst and they all fell on the other side of the village. Our hut, now that most of the occupants have left it, is very comfortable, and is lived in only by Torrie, Menzies, Penn, Griffin, Luxmoore and myself.

THURSDAY MAY 20

A fine summer's day. After breakfast we heard that we were to return tomorrow to our billets at Wallon-Cappel. Good news for we are rather fed up with Vlamertinghe.

Reports concerning Italy's intervention are becoming more frequent. There is no doubt that her entry into this war will cause a good deal of difference, for she is the only Neutral worth considering.

Italy has had months in which to prepare for war. Italian tradition wishes the establishment of Italy as a Great Power. They also feel that the Adriatic should be an Italian Sea.* When Italy comes in, she will bring about a million men, properly equipped with ammunition and well gunned.

---

* Lavish promises had been made at the secret Treaty of London to coax Italy into the war and were in line with her ambitions around the Adriatic. But Anglo-French promises were not all kept at the Treaty of Versailles (e.g. Dalmatia went to Yugoslavia, not to Italy). This did not improve relations between Mussolini and his erstwhile allies in the interwar period.

The British graveyard in front of Vlamertinghe church (later destroyed), in May 1915.

The new church and immaculate cemetery as it is today. (*Author's Collection*)

We were again shelled during the afternoon with the usual result. About 6 o'clock a Taube which had been flying over our lines for some hours was hit twice with shrapnel by a French battery. It seemed to stagger along, and then turning upside down, it fell rapidly nose downwards, towards the ground, the smoke of the petrol gas streaming from its exhaust pipe.

A tremendous cheering arose from miles round, from all who were looking on. The plane fell rapidly and was lost to view behind some trees, and we heard later that it fell between the English and German lines to the NE of Brielen. Here, to make sure, it was shelled and finally smashed by a French 75mm battery, which also killed a lot of Germans who ran out to help it. During dinner we were again shelled, so hastily finishing we retired again about 8.30 to the dugouts.

FRIDAY MAY 21

A glorious day, and we hope our last one in this beastly camp of Vlamertinghe. With luck we are to embus at 9 o'clock tonight en route to Old Wallon.

Orders came through during the afternoon that we were to embus on the Poperinghe road at 8.30 pm. Torrie told me to go on there about 8 o'clock, and mark our 10 buses, which had been allotted to us. We put 24 men in each, and the leading bus we earmarked for the officers. The men didn't take long to embus. It was nearly dark when the Regiment arrived at the rendez-vous, but we were soon on board, and I secured the front left-hand seat on the top. The night was splendidly fine and clear.

The 1st Life Guards were immediately ahead of us and in front of them was the 6th Brigade. Behind us was the Leicestershire Yeomanry and behind them the 8th Brigade. We started on our return journey by 9.20 and bowled steadily along, with a distance of 50 yards between buses. It was very dark when we entered Poperinghe, and the Germans must have been well aware of our movement, for hardly had the leading bus reached the station outside the town, when whiz bang, a shell flew over and burst in the field beyond.

This seemed nice and we saw that we should have to run the gauntlet through Poperinghe. The Military Police outside the town stopped our bus, and ordered all lights to be put on, and a distance of 200 yards between buses to be taken, so they could dash at full speed across the town. Our bus seemed to go very slowly. Creaked and bumped a good deal, which made us afraid that she would break down in the Square and leave us there for some time. However, we kept going and got into the street leading from the town. Seven or eight shells whizzed over and burst beyond, but how near they were I could not say. They seemed to be very close. About 2 miles from Abeele we slowed down, and an examination was made to see if anyone was hit, but I believe there were no casualties.

About 11.30 we reached Hazebrouck, and turned to our right and took the road to Wallon-Cappel, which was reached at midnight. We dropped C Squadron behind, and we ourselves got out at the end of the lane leading up to our billets. The 1st went on to Ebblinghem.

Very glad to be back. Our valises looked very good.

SATURDAY MAY 22

Went for a ride in the morning, country looking very pretty, every farm is a mass of mauve lilac and yellow laburnum. I have never seen a greater change in any part of the world, than there has been here since the winter months. Then the country looked treeless and bare, yet now everything is out. It seems as well wooded and as shady as any part of England.

Since the Russian disasters in Galicia, these operations in the Dardanelles have become more vital than ever. This opening for Russia's supplies must be forced at all costs but I fear that it will be a very tedious and lengthy job. We suspect that some of the divisions of Kitchener's Army will be sent there. Anyhow the force operating there now must be considerable.

We hear that a draft of 150 men and 10 officers have arrived for us at Rouen, and will shortly appear here.

SUNDAY MAY 23

Whit Sunday. A very fine warm bright day. Service at 9.30 in a barn in the village from which, a fortnight ago, we had been so hurriedly summoned to go up to Vlamertinghe. Great news today. Italy has, at last, declared war on Austria. *The Times* reports:

> *Rome, May 23*
> It is officially announced that Italy has declared war against Austria.
> The *Tribuna* says that Baron von Macchio, the Austrian Ambassador, was handed his passports at 3.30 this afternoon. He will leave this evening or tomorrow morning. The Italian Ambassador at Vienna has been recalled – *Reuter*.

> *Amsterdam, May 23*
> A Vienna telegram says:
> The Italian Ambassador, the Duke of Avarna, this afternoon presented a formal declaration of war to Baron Burian, the Foreign Minister.

Now the Italians are committed, there remain few important Neutrals to impress.

About 11 o'clock our new draft arrived. It came under Gurney* who has been in England since November 12 last, and included Hoare, Graham,** Pendarves, two officers belonging to other regiments and 100 men, who seemed of extremely good quality. Amongst them were two coloured gentlemen, solicitors from Trinidad, who at their own expense came over to enlist last September in Kitchener's Army. I believe they are excellent fellows, very quick and intelligent.

MONDAY MAY 24

The French have captured some German trench signalling devices. When the Germans capture a trench line they plant a flag, formed by a double strip of cloth fixed on two sliding handles. The double strip is composed of the red, white and black German flag with a backing of greenish grey cloth. When the signal is planted the inconspicuous grey side is turned towards the front, and the light coloured flag towards the rear. Their artillery see this signal and cease firing on the ground gained. The French have lately captured several of these flags.

Miller Mundy of the 1st Life Guards went home last week. This leaves Penn the sole survivor of the Composite Regiment who has been out since August 14. Not counting Hidden the Quartermaster and Walker the Vet, Stewart Menzies is the only officer who came out on October 6 who has been here all the time. Probably other Cavalry Regiments have a similar record. Yet people in England imagine that the Cavalry has not been much employed!

TUESDAY MAY 25

Very hot and bright. Went for my usual ride in the morning. We hear that we are to move our billets on Friday next towards Aire and St Omer, leaving these present ones to the 2nd Cavalry Brigade, which is coming back from the trenches.

In the afternoon we motored over to our new area to have a look round. We went to Racquinghem, which is to be our centre. There will be nice rides round for St Omer is only 7½ miles off to the NW and Aire about 4½ miles off to the SE. However, we are not there yet, and there may be further changes.

---

* See 15 December for further details of Capt T.C. Gurney and Capt A.S. Hoare.
** See 15 November.

The new Government seems a strong one, and is badly wanted. The leading members of the new Cabinet are:

Prime Minister and	
First Lord of the Treasury	Mr Asquith
Chancellor of the Exchequer	Mr McKenna
Secretaries of State:	
Home Affairs	Sir J. Simon
Foreign Affairs	Sir E. Grey
Colonies	Mr Bonar Law
India	Mr Chamberlain
War	Lord Kitchener
Minister of Munitions	Mr Lloyd George
First Lord of the Admiralty	Mr Balfour

We are all glad to see that Churchill, who was rapidly getting a danger to the State,* has been relegated to the Duchy of Lancaster, where he can cool his heels by administering the Insurance Act, and where he can't do much mischief. A Coalition Government will also show Germany that Public Opinion is united in England, on the question of the war.

WEDNESDAY MAY 26

Another very hot day. Worked out a signalling scheme in the morning.

We hear that the Germans have made another attack on the NE of the Ypres Salient and have tried to gas the 1st Cavalry Division which is holding that part of the line. The Germans have gained the château at Hooge. They will go on I expect gaining little bits until most of the Salient has gone. The 1st Indian Cavalry Division** is going up to the front from Aire, where it has been since November last. I wonder if the native troops will stand the gas?

The Cavalry badly wants a month to get together again, after the last month's movements, but whether we shall get any time it is impossible to say. Probably not!

* This was a popular view. As First Lord of the Admiralty, Churchill was held responsible for the Dardanelles Campaign. Asquith now demoted him to the medieval sinecure of the Chancellorship of Lancaster. 'Almost his only departmental duties were to appoint magistrates for the county of Lancaster', writes Roy Jenkins in his masterly biography, *Churchill*, p. 276.
** The Indian Cavalry Corps (originally the Indian Expeditionary Force) had been formed on 18 December 1914 at Aire and comprised Gurkha, Indian and British troops.

A Zeppelin is believed to have come over Cassel last night, and dropped bombs, but I don't think very much damage was done.

THURSDAY MAY 27

Went into Hazebrouck and bought a nice pewter jug, also a pair of pyjamas for which I had to pay a most exorbitant sum. They would have cost about 7s 6d in the Burlington Arcade, whereas here I had to pay 22 francs, or 18s 4d. The reason for this extortion, I was told, was the War, and then the fact that they were English luxuries made them very expensive.

When I got back to tea, I heard that we are to go up in the trenches again on Saturday. What a nuisance it all is. I had hoped that we should have had a quiet time in Racquinghem. We are to move over there tomorrow as the 2nd Cavalry Division require our billets here. Apparently we are to go up again in motor buses on Saturday.

FRIDAY MAY 28

Cold, but fine day. Breakfast at 7.30, at which Torrie told me to go forward with billeting party to take over the château and house at Wardrecques – our next port of call. Started off at 9 o'clock with Walker. We went via La Belle Hôtesse and Blaringhem to avoid the hills.

Was not sorry on the whole to leave Wallon-Cappel. Although it was better latterly than it was when we first went there in April, it really is an unhealthy village, and we were not too comfortable in billets. Our old landlady seemed sorry to lose us, but she 'manfully' repressed her tears when we gave her two tins of ration jam.

I believe that the 9th Lancers are to take our place at Wallon-Cappel. They suffered very heavily from the gas in the trenches last Wednesday, chiefly owing to laziness on the part of the officers and men in not taking the trouble to put on respirators.

Noel Edwards (the polo player who played in America, in the Polo Team taken over by Wimborne last year)* never bothered to put either a respirator or mask on, with a result that he was badly gassed, and although he succeeded in walking back through Ypres, he died some hours afterwards.

* Capt Noel Edwards, who was commissioned into the 9th Lancers in 1903, was a star polo player. He did not take part in the 1914 tour organised by Lord Wimborne. But he had toured the USA with the England team in 1911 and scored all the goals for his side, four in each match. 'He will be remembered as one of the finest polo players of his time.' *Polo Monthly*, June 1915, p. 232.

The mess billet at Wallon-Cappel. Left to right: Capt J.B. Walker, Surgeon Capt E.J. Luxmoore and Capt S.G. Menzies.

Walker and I reached Wardrecques about 11 o'clock, the Regiment following soon after. We have got for a Mess here a very modern but comfortable house next door to a large paper factory. The owner of the factory lives here and he and his wife gave us a large and well-furnished dining-room.

The lady of the house seems very dissatisfied with the conduct of the war. She says that she expected that it would only last a month. I told her that it very nearly did only last a month, and that if the Germans had taken Paris, the war would have been over long ago. She said she didn't think the Cavalry did much, but she cheered up when I told her that my Regiment had used up 70 officers and about 400 men since August. She will, I expect, get better on acquaintance.

SATURDAY MAY 29

Another glorious day. It was lovely waking up in my nice room, and looking out of the windows across the park. The War seems miles away. For the first time for seven months I hardly hear any cannonading going on. What a relief. It is quite like staying in a nice country house at home. One feels one ought to get into tennis shoes and flannels instead of this shabby and dirty khaki.

Torrie gave me orders to stay behind and look after the horses while the Regiment was in the trenches. Only 3 Officers per squadron were to go up, and Gurney and I and about 10 others are to stay here. At 12.30 twelve motor buses arrived and took 250 of our men and about 11 Officers under Torrie up to Ypres again. We heard that they were to go into dugouts in the fortification there, as supports. But at breakfast today, orders came that we were to relieve the 3rd Hussars in the front line trenches near Hooge, to the E of Ypres.

We shall be anxious about them while they are up there, and anxiously watch the wind to see if it is favourable for gas.

VOLUME VI

MAY 30 – JUNE 18, 1915

SUNDAY MAY 30

A beautiful summer day. Had a long walk round the ground here. Had a long talk with Madame. She really is rather a nice little thing, but of course with very uneducated ideas about the war. They have a house in Lille too, but she does not know whether it is destroyed or not. Her husband apparently is something to do with French motor transport.

There are some quite good pieces of furniture in the house, chiefly Second Empire. What a luxury once more to have a bed with sheets. For the time being I have relegated my fur sleeping bag and well-worn jaeger blankets* to the limbo of the past.

In the afternoon rode into Aire along the canal banks. Quite a pretty ride; took some photos of part of the canal. There is a lot of traffic on it, all to do with the supply in Aire. Every barge we saw was crammed with hay or oats. They are quite the biggest barges that I have ever seen, standing when laden quite 8 feet out of the water. Their length is about 100 feet, with a beam of 10 feet.

Aire was about 4 miles off, and Walker and I got there about 3.30. The Headquarters of the First Army are settled in Aire. I hadn't been there since November 26 last, and even then it looked attractive, but now, with all the trees out, it looks particularly so. The dominating feature of the town is the XV Century church of St Pierre. We went inside and found several beautiful glass windows. Trophies of the Allied flags hung from every pillar, banners expressing every kind of patriotic sentiment were placed all over the church and gave every military appearance to the interior.

The streets are very old fashioned with houses dating from 1570. There are several good shops now largely full of English goods. One can buy almost anything that one wants there. I bought some Vinolia soap.

---

* Derived from the German *Jäger* ('hunter'), a jaeger is a predatory seabird, but most readers will be more familiar with its use as a brand name for quality garments and, as here, bedding.

The *Place* is surrounded by very old houses, one of the most picturesque being the old Guard House, dated 1597, at the corner. I thought it a little gem. The Eastern side of the square is taken up by the Hôtel de Ville, a building dating from Napoleon I. It is decorated with military trophies carved in stone. We had tea in the old Hôtel de la Clef d'Or in the NE corner of the *Place*.

MONDAY MAY 31

A splendid day. What a pleasure to wake up in my nice room, after the bleak schoolrooms and draughty barns in which I have spent so many months.

Menzies arrived back last night from England after his 3 days' leave, bringing with him some news and my telegraphic instrument, on which I wanted to train some more signallers. He said that people in England were still nervous of a raid, but why, heaven alone knows, for where is Germany to get the men? The intervention of Italy will force the Kaiser to send at least 10 Corps (400,000 men) to help the Austrians on that theatre.

Menzies said that he had heard on very good authority, that the total number of men that the British Empire has under arms in England and on the Continent is now over 3,800,000. He seemed to think that the authorities in England were against conscription because of the difficulty of equipping and feeding more men at the Front.

We had news from the trenches this morning. They got in all right without any casualties, and were situated near the Hooge Château. We sent a ham, some eggs and letters and papers up to them today by a motor cyclist. We haven't heard for certain when they return. Went for a ride in the afternoon to Renescure, about 1½ miles from here. General Kavanagh had his Headquarters there in March last, but now it is the Headquarters of General Briggs and the Staff of the 3rd Cavalry Division.*

Renescure has the quaintest old church dating from about 1570, which now looks most picturesque in its setting of lilac and laburnum, with very green grass and millions of buttercups. Close by is the château where General Briggs lives. Its main features are two unique turrets and a fine and very old sundial on the front of the house. The village square backed by the

---

* Maj Gen Sir Charles Briggs had taken over command of 3rd Cavalry Division earlier in the month from Maj Gen Sir Julian Byng. Later promoted to Lieutenant General when commanding British forces in Salonica, he received decorations from Serbia, Greece and Russia for his distinguished service in that theatre of the war.

Gen Sir Charles Briggs' château at Renescure, Headquarters of 3rd Cavalry Division.

church tower is extremely pretty and old world. Lower down the village street stands an old turreted farm dated 1472 with moat and drawbridge which is now the dwelling place of several officers of the Divisional Staff.

A prettier little village would be hard to find anywhere. The houses look very like what they did centuries ago. Except for the presence of a modern barn or two, and new patent farming implements, one could easily imagine oneself back in the time of the *Roi Soleil** or the unlucky Louis XVI.** Many farms built about 1750 are of the same pattern, and I have seen hundreds of barns and old farms in Belgium and the borders of France exactly like the Château of Hougoumont.†

* King Louis XIV (1638–1715) was known as *Le Roi Soleil*. His bed-chamber at Versailles faced east, so that he could rise each day with the sun. He personified autocratic kingship, believing that *'L'Etat, c'est moi'*. Aged only five when he came to the throne, he reigned for seventy-two years, outliving both his son and grandson, and was succeeded by his great-grandson, Louis XV.

** Unlucky, because he was accused of treason by the Convention during the French Revolution and sent to the guillotine on 21 January 1793. His Austrian wife, Queen Marie-Antoinette, was executed later the same year.

† Site of the epic resistance of the Coldstream Guards at Waterloo. They successfully drove the French out of the courtyard at Hougoumont. 'The success of the Battle of Waterloo,' said Wellington afterwards, 'depended on the closing of the gates of Hougoumont.' Elizabeth Longford, *Wellington*, pp. 552–4.

We appear to be having a quiet time in the trenches, and one can now hope that the Regiment will return in a few days without any casualties.

The news on the other theatres of the war interests us most now, especially the Russian affair in Galicia. No decision is gained unless the Russian line is *broken*, for it is then that the Russians can be contained by a relatively small force. Masses of German troops and guns can then be shifted back to this western theatre to obtain a decision here, and incidentally pull off the inconclusive peace.

The fighting over several hundred miles of front continues desperately. The Russians steadily hold the centre intact, while making successes on both flanks, but at the same time the Germans have got perilously near their objective, which is to surround Przemysl. Between the northern and southern lines of attack, two days ago, there was only a space of about 12 miles.

We now anxiously await news of the fate of Przemysl.

TUESDAY JUNE 1

The first day of summer, and a glorious one. Thank the Lord that May is over, it always was an unlucky month. I well remember Mrs Robinson, the palmist, saying to me last January when I went to see her, 'I shall be glad when May is over. It is an unlucky month for the Cavalry.' And so it has been.

May 13 – could anything be less propitious? The numbers on all fronts of killed, wounded or missing for this last month make good reading for the Germans.

	Officers	Men
May	3,600	26,346

Practically 30,000 officers and men, nearly an Army Corps the equivalent of 1½ Divisions. Compared to

	Officers	Men
March	1,081	18,794
April	639	19,158

the May losses are more than double.

Of these casualties, about 130 officers and 2,500 men belong to the 3rd Cavalry Division, and a bit of the 1st and 2nd Cavalry Divisions, and occurred in two days' fighting. I suppose the Authorities here know best, but it seems to us ridiculous to use up our small amount of Cavalry in this way.

We possess out here 3 divisions of Cavalry, and 2 divisions of Indian Cavalry, and this wastage in trench warfare can never be replaced. It is time that reinforcements came out to replace losses because at the present moment the 3rd Cavalry Division is non-existent except for small dismounted detachments now in the trenches, and the 1st and 2nd Cavalry Divisions are not much better.

The best officers, NCOs and men of every regiment are invariably killed or seriously wounded in this trench warfare, and they cannot be replaced. One more show like that of May 13th last, and our reinforcements of both officers and men will have to be scraped together from the four winds of heaven.

Cavalry is a most expensive, highly trained and technical arm and it is being wasted in its present work. Trench work can be performed by a man with but six months' training. It takes two years to produce a cavalryman.

There are masses of infantry out here now, and the whole Cavalry Corps can only supply the number of rifles in the trenches which one Infantry Brigade can. Let them turn us into Infantry by all means if it is necessary, and take away our horses, and organise us as such, giving us proper equipment, and entrenching tools, and providing us with camp cookers, periscopes, flare pistols, and all other paraphernalia for trench work. But at present we are neither one thing nor the other. We are left with 600 horses to feed, water, groom and exercise when we are in the trenches and our equipment is totally unfitted for this work. Our organisation is wrong for it, and we have none of the comforts with which the Infantry are supplied, such as cookers, so that for a fortnight at a time we have to live on tinned meat and cold water.

Each time we are told that it is the last that we shall be so engaged, and then 24 hours after we return to billets, we are hurriedly sent for in motor buses to take the place of some Territorial Battalion which has refused to go in, or else we are stuffed in to fill the gap of some line regiment which has been shelled or gassed out. And we are getting damned sick of it.

We have never been taught to dig or any of the tricks which are always part of an infantryman's yearly training, and every week in the trenches takes us a month to get the Cavalry spirit back. The whole of last winter was spent in eradicating the effects of the five weeks of fighting round Ypres in October and November. Just as we are right again, in we go another three or four times again in April and May.

However, no doubt the Authorities are satisfied with this state of affairs.

WEDNESDAY JUNE 2

A regular summer's day. Not much news from the trenches. We hear that the situation in front of us was quiet, but there was a great bombardment of the

Hooge Château on our left, which was occupied by the 3rd Dragoon Guards. The 1st Life Guards had a few casualties amongst their machine-gun detachment.

About 3 o'clock I set out to ride along the canal bank to St Omer, which lies about 5 miles off. The canal is most interesting and forms an excellent example of the very perfect canal system of France. Every conceivable device is shown on its banks for loading and unloading barges, and the swing and turntable bridges are most ingenious.

To get to St Omer it is necessary to have a pass, otherwise one is turned back at the posts which are situated at the entrance to every road leading to the town. On the road to St Omer, about 2 miles outside the town lies the old town of Arcques which is now full of Territorials and the new 12th Division, which belongs to Kitchener's Army, which is now beginning to come out very fast.

St Omer is a very attractive old town, and is now very important as the Headquarters of Sir John French. Hence the care with which the town is guarded. There is a sort of modern suburb round the town, outside the old glacis of the fortifications, but inside it seems very old.

The town is full of English and French Staff Officers. Most of them I imagine are doing absolutely nothing, but every General Headquarters Staff has, I suppose, a certain number of fawning deadheads on it.

There are two or three nice old churches. One of them, the Chapel of the Jesuits' College, is used as a motor garage, and is always full of cars, standing in pairs between the pillars up the aisle. A screen with curtains hides the altar. The College Saint-Bertin has been given over to the Map Section of the General Staff. It is there that anyone requiring a map of any description applies.

In the centre of the town is the Hôtel de Ville, a not very attractive building. Out of the *Place* runs one of the fashionable streets, the rue de Dunkerque, in which you can buy almost anything. However, the shops sell practically nothing but English goods. They must be making a harvest. We stayed, had tea at the Café Harmonie and rode home in the cool of the evening.

THURSDAY JUNE 3

A scorching day. One wonders if we shall ever again have any rain. The country is inches deep in chalk dust, churned up by the heavy lorries which come here daily to the enormous reserve park of supplies, stored in the paper manufactory. We have now had no rain for over four weeks, except a few very local showers, and there will soon be a scarcity of water. Fortunately for us our horses are on the banks of the canal, but if it is like this in June what will it be like in August? We shall shortly have a million men in the country, and any lack of water will have serious results.

Not much news from the trenches. The section on our left, which was holding the Hooge Château had an awful shelling yesterday, but our fellows didn't get in to it fortunately. I believe that the 3rd Dragoon Guards suffered very heavily there.

FRIDAY JUNE 4

Another scorcher. Whew!! Rather a different Fourth of June* to most years. We expect the Regiment back tomorrow.

When Joffre is ready for his great push, and when the German line has been thinned out sufficiently, then we shall hope to see them forced rapidly back. It is getting very tedious all this hanging about, and then being sent into the trenches. The grand advance would be welcomed on all sides.

We hear Asquith came over to St Omer, and rumour has it that it was to give French a dressing down. I wonder if he will stay on here and finish the war. I think that Douglas Haig would make a better Commander-in-Chief now.**

SATURDAY JUNE 5

No difference in the temperature again today. What *will* August be like? The Regiment is by way of coming out of the trenches this afternoon, but one never knows if they really will come. The Infantry is being re-organised round the salient at Ypres, and III Corps is being mixed with the 27th and 28th Divisions of the V Corps. These two divisions have never been satisfactory. They came over here in February last, composed entirely of British Infantry from India. They arrived, of course, at the worst possible season for troops who had been for long in tropical climates.

They were sent about February 1 into the trenches, trenches which were execrable, trenches which had only just been taken over from the French, badly sited, villainously built, with no wire entanglements in front. They were not provided with periscopes, or Verey pistols for firing flares. The cold was intense and the trenches were feet deep in water. The French had left

*A reference to 4 June (birthday of King George III) celebrations at Eton.
** Sir Douglas Haig was appointed Commander-in-Chief by Asquith shortly before Christmas 1915. Crofton's comment not only reflects growing disillusion with Sir John French, but leads into his impassioned diatribe (5 June) against 'sleek deadheads' in which he gives full vent to his anger at the decision to hold on to Ypres at all costs.

the trenches in a condition of indescribable filth. It was impossible to dig down a foot, in order to improve the trenches, without turning up a dead body. The sanitary provisions were nil.

In these conditions it is not surprising that these divisions lost 10,000 men in a month from sickness and frostbite. Their morale was sapped and, as troops, they were for the time being valueless. They did not understand trench work, they had never been trained to do it. They lay inert in their trenches dying like flies, and the only signs of life they ever showed were the nervous bursts of rifle fire which they hysterically kept up all night long. It seemed to soothe their shattered nerves to pump lead over the parapets. They must have wasted millions of rounds.

On the night of February 5, they were on the right flank next to us and we regarded them as of such doubtful steadiness and suspicious behaviour, that we posted an officer in their trenches with them to keep us informed of what they were doing. This kind of behaviour was all the more astonishing, because these divisions were composed of regiments with the highest traditions, and were straight from India.

Shortly afterwards they were withdrawn and broken up into brigades which were mixed up in other Corps. About April these brigades were once again collected together and the old 27th and 28th Divisions were re-formed into their original state. These were the divisions which we relieved in the Salient about May 12th. They had been there some time and their losses had again been very heavy.[*] The remnants were relieved about a fortnight ago.

There is no doubt that the Salient at Ypres is simply an inferno. It is not war, but murder pure and simple. The massacre which has been going on there since April 22 is not realised at home. From May 1–16 we were losing men at the rate of 1,000 a night. Our casualties for May show we lost 3,600 officers and 26,346 men.

This is all the Ypres Salient. Why we don't give it up now, God alone knows. As a strategic or tactical point Ypres is worthless. As a political centre it does not exist.

The town is a mere heap of rubble, cinders and rubbish. Not a cat lives there now, it is the abomination of desolation. The fields round the town are crammed with the graves of our dead. The smell is awful, and the hum of myriads of awful-looking flies which have been holding orgies on the putrid bodies of countless dead along the trench lines, is unmistakable. Sometimes

[*] According to Brig Gen J.E. Edmonds, the 28th Division lost 15,533 men of all ranks killed, wounded or missing at 2nd Ypres. *Official History of the War*, p. 354.

an extra-special stench issuing from some pile of bricks, tells where the inhabitants and owners of the dwelling were caught and retained.

The surprising facts about Ypres are the wealth of colour from the flowers and shrubs in the unkempt gardens, and, in the occasional quiet from the cannonade, the beauty of the songs from the birds. How bird life must sneer at human culture. No pagan barbarism ever showed anything to touch this. And it is to preserve the sentiment of this muck heap that we lose nightly 1,000 men.

We cannot conceive why the Salient is not straightened and given up. Sentiment is nothing to modern Commanders. Now Italy has come in there is no powerful neutral to impress. Rumania and Bulgaria will come in anyhow after the harvest, Greece is utterly useless, and the United States are still spectators.

Hence why keep Ypres to impress people? We need not give it to the Germans, it can lie between the two lines and be made untenable by our guns. The effect on morale would be nil, in fact it would cheer up our Army, and be forgotten in a week. The Germans have practically no men there, nothing but gas cylinders and heavy guns. Of the latter they have about 35. We know where they are, they are marked down on the maps of our heavy batteries round Vlamertinghe and Brielen. But owing to lack of 8 inch and 9.2 inch ammunition, not a shot is ever fired.

Our men are pulverised, their trenches blown in, and not a shot in reply. If only Sir John French and all the sleek deadheads of the Headquarters Staff could spend an hour in the front line, when one of these bombardments is going on, they would return gibbering idiots.

The German line is strained to bursting point, they haven't a man to spare. Their infantry now is beneath contempt. They are so dependent on the gases and their stores of high-explosive shells that unless they have these things, they won't advance a yard. They are what drugs are to the hypochondriac, and the Germans, once they have had them, want more and more. This method of warfare sins against the military spirit, and they will suffer for it later. If only we had shells, we would push through to the Rhine.

Last week when the French assaulted at Arras, they kept up a preliminary bombardment of 30 hours on German lines. When the assault came, there was nothing there and the French line swept ahead, led by officers on horseback waving swords. On the same day we tried the same game at Festubert, but could only boil up a bombardment for 50 *minutes*.* Result – 9,000 casualties and nothing achieved.

---

* The disparity with French resources is striking. *The Times*, on 14 May, had carried a highly critical article on the 'shells scandal', a factor which contributed to the fall of the Asquith Government – the last purely Liberal Government.

Still one day we shall have shells, if there is anyone here left alive to profit by them. The only reasons that I can see in favour of retaining the Ypres Salient are:

a.   That it takes up more Germans to hold than a straight line would, and so helps to keep them stretched out on a longer line.
b.   That it detains Germans here who might do more mischief elsewhere.

But whatever it is, the fact remains that it is damned unpleasant to be anywhere near the place.

SUNDAY JUNE 6

The fine weather now is almost as monotonous as the wet of last winter. If we don't get rain soon it will be very serious. We have heard that the Regiment is not coming out until tomorrow morning. They will arrive here about 3 am. The relief was so delayed that it was broad daylight before it could be completed and so the Regiment had to stay on in the dugouts until dark.

Went for a ride in the afternoon along the canal banks to St Omer. These banks are so pretty. On the way there I passed a small group of men trying to restore a drowned man to life. He was lying in the grass by the side of the water, and a man was making frenzied efforts to restore him by artificial respiration. I fear however that he was dead. The contrast seemed extraordinary. The green trees, the lilac bushes, the placid water without a ripple, the songs of the birds, the strong sunshine, and the white still body lying in the long rank grass by the water's edge.

Reached St Omer about 3.30, found it very hot and stuffy. Bought some papers and came slowly back. Not a great deal of news.

Am very glad that, on the whole, the trenches have been very quiet. But one unfortunate thing happened yesterday. A rifle grenade fell into our trench and hit one of our best Corporals, Wilkins, on the left thigh, a man who did most awfully well on the Retreat from Mons, and got the DCM. The grenade exploded, nearly blew his leg off and severely wounded him on the other leg, in all making 40 wounds. He was in dreadful pain, and very hard to move out of the trench. I hope his life will be saved but it is doubtful.* Anyhow he will lose his leg at the hip joint. He was engaged to such a pretty young woman in the dress department of Marshall and Snelgrove.

---

* Corporal of Horse Arthur Wilkins DCM of Bedminster, Bristol, joined the 2nd Life Guards in 1906. He did not survive these horrendous wounds, but died at 1st Canadian Hospital, Etaples, on 16 June.

MONDAY JUNE 7

Having heard that the Regiment would return at a very early hour this morning, I kept a look out for Luxmoore to let him know. About 3.45 am I was awakened by the sounds of Luxmoore's bike going past, so I looked out and there he was, disguised as a Christmas tree, and looking very soiled and dirty. I let him in, and after a conversation concerning what he had done in the trenches, we both went to bed and slumbered again.

Went to breakfast at 9 o'clock. Another swelterer. The heat is really getting most unpleasant. Leave has again started, and Wallace, Griffin, Fenwick-Palmer and Wilson went off to England. The people who have returned from the trenches are to have first go. I believe I am to go on Tuesday 15th with Torrie and Luxmoore.

The Regiment has been just eight days in the trenches, and very fortunately has had very few casualties. I hear that the same rifle grenade which wounded poor Wilkins so badly, also killed my late groom Tyler. I got rid of him at Staple in February last, as he was always ill and I tried to get him sent home. However, he was kept in hospital in this country, and returned in about a month. As I had replaced him, I got him a place with Wilson.

How time goes. Several people who got terms of six months imprisonment at Staple months ago are now returning. I fancy that a good many would prefer going on doing imprisonment. Certainly amongst the Infantry, acts to get imprisonment to avoid this horrible trench life are becoming so common and numerous, that now the imprisonment is suspended until after the war. A man on being sentenced returns to duty, and if he does well, his punishment is remitted, but if he does badly he gets it added to. The men all had an idea that all terms of imprisonment would be remitted, as soon as the war stopped. This idea has been knocked on the head.

Many amusing incidents have happened on the return of delinquents, for after this time no one remembers whether a man returns from prison or hospital. A case occurred today. A Corporal went up to a returned man, and shaking him warmly by the hand, said, 'Well we are very glad to see you back after your nasty wound.' To which the man replied 'I never had any nasty wound, I've just come back from six months in prison.' Roars of applause.

Had a nasty accident tonight. Was biking home to this château after dinner, when the handle bars twisted, and I was shot violently on to my face in the road. Felt very stunned, and found I had cut my right cheek rather badly. Resumed the rest of the journey on foot, and when I got in found Luxmoore, who had gone to bed at 6 feeling rather seedy, fast asleep, so had to bandage myself up. Fortunately got a good wash but found a very nasty place on the right cheekbone. Bled a good deal.

TUESDAY JUNE 8

Dull day, very close and stuffy, looks like thunder and rain.

Face felt very sore. The Pill looked at it, but said that it was all right. On the way to breakfast looked into his medical inspection room, and had the wound properly cleaned and painted with Iodine. Very painful. As I had fallen on a dusty and dirty road, I thought I would have an injection for Tetanus. It would do no harm, and as I have once lost a pony from lockjaw who had cut its knees, I didn't mean to take any risks. So at 11 o'clock, Luxmoore and I went off to the 7th Cavalry Field Ambulance to be done. They give you a pretty good dose, twice that of typhoid inoculation. Pill did it, plunging a syringe the size of a garden one into my left chest.

After lunch, clouds rolled up and a violent thunderstorm broke over us. It poured in torrents, but the storm cleared the air which had been insufferable. The force of the storm brought a huge branch off an elm in the drive.

Prince Arthur of Connaught* came to dine with Gurney tonight. His advent caused the greatest excitement to the owner of our house and his wife. The latter determined to do us well, so we were all turned out of the dining-room at 5 o'clock, so that it would be prepared. She lent us a white cloth, and lots of flowers were put on and some highly decorated glass. The Landlord did nothing much, but walk round and round the table and talk in a loud voice. For this share in the proceedings, when the table was laid he demanded a glass of whisky. Under the influence of which, he then rushed to the looking glass over the fireplace, and, mounting in a very shaky manner on a chair, he wrote *Vive l'Angleterre* on it with a piece of soap.

Connaught, accompanied by Bonham,** arrived at 8 o'clock, and the dinner was a great success. Our landlord and his wife were presented, which pleased them very much.

Owing to my face, which made me look rather like 'Chirguin, the White Eyed Kaffir', I could not do full justice to the wine, which was very comprehensive.

---

* Prince Arthur (1883–1938), only son of the 1st Duke of Connaught, was at this time ADC to Sir John French (later also to Sir Douglas Haig). In 1920, he was appointed Governor General of the Union of South Africa, in succession to Earl Buxton. In 1921, he became Colonel-in-Chief of the Royal Scots Greys.
** Maj Sir Eric Bonham (1875–1937), Royal Scots Greys, was Comptroller and Equerry to Prince Arthur from 1911 to 1926.

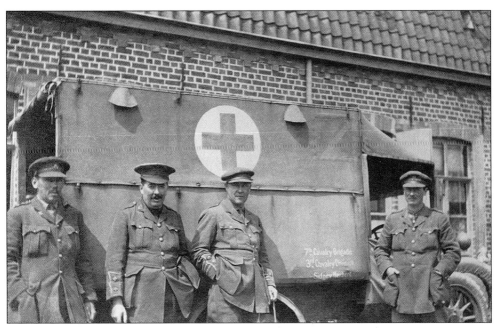

7th Cavalry Field Ambulance crew: Surgeon Capt E.J. Luxmoore, Lt W.J. Maloney (officer in charge of water purification), Maj H. Herrick and Surgeon Capt J.D. Anderson.

WEDNESDAY JUNE 9

The French seem to be doing well near Arras; they took more prisoners yesterday and killed over 2,000 Germans. I wonder if this is really their boost or not? The Germans seem to be very pressed to get reinforcements. They are bringing them up in motor vehicles from distances 80–100 miles off.

The Italian intervention should make a substantial difference to the general conduct of the War. Italy has adequate supplies of guns and ammunition; whereas it is doubtful whether Austria and Germany can really spare the men to make full use of their defensive advantages.

THURSDAY JUNE 10

Fine again and cooler. The rain has done a great deal of good. The crops are coming on well. Torrie tells me that Luxmoore, he and I can go home on three days' leave on Tuesday next. Praise the Lord!

Not *very* exciting here. The Regiment is having an easy time after its adventures, which have really stretched continuously from April 23–June 7. Officers and men are going home for 3 days' leave in batches.

Beyond spurts of shelling along our front, we seem to be waiting chiefly for ammunition. The Germans are said to be concentrating again near Dixmude.

But it is difficult to believe that they can make a violent offensive there, as they have all they can do to reinforce against the French effort at Arras which every day seems to get more formidable. Still we hear that the Dutch–Belgian frontier has again been closed hermetically, an act which always points to a move in these parts.

Nous verrons. We are very strong now in this area. The British front is about 40 miles long, and it is being extended still further. We have now 21 Divisions of Infantry out here, at least 500,000 men, who are now being organised into 7 Corps of 3 divisions each. In addition there are 2 Cavalry Corps, a total of 5 Cavalry Divisions, about 23,000 men and besides this an enormous number of Artillerymen and Engineers. Exclusive of supply columns we must have nearly 800,000 men out here.

Very different to November last when we were hanging on to the ground in front of Ypres by our eyelids, with only 120,000 men in the country.

FRIDAY JUNE 11

Fine. The 14th Division of Kitchener's Army[*] marched through here today. The men looked extremely good and useful.

A youth called Bury turned up here in one battalion of the Essex Yeomanry. I hadn't seen him since we used to play Bridge at the Marlborough.

This is the third Division of Kitchener's Army that I have seen. We hear that 3 more are now coming over, so that will make up the whole of Kitchener's First Army of 120,000 men. This will be *in addition* to those numbers that I mentioned yesterday. Kitchener's Second Army, also of 120,000 men, is quite ready to come out. It is only a question of the transport.

To avoid submarines these divisions are being shipped over in bursts, and not in a steady stream. Two battalions are brought over every night now, on each of the Folkestone to Boulogne mail boats. Some of Kitchener's divisions we believe have gone to the Dardanelles, but not much information can be gathered.

The ammunition question is progressing better. Stanley,[**] commanding the 1st Life Guards, returned yesterday off leave. He told us today that

---

[*] Kitchener's Army consisted of the hundreds of thousands of men who responded to his imperious call for volunteers in the autumn of 1914, 'Your Country Needs You'. This proved to be the most effective recruitment campaign ever launched. Kitchener's expectations were swamped in a tide of patriotic fervour which brought in ½ million volunteers in the first month. A.J.P. Taylor, *First World War*, p. 53.

[**] Lt Col the Hon. Algernon Stanley, youngest brother of the 17th Earl of Derby.

someone in the know, presumably Lord Derby, his brother,* had told him that our daily output of shells now was 4,000, and that shortly it would be increased to 10,000 a day or 70,000 a week. But the daily expenditure of shells in a battle on this side is now about 40,000, so there is still great leeway to make up.**

The official casualties mentioned by Mr Asquith in the House of Commons, two days ago, are larger that one would have imagined. They are:

Up to May 31

	Officers	Men
Killed	3,327	47,015
Wounded	6,498	147,482
Missing	1,130	52,617
	10,955	247,114
TOTAL	258,069	

This is more than double the number of the entire original Expeditionary Force which embarked in August and September last.

So far, from April 11 to May 31, our losses have been 119,000 officers and men. These numbers show the cost of Hill 60, 2nd Battle of Ypres, the fighting at Festubert, the Canadian and Gas casualties and also the fighting in the Dardanelles.

The fighting from June 1–10 will probably add another 20,000. Thus roughly we lose the services of 3 divisions a month. But most of the

---

* A bluff, genial figure, Lord Derby (1865–1948) was Director of Recruiting in October 1915. When not enough men came forward via his 'Derby Scheme', whereby men voluntarily attested their readiness to serve, the first Military Service Act, limited to single men under forty-one, brought in conscription in January 1916. In the Commons, Asquith quoted King Henry V's words to the Lord Derby of the day in the year of Agincourt:

> Go 'cruit me Cheshire and Lancashire
> And Derby hills that are so free
> No married man or widow's son
> No widow's curse shall go with me.

See The Times, 5 February 1948.
** Thanks to Lloyd George, some leeway would soon be made up. 'The military had underestimated the enormous number of shells required for the war of attrition on the Western Front. Asquith mitigated his blunder by appointing Lloyd George Minister of Munitions in his new Coalition Government.' Roland Quinault, Modern History Review, April 1993, p. 6.

wounded, numbering 6,498 officers and 147,482 men, return to the fray. They include people who have been wounded twice or three times, and thus count as 2 or 3 wounded men. Also a great number of the wounded are very slightly injured and soon return.

The total loss to the Empire in ten months has been roughly 65,000 persons (or 6,500 a month). That is about 3,800 officers and 61,200 men, or 1 officer to about 16 men.

SATURDAY JUNE 12

A nice summer's day. Torrie said today that the Regiment seemed very short of instructors at Windsor. Therefore I might return to the Depot there for a spell of duty where he thought that I should be most useful. As we seem to be going to sit in billets for eternity here, I quite agreed that I should like to return for a bit.

The worst of war is that one is either bored stiff in billets, or scarified out of one's existence by high-explosive shells. There is no happy medium and seven and a half months of this existence makes a change at home very acceptable. Torrie is to come home on Wednesday next, and he and I will then square matters up. Luxmoore and I are to go home on leave on Tuesday.

SUNDAY JUNE 13

Went to lunch with Joicey and B Squadron. Took some photos of their billets.

Afterwards we adjourned to the canal, and watched some swimming sports which Joicey had arranged there. The sports were rather amusing. The boarding by a perfectly nude man of a barge which was being steered by a lady, was the occasion of considerable levity.

In the evening I gave an outdoor lecture to this squadron on the War in general and the Russian retreat in particular.

The list of the total Casualties at the Dardanelles during the month of May was issued today. They seem heavy, but the feat of landing troops below the cliffs of Gallipoli might easily have been more costly. The landing is an eye opener to the authorities in Berlin. The total was made up as follows:

	Officers	Men	Total
Killed	496	6,927	7,423
Wounded	1,134	23,542	24,676
Missing	92	6,445	6,537
	1,722	36,914	38,636

Of these I fear that most of the Missing will eventually prove to be dead, as many of them were the men who were killed on landing and probably fell into the water.

MONDAY JUNE 14

Very fine and hot. Getting ready for my departure tomorrow. I decided to take all my saddlery and kit back with me, for Torrie tells me that he will arrange when he is home for me to go straight down to Windsor, and start instruction there.

Lunched with C Squadron at their billets, and took some photos afterwards. The Officers Mess is rather a nice old house in a dreadful state of decay.

In the afternoon gave a lecture on the War to D Squadron. I have now lectured exhaustively to all three squadrons. The men always seem very keen to hear any bit of news, and take the greatest interest in any lecture on the subject. These lectures are very useful because they keep the men from getting too pessimistic, which they are very apt to do, as the papers don't tell them much. It requires a broad view of the war to prevent pessimism.

Later went for a ride round by the Aire–St Omer road. The country looks delightful, and I regret very much having to return to Windsor. However,

C Squadron officers enjoy some time out. From left to right: Capt the Hon. Malcolm Bowes-Lyon, Capt F. Penn, Lt J.S. Pendarves and Capt D.J.N. Blair.

C Squadron kitchen at Wardrecques. Crofton wrote on 1 June that the Cavalry were poorly equipped for trench work and still had no camp cookers.

I imagine that the Regiment will sit tight here for some months. With the Russian retreat there is not likely to be a grand offensive for some time, so I don't suppose I shall miss much.

TUESDAY JUNE 15

A topping day. Felt very like a schoolboy going home for his holidays. The leave papers were a very long time in coming from the General's Office, and we began to get very nervous concerning them.

Luxmoore and I were travelling together, and Herrick, who commanded our Field Ambulance, sent it to say that he would motor us to Boulogne to catch the 3 o'clock boat. The padré Pelling was also going.

At 11 o'clock the leave papers were still missing, so we decided to go ourselves to the office at Wardrecques to get them. Having said goodbyes all round we started at 12 o'clock for Wardrecques. Our kit was piled into the Field Ambulance car, on the top of which Herrick, Pelling, Luxmoore and myself climbed and we reached Wardrecques about 12.15. Here we had some difficulty in penetrating into the General's Office for the leave papers. However, at last we succeeded in getting them and started off.

The road was very dusty, the motor was very stuffy, and the day was sweltering, but none of us cared twopence about such trivial irritations, and we hummed merrily along towards Boulogne and our boat. Halfway there a tyre burst with a terrific report. This was jolly and for half an hour we sat by the side of the road in the dust and glare waiting for repairs. Motor after motor rushed by covering us with a thick stifling powder, and about 2 o'clock we resumed our journey *ventre à terre*.

We fetched up at Boulogne about 2.45, and at once boarded the packet *Invicta*. The sea was fairly calm, but there was a stiff breeze blowing. There were not very many people in the boat, less than on any other occasion on which I have been over.

About half way across a mine which had broken adrift was sighted. It was impossible to say if it was English or German, it was a round and very rusty iron ball, and it turned over and over and bobbed up and down like the float on a fishing line. Great excitement followed on deck and several people had shots at it from rifles. At one time it was less than thirty yards off. The packet boat made two circles round it, heavy firing going on all the time from the deck. This manoeuvre evidently was an arranged signal, for very shortly we saw two trawlers approaching which had 3 inch guns fixed in the bows, and soon made short work of the mine. The Captain said that they very often saw floating mines, especially after a gale, and they were invariably sunk by the trawler fleet which was kept handy for that purpose.

We reached Folkestone about 5 o'clock, and at once boarded the London train which left at 5.30. Luxmoore, the padré Pelling and myself shared a compartment and had an excellent dinner en route. Reached Victoria about 7.15.

WEDNESDAY JUNE 16

Got my hair cut, and had a general clean up. Did a lot of shopping.

Went to see George Arthur at the War Office.* He thought it an excellent plan that I should go to Windsor for a bit and help with the training of the large number of recruits there. Instructors are very badly needed now at home. We have over 800 men there being trained as drafts for the Front, and there is nobody at Windsor with any experience of this War. Arthur said that I had better take an extension of 4 days' leave, during which period my transfer to Windsor would be carried out.

Asquith made the announcement in the House that the *daily* expenditure since April 1 on War Services amounted to £2,660,000.

---

* Sir George Arthur, Lord Kitchener's PPS. See 4 December.

THURSDAY JUNE 17

Lunched with Torrie at the Cavalry Club, who said that he had fixed up my transfer to Windsor. He gave me a lot of instructions on the work which he wished done for the drafts.

FRIDAY JUNE 18

The Centenary of Waterloo.

The Russians announce that the German Casualties for a month on the Dniester front* over a distance of 40 miles are from 120,000 to 150,000 men.

During the afternoon received at the Marlborough Club a telegram from the Adjutant General telling me to postpone my return to France.**

---

* The River Dniester flows into the Black Sea south of Odessa.
** After a few months at Windsor, Crofton was posted to Dar es Salaam. See 'Biographical Note'.

EPILOGUE

First Ypres saw the apotheosis of British regular soldiers, but also their end. A large part of the 'Old Contemptibles' was dead, and what was left was soon to be distributed among 1,000 new battalions.

But the memory of the type remains – perhaps the most wonderful fighting man that the world has seen. Officers and men were curiously alike. Behind all the differences of birth and education there was a common temperament; a kind of humorous realism about life, a dislike of talk, a belief in inherited tradition and historical ritual, a rough-and-ready justice, a deep cheerfulness which was not inconsistent with a surface pessimism. They generally took a dark view of the immediate prospect; therefore they were never seriously depressed. They had an unshakable confidence in the ultimate issue; therefore they never thought it worth mentioning. They were always slightly puzzled; therefore they could never be completely at a loss; for the man who insists on having the next steps neatly outlined before he starts will be unnerved if he cannot see his way; whereas others will drive on cheerfully into the mist, because they have been there before, and know that on the further side there is clear sky.

It was the end of an old army, and an older and freer mode of war. For now a huge, cumbrous mechanism had cast a blight of paralysis on human endeavour. The fronts had been stricken by their vastness into stagnation. Already a man could walk by a chain of outposts from Switzerland to the Vosges, and in a ditch from the Vosges to the North Sea.

John Buchan – *The King's Grace, 1910 – 1935*

SELECT
BIBLIOGRAPHY

This list gives details of books cited in the footnotes. Many other biographies, historical works and regimental histories were consulted. The place of publication is London unless otherwise stated.

Anglesey, The Marquess of, *A History of the British Cavalry 1816–1919*, vol. 7, Leo Cooper, 1996

Arthur, Sir George, *The Story of the Household Cavalry*, vol. III, Heinemann, 1926

Arthur, Max, *Forgotten Voices of the Great War*, Ebury Press, 2002

Ascoli, David, *The Mons Star*, Harrap, 1981; republished Birlinn, Edinburgh, 2001

Ashley, Maurice, *Louis XIV and the Greatness of France*, EUP, 1960

Ashmead-Bartlett, Ellis, *The Uncensored Dardanelles*, Hutchinson and Co., 1924

Baker, Anne, *From Biplane to Spitfire*, Pen & Sword, 2003

Barker, Ralph, *The Royal Flying Corps in France – from Mons to the Somme*, Constable, 1994

Beckett, Ian and Simpson, Keith, *A Nation in Arms*, MUP, 1985

Bennett, Geoffrey, *Naval Battles of the First World War*, B.T. Batsford, 1968

Brereton, J.M., *The 7th Queen's Own Hussars*, Leo Cooper, 1975

Brown, Malcolm, *The Imperial War Museum Book of 1914 – The Men Who Went to War*, Sidgwick & Jackson, 2004

Buchan, John, *The King's Grace, 1910–1935*, Hodder & Stoughton, 1935

Campbell, John, *Jutland – An Analysis of the Fighting*, Conway Maritime Press, 1986

Churchill, Winston, *The World Crisis, 1911–1918*, Odhams Press, 1938

Clemenceau-Jacquemaire, Madeleine., *The Life of Madame Roland*, Tellandier, Paris, 1929

Corbett, Julian, *Official History of the War: Naval Operations*, vol. II, 1921

Dendooven, Dominiek, *Menin Gate and Last Post*, De Klaproos Editions, Belgium, 2,000

Edmonds, J., *British Official History: Military Operations France and Belgium, 1914–15*, Macmillan, 1925

Egremont, Max, *Under Two Flags – the Life of Major General Edward Spears*, Weidenfeld & Nicholson, 1997

Falls, Cyril, *Life of a Regiment. The Gordon Highlanders in the First War*, Aberdeen University Press, 1958

Ferguson, Niall, *The Pity of War*, Allen Lane, Penguin, 1998

Fisher, W.G., *History of Somerset Territorial Units*, Phoenix Press, Taunton, 1924

—— *A Short Report on the North Somerset Yeomanry*, A.S. Flower, Bath

Gilbert, Sir Martin, *Winston S. Churchill*, vol. III, Heinemann, 1971

—— *First World War*, Weidenfeld & Nicholson, 1994

—— *The Routledge Atlas of the First World War*, Routledge, 1994

Gray, Edwyn, *British Submarines in the Great War*, Charles Scribner, 1971

—— *The U-Boat War, 1914–1918*, reprinted, Leo Cooper, 1994

Haber, L.F., *The Poisonous Cloud – Chemical Warfare in the First World War*, Cleveland Press, Oxford, 1986

Hawkey, Arthur, *The Amazing Hiram Maxim – An Intimate Biography*, Spellmount, 2001

Helmreich, Ernst, *The Diplomacy of the Balkan Wars*, CUP, 1938

Hickey, Michael, *Gallipoli*, John Murray, 1995

Hills, R.J.T., *The Life Guards*, Leo Cooper, 1971

Holmes, Richard, 'The Last Hurrah – Cavalry on the Western Front, August – September, 1914', – in *Facing Armageddon*, ed. Peter Liddle, 1996

Household Brigade Magazine, Autumn, 1955

Jenkins, Roy, *Churchill*, Macmillan, 2001

Keegan, John, *The First World War*, Pimlico, 1999

Kershaw, Ian, *Hitler, Vol. I – Hubris*, Penguin, 1998

Liddell Hart, Basil, *History of the First World War*, Faber & Faber, 1934

Lomas, David, *First Ypres 1914*, Osprey Publications, 1999

Longford, Elizabeth, *Wellington, The Years of the Sword*, Weidenfeld and Nicholson, 1969

Lopez, Jean, *Le Calvaire des Poilus*, Editions Le Sir, Montpellier, 2,000

Lunt, James, *The Scarlet Lancers*, Leo Cooper, 1993

Macdonald, Lyn, *1915 – The Death of Innocence*, republished Penguin, 1997

Marshall-Cornwall, Sir James, *Foch as Military Commander*, B.T. Batsford, 1972

Massie, Robert, *Dreadnought: Britain, Germany and the Coming of the Great War*, Pimlico, 2004

Maze, Paul, *A Frenchman in Khaki*, William Heinemann, 1934

Meyer, Jacques, *La Vie Quotidienne des Soldats pendant la Grande Guerre*, Hachette, 1966

Miquel, Pierre, *Les Poilus – La France Sacrifiée*, Terre Humaine, Plon, 2,000

Modern History Review, April 1993

Official War Diaries of the 2nd Life Guards, PRO, Kew, ref. WO 95/1155

Pollock, John, *Kitchener*, Constable, 2001

Ponsonby, Sir Frederick, *The Grenadier Guards in the Great War*, vol. I, Macmillan, 1920

Rimell, R.L., *Zeppelin! A Battle for Air Supremacy in World War I*, Conway Maritime Press, 1984

Ryan, W. Michael, *Lt Col Charles Repington, A Study of the Interaction of Personality, the Press and Power*, Garland, New York, 1987

Sassoon, Siegfried, *Memories of a Foxhunting Man* – Faber & Faber, 1928

Shurtleff, Leonard, 'Canada in the Great War, a Statistical Summary', *Stand To!*, January 2003

Smith, Anthony, *Machine Gun*, Piatkus, Aldershot, 2002

Spears, E.L., *Liaison 1914*, Heinemann, 1930

Strachan, Hew, *The First World War, Vol. I – To Arms*, OUP, 2001

Taylor, A.J.P., *The First World War, an Illustrated History*, George Rainbird, 1963

Upton, Peter, *The Cherrypickers*, BAS Printers, Stockbridge, 1997

Warner, Philip, *Field Marshal Earl Haig*, Bodley Head, 1991

Wheeler-Bennett, Sir John, *King George VI, His Life and Reign*, Macmillan, 1958

Winthrop Young, Geoffrey, *The Grace of Forgetting*, Country Life Ltd, 1953

Woodham-Smith, Cecil, *The Reason Why*, Constable, 1953

Wyndham, Humphrey, *The Household Cavalry at War*, Gale & Polden, Aldershot, 1952

Ziegler, Philip, *Edward VIII – The Official Biography*, William Collins, 1990

INDEX